KOOTENAI BROWN

Canada's Unknown Frontiersman

by William Rodney

Photo Credits

Front cover color photo by Merv Syroteuk
B.C. Provincial Archives: 41, 44 (bottom), 51 (top), 163 (top); Fort Macleod
Museum: 204 (top); Glenbow Archives: 106 (top), 121 (bottom), 129, 139,
146-147, 151, 158, 167, 172 (bottom), 179, 191, 213, front cover (inset),
back cover; Heritage House: 44 (top), 51 (bottom), 121 (bottom), 163 (bot-
tom), 204 (bottom), 218; Historical Society of Montana: 121 (top and inset);
Manitoba Archives: 63 (bottom), 106 (bottom) 187 (center); Provincial
Archives of Alberta: 63 (top) 81 (top), 187 (bottom); Public Archives of
Canada: 81 (bottom); RCMP: 112 (bottom); Saskatchewan Government: 172
(top), 187 (top).

Canadian Cataloguing in Publication Data

Rodney, William, 1923-
   Kootenai Brown

   Includes bibliographical references and index
   ISBN 1-895811-31-7

   1. Brown, John George, 1839-1916. 2. Frontier and pioneer
life – Alberta. 3. Pioneers – Alberta – Biography. 4. Alberta –
Biography. I. Title.
FC3672.1.B7R6 1995   971.23'02'092   C94-910601-1
F1078.B7R6 1995

First Edition – 1996

HERITAGE HOUSE PUBLISHING COMPANY LTD.
Unit #8, 17921 55th Ave., Surrey, B. C., V3S 6C4

Printed in Canada

Contents

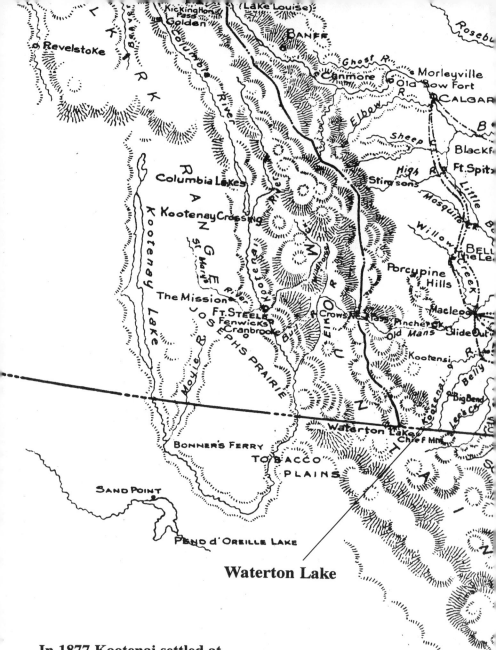

Waterton Lake

In 1877 Kootenai settled at
Waterton Lake in the Northwest
Territories. In 1905 the area
became part of the new provinces
of Alberta and Saskatchewan.

4

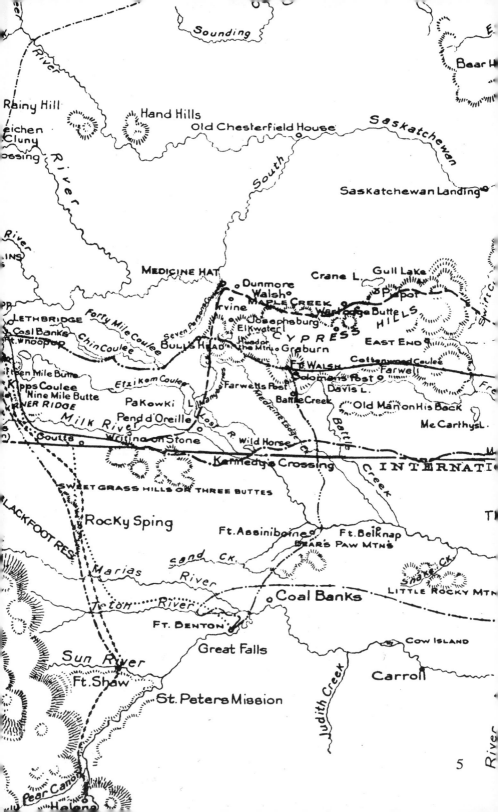

Acknowledgments

Every book is the crystallization of the assistance and interest of many persons, and this study of "Kootenai" Brown is no exception. While on the trail of Kootenai, I have been helped by many people who gave generously of their time, and who drew willingly from their experiences and memories. Without their help this book would have been the poorer, and no acknowledgment can adequately express my debt to them.

To the Archivists, Librarians and staffs of the National Archives, Washington, D.C., the Public Archives of Canada, the Public Record Office, London, the Provincial Archives of Alberta, the Montana State Historical Society and the North Dakota State Historical Society, my thanks for unfailing courtesy and efficiency in helping me to run down information that was at times elusive and unpredictable as to origin and source. To Mr. Willard E. Ireland, the Provincial Archivist of British Columbia and his deputy, Miss Inez Mitchell, I owe particular thanks for their assistance and for providing photographs which illustrate the text.

Two research grants from the Glenbow Foundation, Calgary, Alberta, enabled me to examine documents, to talk with old-timers who knew Kootenai, and to travel over, however superficially, some of the country in which Brown ranged almost a century ago. Without the Foundation's assistance I should not have had the opportunity to meet Mr. W. McD. Tait, Fergus, Ontario, and to divine something of Kootenai through his recollections, as well as from his writings. The interest and assistance of the Foundation's Librarian, Mr. T. R. McCloy, and its Archivist, Mr. Hugh Dempsey, has enhanced the work in terms of detail and illustration.

To the National Parks Service of the Department of Indian Affairs and Northern Development I owe a particular debt for it was while on temporary service during three happy summers that my interest in Kootenai and my affection for that most beautiful of Canada's National Parks, Waterton Lakes, were kindled. The late H. A. de Veber, then Superintendent, did much to encourage that interest, and introduced me to Mr. F. W. Lothian, whose knowledge of the development of Canada's National Parks is unrivaled. Through the courtesy of Mr. A. J. Reeve, Assistant Director of the National Parks Branch, I was able to examine early records without restriction.

I am particularly pleased to acknowledge the contribution to this book of the Commissioners and men of that unique and gallant body, the Royal Canadian Mounted Police. Their co-operation made it possible to pinpoint Kootenai's connection with the North-West Mounted Police, and to draw upon the rich resources of their photographic library. Two awards from the Arts Research Grants Committee, Royal Roads Military College, indicate the lively interest of the Director of Studies, Dr. E. S. Graham, and my colleagues.

No acknowledgment can reflect the depth of my appreciation of my wife's part in the completion of this book. Her professional advice was, throughout, invaluable for its precision, and she has been my principal typist as well as my sternest critic. In the latter respect she has been joined by my children, Helen and Greg, whose final approval of Kootenai's tale compensates for the times we could not share during the long search.

William Rodney
London, England.

Introduction

Since his death on July 18, 1916, stories about John George "Kootenai" Brown have multiplied enormously. With the advent of radio, television, and films, and discovery by governments that tourism is a major source of revenue, accounts of Brown's life and adventures have achieved a currency that is constantly increasing. Thus, it comes as no surprise that the Lieutenant Governor of Kootenai's own province, Alberta, speaking to a convention of United States businessmen, puts Brown at the top of his list of ten Canadian heroes. The criterion, apparently, was that all choices had to have a touch of mischievousness and a courageous personality. These are qualities that Kootenai certainly possessed. Again, in the wider context of the cinema, Kootenai is mentioned in that brilliant National Film Board production *Helicopter Canada*. As the camera threads its way among Alberta's oil wells the audience is reminded that "the search for oil has come a long way since 'Kootenai' Brown mixed molasses with kerosene, served it as a cocktail to the Stoney Indians, and told them if they ever tasted anything like it, to be sure to let him know."

With the passage of time, such tales about Brown – most of them apocryphal – have taken on the patina of authenticity. With each projection on the screen, in print, or by recorded word they become more permanent and, in some respects, more plausible. For example, it is widely believed that " 'Kootenai' Brown was an Eton and Oxford man, who had been a member of the Guards." An even more romantic story appeared in the *Lethbridge Herald*, July 9, 1936:

> In Queen Victoria's garden on any sunny day in the late 1840's, a middle-aged man could be seen leading an amiable donkey laden with two heavy wicker baskets, and in each basket a happy child uttered shrieks of delight over the morning's fun. One of the children later became Edward VII of England, the other Louise Duchess of Argylle. [sic].
>
> A third party in the morning's activities could often be seen peering through the tall bars of the gateway watching his father, John George Brown,

gentleman, as he performed his duties as Queen's Overseer, and companion to the Royal children.

The boy who was born in the shadow of Balmoral Castle, whose life was destined to reach both the heights and depths beyond a wanderer's wildest fancies, never dreamed that he would become a trusted member of the Royal Household, and a wandering squaw-man on the lonely reaches of Western Canada.

This improbable account is just the sort of story that Kootenai would have relished for it contained enough of the might-have-been to make it credible to those who are less than critical. Certainly Kootenai's name was the same as that of Queen Victoria's famous ghillie, and he indeed may have visited Scotland briefly at one time in his life. But depots of the 93rd Highland Regiment at Paisley, Stirling, or Fort George are not Balmoral, and Victoria's John Brown, born in 1826, and never married, certainly would have created a legend if, at the ripe age of 13, he had sired Kootenai.

Stories such as these have become commonplace, and it is not to denigrate their authors that attention here is momentarily focussed upon them. Both have their place in the warp and woof of society and of every personality. The point rather is that such accounts about Brown have tended to obscure the real man, an unusual person in his own right. In turn, the real stories about Brown begin with the basic questions: Who was Kootenai Brown? Did he have an interesting life, one worth noting? Was he English, a public school graduate, a squaw man, the last of the old frontier scouts?

The fact that the answers to these and many other questions have varied over the years and are now compounded into an amalgam of half truths or wild nonsense and fixed by time is not surprising. They were already in the making during his lifetime, particularly after he became a civil servant in Waterton Lakes National Park. Most of the contemporary details about Brown were handed down second hand, as it were, by a growing number of visitors who glimpsed him as he toured the area during the course of his duties as acting Superintendent. Those who got to know him, and who later wrote about him, did so towards the end of his life. In many cases they were new to the West, and the age differential was marked.

To the newcomers, Kootenai, with his long white hair and his fringed jacket, represented the old west, a period about which they knew little and about which they tended to romanticize. Kootenai himself did little to dampen their interest in him or their enthusiasm for the western past. His stories of adventure on the plains, the rowdiness of Cariboo saloons, the thrills of hunting in the mountains or on the prairie were touched with an authenticity that compelled the attention of those who stayed to hear. His age, his position in the Park, his evident education, and the very contrast he afforded with contemporary society of the early twentieth century, all tended to give his stories an acceptance value that was rarely questioned. Again, the lack of skepticism was due, at least in part, to the prevailing climate of opinion which held throughout the west during its heyday: a man was accepted for what he was. Michael Holland, who acquired a ranch in the Porcupine Hills near Fort Macleod in 1890, and who knew Brown, summed up the prevailing attitude with admirable succinctness: "...in those days we did not enquire into the family history of strangers in the west of Canada."

Although Kootenai Brown was an unusual man in every respect, he also epitomized the traits which were essential to life in the American-Canadian west. Strong character and toughness of mind and body were basic to survival on the frontier. What makes Brown unusual is that he not only survived the turbulence of a rapidly changing frontier society, but that much of the record of his adaptation and progress has also survived. Too often in the history of western Canada and its pioneers, leads that appear full of promise or excitement peter out, leaving in their wake gaps and disappointment. To be sure, the points of contact with the past, and particularly with the quicksilver of an individual life, are all too rarely preserved in any detail. Certainly no Boswell recorded Brown's daily life, and whatever correspondence or other exchanges took place between the man, his family, friends or official organizations were not preserved with Lytton Strachey-like care. Even if such were the case, the biographer can only be humbled by Plutarch's reminder that "...very often an action of small note, a short saying, or a jest shall distinguish a person's real character more than the greatest seiges or the most important battles." Who was present in Kootenai's company to record the significant action or saying or jest, and to preserve it for future use? Obviously, no one. Nevertheless, much has been preserved, enough to fix the man in terms of time and place, and to enable the researcher to divine something of his personality. R. G. Collingwood, the historian, has put the problem of doing so into a perspective that applies with particular validity to the story of Kootenai Brown and his times:

> The historian's picture of his subject, whether the subject be a sequence of events or a past state of things, appears as a web of imaginative construction stretched between certain fixed points provided by the statements of his authorities.

The "fixed points" in the history of Western Canada and its pioneers tend to be limited and few. Conditions of life were hard, and personal records were rarely preserved. In Brown's case, however, they exist in greater quantity than for most of those who sought adventure and a new life in the West. In terms of significance to Canada and the Canadian west, the most important of Brown's "fixed points" is his interest in conservation and his part in the establishment of Waterton Lakes National Park. That alone is reason enough for remembering Kootenai. That he was, in his own way, an epitomization of the old west, adventurous, courageous, hot-tempered and lucky is, in a sense, an incidental bonus.

This book is based primarily upon original sources, and whenever possible, Kootenai himself tells his story. Where lack of direct or reliable evidence has made it necessary to project an "imaginative construction stretched between fixed points" the attempt has been clearly delineated. The difficulties of scholarship and writing that face every biographer are, even under ideal circumstances, formidable enough. One can only take comfort in the realization that the proper problem of any biographer is to assess the role of men in history and that the object is not a picture of the complete man or the complete society, but the "point" at which the two interact. In writing about an individual of less than front rank significance the problems of sources and interpretation are, if anything, even more challenging.

It is to be hoped that in Brown's case the portrait of the man and his times approximates at least a facet of reality.

Chapter 1

Brown's Early Life

On October 10, 1839, in Ennistymon, County Clare, Ireland, was born John George Brown, the "Kootenai" Brown of southern Alberta. The town, which is small and grey, sits brooding on the side of a hill overlooking the valley scooped out by the Cullenagh River tumbling over rocky slabs and waterfalls on its way to Liscannor Bay and the Atlantic some five miles away. On the coast the cliffs of Moher burst through the sea, rising to a height of over 700 feet. For almost five miles this great "Wall of Thomond," a skirt of foam constantly at its base, stands supreme, a stupendous bulwark against the ocean's ceaseless onslaught. Along its face ledges make ideal nesting sites for sea birds, and in the same context provide a refuge for flowers – sea pink, sea lavender, chickweed – from the wind and salt spray sweeping in from Galway Bay. From the cliff tops the Aran Isles appear like dark shadows against the background of ever-changing colour of the sea, while fulmars, herring gulls and puffins soar, wheel and whirr in the foreground.

Although the sweep of the landscape is wild and exciting, it is everywhere tempered by evidence of man's presence. Horses graze serenely upon the rolling grassy slopes of the cliff heights against a backdrop of stone fences and tumbled ruins. On the highest point of the cliffs the crumbling ruins of O'Brien's Tower, built originally to give warning of the approach of the wild Galway tribes, stands as a grim reminder of earlier, less settled days. It was into these surroundings that Brown was born, and it is against these contrasts that we see him at play for at least part of his childhood and early boyhood.

Little is known of Brown's parents. Ellen Finucane, his mother, was the daughter of Charles Finucane, a country doctor who practiced in that westernmost portion of County Clare. Little else in the way of direct family traces remain. A ruined church and old tomb-stones located above the town link the present with the past and indicate that Finucanes, at least one of whom was an M.D., did indeed live in or near Ennistymon.[1] For the rest, parish and other local records which may have revealed more about the family have been lost, destroyed in 1922 when many of Ireland's fine old houses and the country's Public Record office were sacked during the civil disorders.

From Kootenai's side, however, the picture is considerably clearer. His father, after whom he was named, was the second son of an Army officer, Captain John Brown, who served for 31 years "in the active and zealous discharge of his duties."[2] Indeed, and indicative of that service, Kootenai's father was born in South Africa on May 29, 1812, when John Brown senior's unit, the 93rd Highland Regiment, was stationed in the Cape of Good Hope during the Napoleonic wars.[3] Records show that the 93rd removed from Scotland to Ireland in February 1803, and that "on 30 July [1885]...embarked at the Cove of Cork for the Cape of Good Hope...where they landed on 6 January 1806."[4] There the unit remained in garrison until 1814.[5]

Interestingly enough, the year before the 93rd moved to Ireland, Kootenai Brown's grandfather, then with the Nottingham Fencibles Regiment, made the connection with Ireland a permanent and personal one by marrying Bridget Sophia Butler at Cashel, County Tipperary, on February 6, 1802.[6] As customary, he had his Colonel's permission to marry. Since there is no indication in military records of where John Brown was born, his connection, first with the Nottingham Fencibles and then with the Sutherland Highlanders, strongly suggests an English or Scottish family background. Ireland thus became a part of Kootenai Brown's life through his grandmother and the turn of her circumstances.[7]

When Kootenai's grandfather died on January 4, 1828, "from over-exertion in the good of the Service" in St. Kitts, British West Indies, where he commanded the Island garrison, he left his widow and six children, three girls and three boys, "wholly destitute."[8] Because it was clearly impossible to remain in the Caribbean, Bridget Sophia returned to England by the first available military transport and, after landing in Portsmouth in April, set about providing for her large family. From her temporary quarters at Milton Place she applied for a widow's pension, and for allowances for her children. At the end of July, having supplied the authorities in London with a memorial, proof of marriage, and the children's baptismal certificates, she was granted a provisional pension of fifty pounds per annum. That sum remained constant until her death on January 31, 1862.[9] Bridget Sophia's application on behalf of her children, however, did not fare as well. A letter from the War Office dated August 13, 1828, summed up the position with chilling candor:

Madam, I am directed...to acquaint you that your daughters Margaret and Sophia being above 21 years of age and your son James being more than 19 are ineligible for the Compassionate List. The other three children appear to be within the prescribed ages but as the amount of the Comp. [sic] Fund is limited, Sir H. Hardinge regrets that it is not in his power to grant them any allowances at present. Vacancies, however, on the Compassionate list will in all probability occur in the course of the year, affording him an opportunity of placing one or two of the children thereon, and after Christmas [Hardinge] will communicate to you his final decision and he trusts that at that time the state of the Compassionate Fund will be such as to enable him to meet your wishes without prejudice to the claims of others....[10]

While the news was disappointing, it was not entirely lacking in hope. In turn, the compartmentization of the War Office and slow administrative processing did not take into account changes in the family fortunes which by August, had already taken place.

Bridget Sophia, obviously a woman of resource and much determination, did not resort to or count upon receiving allowances for all of her children. Almost immediately upon arrival in Portsmouth she petitioned the Commander in Chief of the Army, Lord Hill, on behalf of her eldest son, James Montagu, who had been "born at sea on passage to Cape of Good Hope" in May 1809. Her case was a strong one:

The eldest son...received a liberal classical education and was noted in the year 1823 for an Ensigncy on the list of his late lamented Royal Highness, the Duke of York, with repeated assurances of being appointed to an Ensigncy in the 93rd Regt. and subsequently strongly recommended by Lieut. Colonel the Honbl. [sic] Sir Charles Gordon through General Sir Hudson Lowe, and after the demise of his Father...strongly recommended by Lieut. Colonel McGregor commanding the Corps through Major General Mainwaring commanding His Majesty's Forces in the West Indies, as a young man worthy of succeeding to the Ensigncy in the Regiment caused by the death of his Father. He was, however, destined to see [upon] his arrival from the West Indies another appointed in his stead. There is now a vacancy caused by the demise of Lieut. Smith at Antigua in the 93rd Highlanders, and as my son has so long been held in expectation of being appointed, Humbly Trusts your Lordship will kindly interest yourself in his behalf and appoint him to the vacant Ensigncy."[11]

The appeal struck home. Written in Portsmouth on April 15, within days of disembarkation, it resulted in James Montagu's appointment as Ensign without purchase in the 93rd Regiment two days later. In her straitened circumstances the happy result must have given Bridget Sophia great satisfaction. It also foreshadowed an even more determined and protracted correspondence with high military authorities many years later on behalf of her grandson, John George "Kootenai" Brown. In the immediate sense, however, Bridget Sophia's plight, thus lightened, was further relieved when the War Office, as intimated by Sir Henry Hardinge's secretary, in July 1829 granted each of the three younger children, John George – Kootenai's father – 17, Charles 15, and Isabella Marion, an allowance of twelve pounds per annum.[12] Her family thus provided for, Bridget Sophia sometime during this period returned to Ireland, settling in the vicinity of Clonmel, Tipperary.

The choice was a sensible one. She originated from the region and, although records are lacking, there is always the possibility that members of her family were still in or near the town. Certainly some of her friends still lived in Clonmel, including a Mrs. Catherine Fitzgerald, also widowed, at whose house Bridget Sophia and John Brown were married.[13] Then, too, the area is a pleasant part of Ireland – Clonmel means, literally, land of honey – a region of contrasting, fertile farmland and hills, with the town nestling at the base of the Comeragh Mountains. In those days, too, British Army units frequently were stationed in the vicinity of the county's principal towns, Cashel and Clonmel amongst them. Bridget Sophia' s residence, Munroe House, in the parish of Ardfinnan, soon became the focal point for the children: for the eldest daughter Margaret, a spinster, who remained at her mother's side; for James Montagu, who also never married, during his leaves and a long period on half-pay between regimental appointments; and, eventually, for Kootenai Brown. It is from this point that the story of Kootenai Brown begins to emerge from the base of family background.

The exact date Kootenai's father married Ellen Finucane in 1838 is not known since the original marriage bond was destroyed in 1922, and only the index to Killaloe and Kiffenora Marriage License Bonds remains. Similarly, it is not known if the couple had more than the one child born on October 10,

1839. Tragedy, however, is known to have struck the family, for when Kootenai was still very young he was orphaned. Although the circumstances are not known, the possible causes of the parents' death are not difficult to surmise. Ireland throughout the 1840's was a land seething with political discontent.

The demand to repeal the Act of Union passed in 1801, which was organized by "Swaggering Dan" O'Connell, reached a peak in the autumn of 1843, symbolized by huge mass rallies and the great Irish leader's arrest by the British authorities. Although O'Connell was released, Ireland became a sullen land of hostile, lawless, oppressed and poverty-stricken people. With the failure of the potato crops through disease, disaster in the form of famine and unusually severe weather reached into every corner of the country. It is against the spectacle of the soup kitchens, the starving bands of beggars bringing with them the horrors of relapsing fever, louse typhus, and baccillary dysentery, and wholesale emigration triggered by hunger, that we must accept the deaths of Brown's parents.

It is against such a backdrop that we see the young Kootenai removed to his grandmother's house, there to be brought up under the surveillance of Bridget Sophia, her eldest daughter, and from 1847 until he rejoined his regiment eight years later, the continuing presence of James Montagu, chafing under the limitations of a Captain's half pay and a gnawing desire to return to his unit.

Munroe House must have been a haven of security and comfort compared with the hunger, turbulence, and unrest which was the lot of the majority of Ireland's eight million people. At the same time, Bridget Sophia's household provided Kootenai with two advantages that were singular factors in his life: a knowledge and awareness of the wider world as seen through the eyes of his grandmother, aunt, and uncle, and an education that directed him towards a career in the British Army. As Bridget Sophia's letters to the War Office make clear, young Brown's education was achieved at considerable expense and sacrifice on her part. Writing to Lord Hardinge in June 1855, when Kootenai was on the threshold of coming of age, she made her position perfectly clear:

...I am most anxious to obtain an Ensigncy in Her Most Gracious Majesty's service for my grandson Master John George Brown who is now of an age and fully qualified to enter the Military Profession. I have not the means to purchase for him. All I can do is to give him a good education which, with the long services of all his progenitors both in the Army and Navy, will, I trust, place his cause with your Lordship and induce you to place his name on your list of candidates for a commission in Her Majesty's service without purchase.[14]

Bridget Sophia's difficulties in bringing up young Kootenai and her anxiety over his future are revealed more clearly the following year in a letter to the Military Secretary, Sir C. Yorke:

I am anxious that his labours and exertions to qualify himself for the Army, to say nothing of all the expense and trouble I, his widowed Grandmother, have been put to in order to educate him for the military profession should not be overlooked....[15]

Because of the family background and despite financial limitations, young Kootenai may have been educated in much the same way as his contemporary and future travel companion, A. W. Vowell. The son of a lawyer in Clonmel, Vowell attended local grammar schools and rounded out his education under a private tutor, before being commissioned in the Irish Militia.[16] Even if Bridget Sophia's means did not permit employment of a tutor, her own experiences of travel and life in South Africa and the Caribbean, supplemented by those of Kootenai's uncle, James Montagu, must have had some impact upon the boy.

James Montagu not only brought with him the experiences of soldiering with the 93rd Highland Regiment in distant parts of the British Empire; he also brought to the household "a liberal classical education" that could be related to the social and military experience of service at home or abroad. "Born on board ship on passage to the Cape of Good Hope" where the regiment was posted on its first foreign tour of duty, James Montagu, through his service, epitomized the family's military background as well as the restlessness that later characterized his nephew.[17]

When he arrived at Munroe House at the end of 1846, James Montagu had spent four years on duty in the West Indies, and three years in Upper Canada (1838-1841) following the rebellion led by William Lyon Mackenzie. There, while stationed in Toronto, Brown's uncle undoubtedly saw the ebb and flow of traders, trappers, settlers and Indians as the frontier community pushed its way stubbornly north from Lake Ontario into the surrounding wilderness. The opportunity of "travelling with dispatches to New York" provided further contrasts, and these experiences, together with a multiplicity of others, undoubtedly became a natural part of conversation in Bridget Sophia's household during James Montagu's prolonged residence.[18]

Apart from introducing the glamour of Army life and far off places into Munroe House at Clonmel, the presence of James Montagu for eight years was symptomatic of the prime problem all serving officers with limited means had to face since the creation of a permanent force in the seventeenth century: promotion by means of purchase. Under the purchase system a man bought his commission and then paid for each subsequent advance in rank. Exceptions to this general rule were few.

Resting as it did upon the theory that rank and responsibility could only be entrusted to those who had a substantial stake in the country, the system was rarely breached. Only in times of emergency, or in unusual circumstances and generally upon compassionate grounds were exceptions made, and they were relatively few in nature and number. Thus, when Kootenai's uncle went on half pay as a Captain in January 1847, he did so simply because there was no vacancy for his rank in the 93rd Regiment's establishment, and because he lacked the means to transfer to another unit where there was a place.

In addition, because he did not have money enough to transfer, he certainly did not have enough money for the more expensive matter of purchasing a promotion. As a result, like many other officers who were forced to leave their regiments, he had to wait in enforced idleness until an emergency brought a recall to the colours, or until fortune or talent provided enough capital to make possible a return to active service. In James Montagu's case, it was Britain's involvement in the Crimean War which triggered his return to active service with the 93rd Highlanders.

Resentment against the purchase system was widespread and opposition, beginning soon after the Napoleonic wars ended, mounted steadily. Indeed, the very year that James Montagu became "unattached," *The Times* of London spoke out thunderously against the purchase system:

Society abounds with military men who attribute their low positions in the Army, or their retirement from it in disgust, to nothing but the purchase system – they had no money so how could they get on?

18

Despite mounting opposition from all quarters, influential and conservative-minded men such as Palmerston and the Duke of Wellington, remembering that the system was introduced originally to prevent the Army from being a stronghold of military adventurers, resisted change, maintaining that "if the connection between the Army and the higher class of society were dissolved then the Army would present a dangerous and unconstitutional appearance."[19] The system, as its numerous critics constantly pointed out, lent itself to many abuses, and Kootenai's uncle through his service and by his presence in Clonmel, illustrated them to a nicety.

One particular and common abuse centered upon the custom of avoiding uncomfortable service abroad either by voluntarily going on half-pay, or by exchanging, at a price, to another regiment. Again, when a fashionable regiment had to do a turn of duty in some uncomfortable outpost of empire, it was notorious that a different set of officers were posted from that which had been on duty at St. James's Palace or the Brighton Pavilion. When the regiment returned, the overseas duty officers – most frequently from India postings – dropped out and a wealthier set took their place. Discussion of these and similar problems must have been commonplace during James Montagu's enforced sojourn. Initially, they did not greatly concern the young Kootenai Brown. Ultimately, however, the purchase system impinged directly upon his life and, in its own way, profoundly affected his future.

While the presence of James Montagu exemplified one of the most common features of the purchase system, the Captain on halfpay commissioned "without purchase" also provided an example that the system could be breached. As young Kootenai grew older his upkeep and education became increasingly burdensome upon his grandmother's resources. "All his friends could do for him is among them – to allow him a small annuity to help him out of debt."[20] Accordingly, and not surprisingly under the circumstances, the family's thoughts turned more and more to the possibility of obtaining a commission for the boy "without purchase." Soon after James Montagu rejoined the 93rd, leaving Munroe House and his mother, sister, and nephew, Bridget Sophia took the first determined step to establish young John George in a military career. Using her own son's entry into the army as a useful datum, and recalling her husband's long service, she wrote to Lord Hardinge, then Commander-in-Chief, with customary candor and directness:

> Being the widow of the late Captain Brown 93rd Highlan-ders who died in the West Indies from the effects of that pestilential climate after long, arduous, and zealous service of Thirty one Years and being also the mother of Captain J. M. Brown 93rd Highlanders at present employed with his Regiment on active service, I am most anxious to obtain an Ensigncy in Her Most Gracious Majesty's service for my grandson Master John George Brown who is now of age and fully qualified to enter into the Military Profession. I have not the means to purchase for him.[21]

It was the start of a prolonged, stubborn duel with the War Office and, in its own way, a direct assault upon the purchase system.

Ten days later, Bridget Sophia forwarded a copy of her grandson's baptismal certificate to the Military Secretary at the Horse Guards in London "for the information of the General Commanding in Chief."[22] On November 13, a scant month after Kootenai's birthday, she again addressed herself to Viscount Hardinge, reminding the military authorities that "Mr. John George Brown for whom I am most anxious to obtain a Commission in her Majesty's Service without purchase has now fully attained his age of 16 years."[23] As a result, a week later Kootenai's name was "from a statement of his Grandfather's services placed on the list of the General Commanding in Chief for a commission in Her Most Gracious Majesty's Service, without purchase as soon as he has passed the necessary examinations."[24] From this point the level of expectation and apprehension rose perceptibly in Bridget Sophia's household. Ultimately the boy was requested "by a communication from the Horse Guards...to appear at the Royal Military College [at Sandhurst], at 10 o'clock in the morning of the 1st July 1856" to attempt the prescribed examinations.

Information about the nature of the examinations taken by Brown is scanty. The standards and requirements for entry into the Army undoubtedly varied for until 1858, when the Council of Military Education was established, there was no body that dealt with such matters. However, since the examinations were written at Sandhurst – they could be attempted twice – it is reasonable to assume that they were the same papers that were attempted by young men who wished to become officer cadets at the Royal Military College.

The entrance qualifications for the College, an establishment intended for young men whose families could afford fees and maintenance costs of more than one hundred pounds per annum, required candidates to be able to write from dictation in English, to have knowledge of arithmetic, including decimal fractions, the first rules of Algebra, Latin, French, or German, the geography of England, Scotland and Ireland, and an ability for "printing the ordinary Roman Characters with neatness and facility."[25] Merely appearing in Camberley to attempt the papers involved "considerable expense, anxiety and study" for Bridget Sophia and young Kootenai.[26] As it was, the boy "passed with the greatest possible credit, obtaining extra marks for proficiency on several points."[27] With the examinations over and the results known, Kootenai returned to Ireland, hopefully to wait the news of an appointment to a regiment.

Anticipation of a new exciting life, heightened by a brief but tantalizing glimpse of a wider world and tempered by the knowledge that the boy had done well in competition, now began to grip the household in Clonmel. Bridget Sophia betrays the importance that she attached to her grandson's performance. When a month passed and no news came she wrote to the new Commander in Chief, the Duke of Cambridge, pointing out Kootenai's excellent results in the examinations, and that "his Father was born in and his Grandfather and Uncle had served for nearly 50 years in the 93rd Highlanders."[28] She then entreated that the Duke "graciously take the long and faithful service of my husband and son into [his] kind consideration and be pleased to appoint my grandson to the first Ensigncy that may offer in that Regt. [sic]."[29] Her petition failed to move the military authorities and young Brown remained unplaced.

Undaunted by the rebuff and undoubtedly spurred on by necessity, Bridget Sophia, towards the end of October 1856, wrote to General Yorke, the Military Secretary: *"I am anxious that his [ie. her grandson] labors and exertions to qualify himself for the Army to say nothing of all the expense and trouble I, his widowed Grandmother, have put to in order to educate him for the military profession should not be overlooked. I humbly entreat that you will be graciously pleased to lay a statement of his merits and the claims of his family before His Royal Highness, the General Commanding in Chief and use your interest to have Mr. John George Brown appointed Ensign in Her Majesty's Service as soon as possible.*"[30]

The reply, civil as always, pointedly stated that there was no hope without purchase. Still undeterred, Bridget Sophia, on the last day of December 1856, again wrote to Yorke repeating her claims and requesting once more "to have this young Gentleman appointed to an Ensigncy in any Regiment in Her Majesty's Service in or about to proceed to India or elsewhere."[31]

The new year, 1857, began with the standard refusal from the War Office. It also brought about a new tactic on the part of Bridget Sophia and her grandson. Instead of writing on the boy's behalf the old lady instead instructed Kootenai to write a personal memonal addressed to the Duke of Cambridge. Written from "The Cottage, Ennistymon," at the end of May 1857 – the place of writing suggests that relatives on Brown's mother's side still resided at Ennistymon – the appeal repeated the arguments and used phrases put forward by Bridget Sophia from the moment she initiated correspondence with London.[32] It was no more successful than the other petitions, for the reply dated June 1 made it clear that there was little hope of the boy obtaining a commission without purchase.

At this point in the family fortunes, events far removed from Clonmel and the Irish landscape began to impinge upon the personal situation of Kootenai Brown. News of the Indian Mutiny reached the British Isles, and a shudder of indignation ran through the population. Bridget Sophia returned at once to the fray, taking up her grandson's cause asking, with her customary directness, that the boy be commissioned in the 93rd Regiment. A minute noted on her letter of July 4 sums up the military authorities' position with graphic brevity: "already told 'no hope no pur[chase]'."[33] An emergency abroad and Bridget Sophia's determined interest were enough to dismiss London's refusal as a passing phase. Little more than a month later, she pointedly indicated that she was still aware of regimental movements in all their implications:

Having been informed that an Augmentation of 2nd [sic] Battalions to the Regts. [sic] in India is likely to be made, I humbly and most earnestly entrust that you will be so very kind as to bring the claims of my grandson Mr. John George Brown before His Royal Highness the Commander in Chief ... to have this most promising young Gentleman appointed to an Ensigncy in the 93rd or any other Corps in Her Majesty's Service.[34]

Although doomed to refusal like the rest of her appeals, the petition shrewdly struck to the heart of a situation which, in terms of her grandson, grew more favorable each day.

Once the Indian Mutiny became a factor in the battle for Kootenai's commissioning, Bridget Sophia, sensing her opportunity to press the boy's case, did so with renewed vigour. A standard refusal to her letter of August 10 simply resulted in a stronger and longer communication a fortnight later:

He studied hard and obtained extra marks for superior answering, and feels deeply disappointed at not being Gazetted to some Regt.... Were I able to purchase for my poor boy gladly, most gladly would I do so. All his friends could do for him is among them to allow him a small annuity to help him out of debt. Trusting that Justice may be done to us, now that another war has broken out and that the most awful events in the history of India are occurring there and calling loudly on every noble and manly soul to ship for work for its safety and protection of those who are exposed to such unparalleled horrors, I remain...[35]

In the face of such an outburst of eloquence the reply, dated September 4, was, most decidedly, a disappointment. The notation in the Ireland Book epitomizes the prevailing policy for commissioning officers with almost brutal frankness: "Has been told there is no hope without purchase."[36] To Bridget Sophia, by then fully aroused to the justness of her cause, the reply from the Military Secretary merely served as another goad to action. Her reply, after a suitable interval for marshalling her arguments, strikes a note of mounting anger that is absent from her previous correspondence with General Yorke, the Military Secretary:

...as the widow, the Mother, and the Sister of zealous and active officers, who served their Sovereign and country in every quarter of the globe, I feel myself much aggrieved by the way in which the promise made me has been passed over. I was assured that when my grandson Mr. John George Brown should have attained the age of 16 and passed the necessary examinations before the Board at Sandhurst, he would be recommended for a Commission, in the Army *without purchase*. His name was transmitted from the Royal Military College to the Horse Guards as having passed a good examination on the 1st July 1856 and yet he remains unprovided for although each succeeding Gazette presents to the public the names of numerous Gentlemen to be Ensigns without purchase who have been noted for appointment subsequently which I being universally acknowledged that I have been very badly treated.... By this act of justice [Kootenai's appointment] happiness will be restored to the breast of an aged widow whose only and most anxious desire on earth is to see this orphan grandson holding a Commission in Her Most Gracious Majesty's Service. I confidently hope that the Noble and the Great in whose hands the Almighty has been pleased to place the power to grant will bestow the inclination to answer favorably my humble prayer.[37]

Once again, however, Bridget Sophia's eloquence and evidence of unfair treatment were to no avail. The reply from London, dated November 5, 1857, offered no hope to her or to her grandson.

The refusal, if anything, prompted immediate action. Five days later she again wrote the Military Secretary, pointing out that Kootenai was "most anxious to proceed to India."[38] She reinforced her request with a specific and telling reference to the unsettled condition of the sub-continent, and the rising losses as a result of action taken to put down the uprising:

When so many casualties are daily occurring among the British officers in India, some of whom are now neighbors and acquaintances, surely you will be graciously pleased to take our claims into consideration and grant my earnest humble request.[39]

Again, as had happened so many times before, the plea failed to move the authorities. A brief comment on the back of Bridget Sophia's letter, makes the point: "already told no hope."[40] Yet even as the unknown officer who wrote that phrase was preparing to acknowledge Bridget Sophia's letter, concern over the impact of the Mutiny upon Britain's position in India was beginning to manifest itself throughout the British Isles. To the politicians and to the military the situation, coming so soon after the Crimean War, constituted a genuine emergency. Accordingly, the general situation increasingly obtruded in young Kootenai's favour, countering, in effect, the almost routine refusal dispatched from the War Office. A memorandum dated December 7, in which details of Brown's *curriculum vitae* are noted, is marked by the notation "wishes to be appointed," suggesting that a different consideration was at least possible.[41] Less than a week later that suggestion was transformed into reality when John George Brown, on December 13, 1857, was commissioned as an Ensign "without purchase" in the Eighth Regiment of Foot.[42]

That the event brought joy and great satisfaction to a young man and an old lady is undoubted. After the long, dogged, dispiriting correspondence with a military bureaucracy far removed and, for the most part confirmed in its support of the purchase system, the appointment must have been a moment of singular release to all the residents of Munroe House. For young Brown, however, it meant an end to his boyhood and signalled the close of the Irish phase in his life. Once he took up his appointment with the Eighth he, in effect, left Ireland forever.

Before meeting the Examining Board at the Royal Military College, we can see young Brown preparing his subjects, head bent over books, or trudging to and from the classroom. After the journey to Camberley the focus becomes less sharp, and we can only imagine the activities and interests of a healthy, essentially outgoing boy of 16. The Comeragh mountains were there for climbing; the river may have provided opportunities, licit or illicit, for fishing; and there were always games, mischief, and chores around a house that lacked the presence of a male head.

Equally, it is not possible to divine the quality and temper of the relations between the boy, his grandmother, or his aunt Margaret. That they were amicable seems a reasonable assumption; indeed, the suggestion in Bridget Sophia's letter is that she was fond of the boy even though circumstances equally indicate that an appointment was a matter of strict necessity as well as family pride. Whatever may have been the real climate of Kootenai's days in Munroe House, Clonmel quietly and irrevocably faded from his life when he reported to the regimental depot at Chatham, Kent. He was then, as the Returns of Officer Service put it, 18 3/12 years old.

Chapter 2
With the Army in India

When John George Kootenai Brown joined Number 12 Company of the First Battalion Eighth Regiment on January 14, 1858, he stepped into an already half-familiar world, one that was inextricably interwoven into his family's background. Apart from any heightened awareness or possible expectations brought about by his grandmother's, his aunt's, or his uncle's stories of service life, indoctrination and routine at Chatham were certainly different from the particular order and pattern of existence at Munroe House.

His appointment eased the burden of upkeep which Bridget Sophia so pointedly referred to in her letters to the War Office, and the boy, for the first time in his life, enjoyed a regular if limited income of five shillings three pence [about $1.30] per day. Whether any part of that small stipend was allocated to Bridget Sophia is not revealed in the extant pay records.[1]

Whatever the young Kootenai may have thought about his appointment to the Eighth instead of the 93rd, it must have been tempered by two distinct factors: the excitement and anticipation fostered by the knowledge that reinforcements for the First Battalion were destined for duty in India; and, with every passing moment at the depot, growing awareness that the Regiment was a long established unit with an illustrious campaign record. Indeed, soon after Brown's arrival at Chatham the main body of the Eighth, which had been on service in India for almost twelve years, moved to Agra.[2] From there detachments were sent out "to engage bands of mutineers who infested the neighborhood of the cantonment."[3] Great distances and slow communication between the sub-continent and England made news of such developments late in filtering through to the companies readying themselves for service overseas. Whatever details reached Chatham clearly suggested that the Regiment, by taking part in such operations and by its participation in the relief of Lucknow in November 1857, was adding to its list of battle honours.

Formed in 1685 as the Princess Anne of Denmark's Regiment, the Eighth had made its mark in such notable engagements as the Battle of the Boyne (1690), Marlborough's great victories at Blenheim (1704), Ramilles (1706), and Malplaquet (1709), the resounding defeat of the French Army on the hot sands of Aboukir (1801), and, in addition, had seen service in Malta, the West Indies, and British North America. There the unit had stood garrison duty in Nova Scotia, and fought engagements at Ogdensburg and Lundy's Lane in 1813.[4] Thus, through the Eighth's connection with North America and through his uncle's service in Upper Canada, Kootenai was brought into perceptible if not conscious contact with that part of the world to which he was ultimately and finally committed.

During those initial months of 1858 young Ensign Brown, at the regimental depot, learned how to handle weapons and men, acquired a knowledge of the Queen's Rules and Regulations, and, above all, became aware of the unwritten code that in its own particular way is unique to each unit and which, at times, provides a more important datum than anything committed to print. With the exception of a return dated Brompton, Yorkshire, April 1, the monthly record of officers service for the First Battalion show Brown on strength at Chatham.[5] Presumably the exception pinpoints an exercise or a particular aspect of training that is not specifically recorded. In the October notation appear the significant words "Ens. Brown embarked at Gravesend on the 3rd September 1858 for Calcutta."[6]

The prospect of adventure implicit in a military career began to unfold. With it, too, came responsibility, for the young subaltern was put in charge of 21 private soldiers for the duration of the long uncomfortable passage to India, aboard the vessel *Octavio*.[7] Details of the draft, which was dispatched ahead of the replacement contingent, do not give any further information about the four-month voyage through the Tropics, around the Cape of Good Hope, or arrival in the torrid mid-summer heat of Calcutta. A monthly return, dated Camp Bewlee, December 1, 1858, merely notes "Ensign J. G. Brown enroute to join."[8] At the very moment of embarkation and while the new recruits were on the high seas, the First Battalion was undergoing some of its severest trials. A draft of reinforcements, fresh from England, which reached Fattehguhr in the province of Uttar Pradesh on the very day Brown and his men boarded the *Octavio,* arrived "in a most pitiful plight." A. C. Robertson, the regimental historian who commanded the Eighth during this period of its service on the sub-continent, records that "the survivors had no kits; many of them had not even boots on their feet."[9] Nearly half of the contingent was lost through action, and, not surprisingly, through cholera and other diseases.

While Brown and his 21 men were still on the high seas, and therefore unknown to them, the unsettlement stemming from the Mutiny subsided and the First Battalion, taking full advantage of the situation, began consolidating its forces. "The Headquarters of the Battalion ... joined the Field Force under Brigadier Hale, C.B., on the 17th October and marched for Fattehguhr on the 18th Idem."[10] A month later three of the Battalion's companies were "detached to augment Brigadier Barker's column" as the force under Hale continued to be "engaged in the subjugation of the Oudh Territory."[11]

Early in January 1859, almost at the time that the *Octavio* was rounding into port, "The Headquarters [sic] and left wing [of the Battalion] marched to Fattehguhr," which thus became the Regiment's operational base.[12] By the time "Ensign Brown joined [the] Services Companies on 3 February 1859," skirmishing in the region had died away and the familiar pattern of British military life in India started to reassert itself.[13] Instead of exciting patrols and action, the chief hazards which Brown and the other replacements met were boredom, climate and attendant illnesses described in the regimental returns as bowel complaints, fevers, and "venereal affections." For the better part of a year the Battalion, including the Headquarters company to which Brown was attached, remained in Fattehguhr. Brown, his name regularly noted in the monthly returns, carried out his duties in the sweltering heat of the day, attended the dinners that punctuated mess life, observed the landscape and the teeming masses, occupied himself with letters home, took part in shooting parties or hunting trips. Although in his later years he said little about his service in India, the sojourn, relatively brief though it was, made an impact, for Kootenai turned to the doctrines of Theosophy, and Helena Petrovna Blavatsky's writings inspired by her own experiences in India.

Brown's service overseas, as it turned out, was comparatively short – about a year and eight months from embarkation out to embarkation home. Towards the end of the year the Eighth, after almost 14 years of duty in the sub-continent, was recalled to Britain. Accordingly, the forward units of the First Battalion received orders on December 2, 1859, to proceed from Fattehguhr to Calcutta, there to prepare for embarkation, and the Headquarters and five companies reached Cawnpore on December 11. The five remaining companies arrived at the muster point on the first day of the new year.

While the hard work and frustrations of the posting kept the unit occupied, pomp, ceremony and pleasure also crowned the Eighth's last days in India. Before proceeding to Calcutta, the regiment was reviewed by Lord Clyde, who commanded the British Forces during the relief of Lucknow, and a ball was given by Lady Canning, wife of the new Governor General. Young Ensign Brown oscillated between the prosaic practical matters made necessary by the recall and the pageantry and pleasure. It is not difficult to picture him standing stiffly to attention or pirouetting with military precision in review order during the martial ceremonies, or wheeling and swooping his partners at the farewell ball, a glittering affair that contrasted vividly with the heat, grime, orders and activity which are the soldier's inevitable lot.

What memories of those days in India lingered in Kootenai's mind is difficult to establish. Certainly, he remembered and, at times, mentioned highlights of his service days in India. But, like so many things he noted, the details of time and place have been lost and in their stead have emerged romantic amplifications based on a shred of reality. Annette Christie, for example, writing in the *Calgary Herald*, April 13, 1935, claims that Kootenai's career in the Army ended abruptly when he shot a fellow officer. He then, she continues, made his way to Calcutta disguised as a native, boarded a windjammer loaded with nitrates – an improbable cargo to say the least – bound for South America. Equally imaginative is the claim made by Mary Flett, who was in Waterton Lakes when Kootenai died and who attended his funeral, that Brown "had been given an elephant by an Indian rajah in the east." [14]

In actuality, Brown's service overseas and, in some respects his Army career, came to a symbolic end with the regimental review and Lady Canning's ball. These functions, traditional and social, in their own way also signalled the end of an era in the British occupation of India. The Mutiny forced the British government in London to reassess its policies and practices in the sub-continent, and the decisions taken were already in the process of implementation as the Eighth was withdrawing from the land.

Sweeping changes, including measures dealing with sanitation and welfare recommended by Florence Nightingale, were on the threshold, exemplified by the appointment of a Governor General whose liberal outlook already had alarmed old India hands to the extent that he had been nicknamed "Clemency" Canning. Brown, unknowingly, had experienced India in the lingering twilight of the old East India Company's rule, a way of life and administration that altered rapidly as the British raj rose to its full glory in the last quarter of the nineteenth century.

Military reviews and balls, diverting pleasantries though they were, did not seriously impede the regiment's preparations to leave India. Bullock trains, river steamers on the Ganges, and rail were all put to use transporting men and equipment from Cawnpore through Allahabad and, eventually, to Calcutta. The advanced elements of the Eighth reached the port on February 13, 1860, the rest following in waves. While awaiting embarkation, volunteers were called for to serve with other British forces being dispatched to the Second Chinese War but Brown, significantly, did not step forward. Ultimately, on April 5, the first detachment embarked for England on the freightship *Monica*. It was quickly followed by two further detachments which were dispatched in the vessels *Lady Clarendon* and *Sevilla*.[15] Finally, on May 5, 1860, the Headquarters and remaining companies, with Brown as one of the 13 officers, boarded the *Clara*, a full-rigged vessel of 938 tons, for the long voyage home.[16]

Thus terminated fourteen years of Indian service. The four freight ships carried home twenty-one officers and five hundred and nine non-commissioned officers and privates. Among the officers who embarked at Calcutta, only two, Colonel Robertson and Quartermaster Keating, were with the colours when the Regiment left Portsmouth in April 1846.[17]

The attrition rate during service in India, as the Regimental historian suggests, was high.

During the return voyage, the *Clara* twice interrupted its passage by stopping at the East India Company's traditional calling points. Five days (July 1-6, 1860) were spent at Simon's Bay on the southwest coast of Africa. Taking on water and fresh provisions offered relief from the tedium of the voyage and a brief opportunity to stretch legs, have a change of diet and take a breath before tackling the trials of an equatorial crossing by sailing ship. The provisioning and other attendant operations must have been fairly normal for little about the stopover is recorded.

A fortnight later, however, we have the notation that on July 20 the vessel *Clara* called at St. Helena, that speck of an island, rising like a tri-turretted black castle from the wastes of the South Atlantic Ocean. There "the whole of the men were landed and marched up to the tomb of the Emperor Napoleon."[18] The opportunity of such a mass pilgrimage of military men is not surprising. St. Helena was regularly visited by East India ships on their return voyages to take on fresh water or to leave supplies for the British garrison, and in the case of the Eighth Regiment, it made good sense to give the troops a break from shipboard life, their last before disembarkation in England.

Colonel A. C. Robertson, the commanding officer and later the regiment's historian, describes his men, Brown among them, marching from the dock at Jamestown along the winding road climbing its way upward and inland for some five miles to the Valley of the Geraniums where Napoleon originally was buried. Roughly a mile from Longwood, the house where the great commander spent his last days, the tomb, quadrangular in shape, was, by the time Brown and the men of the Eighth arrived, surrounded by tall weeping willow trees.[19] By then, too, the body, together with the vases holding the heart and entrails, had been removed to France, to the formal splendor of Finnish granite and the graceful dome of Les Invalides in Paris.

There can be little doubt that Brown and his companions were moved as they paused before the tomb in that grove. In later years Kootenai spoke of the stopover in St. Helena, but his random recollections were variously interpreted by his listeners to be references to the state capital of Montana, itself the setting for an even more dramatic and unforgettable incident in Brown's life. The pause at St. Helena and the return voyage from India began the process of Kootenai's disengagement from his family and from the army.

During the return, Kootenai's uncle, James Montagu, had embarked with his regiment, the 93rd, in June from Gravesend and the two men passed one another in mid-ocean.[20] They never met again. While James Montagu, by then a Brevet Major, continued his career with the Highlanders, ultimately rising to the rank of Colonel, and commanding the unit before retiring in 1873, his nephew left the army and began a new life of adventure in the mountains and plains of North America.[21]

Early in September 1860, the *Clara* at last reached Spithead and, to their undoubted relief, the men disembarked at Portsmouth on the fifth. Eleven deaths — non-fatal illnesses are not recorded — occurred during the 124-day voyage.[22] Once on land, the Eighth moved to Gosport where it remained until its transfer to Aldershot in August 1861.[23] Apart from the experiences of the long voyage, the journey left Kootenai with a mess fee of five pounds, almost one quarter of his full pay of £23-12-6 for the voyage.[24] [About $100.]

As the regiment settled down in its quarters at Gosport and began the process of rediscovering the duties and practices of soldiering at home, Brown had the opportunity of reassessing his future. At the end of the year he obtained a fortnight's leave over the holiday season.[25] During that brief interval, December 14, 1860 – January 3, 1861, with memories of his recent experiences overseas still fresh in his mind, he travelled to Ireland to spend Christmas with Bridget Sophia and her eldest daughter, Margaret. Assuming that he did indeed spend his leave at Munroe House, Kootenai's recollections no doubt took on added meaning in the knowledge that James Montagu had, by then, reached India and perhaps was experiencing the very sights, sounds, and smells that impinged upon the young man's senses.

Bridget Sophia, well advanced in years, must have listened to her grandson's accounts with interest and, quite possibly, the boy's experiences stirred memories of her own travels, of James Montagu's birth "at sea on passage to the Cape of Good Hope," of the Caribbean, and the pleasures as well as problems of being a soldier's wife. Perhaps, too, she may have been on board a vessel that had also called at St. Helena, and could therefore savour

Kootenai's description of the Eighth's pilgrimage to Napoleon's burial place.

Brown's first leave, in some ways his disembarkation leave, was soon followed by a further two-week interval away from duty in March 1861.[26] Why he was granted further leave so soon is not indicated in regimental sources. The possibility that Bridget Sophia may have taken ill cannot be excluded. Equally, personal interests, or dissatisfaction and disillusionment with army life and the low returns of a subaltern's pay cannot be discounted. He was, at the time, fifth Ensign in seniority in the regiment and, with the purchase system still very much in force, prospects of promotion were obviously limited. In fact, without money, advancement was virtually impossible. The nature of the system ensured that only those who could afford to advance to higher rank did so:

> An officer, once commissioned, did not have to pay the full price for each step in rank; but only the difference in value of his old and new rank – the old commission being sold to someone lower down the list.[27]

With the initial price of an Ensigncy in the order of £450, and with the cost of a Lieutenancy approximately £700 Brown, in order to advance in his own or some other regiment, had to face the prospect of finding at least £300 [$1,500.][28] For entry into and further promotion in the exclusive cavalry or Foot Guards, prices of commissions and advancement were often more than double those for the ordinary infantry units. As *The Times*, February 27, 1860, put it in a discussion of commission costs, the prevailing rates were not the only governing factors in a military career:

> These [the reference is to prices of commissions in the cavalry which were listed as £80; £1901; £3225; £4575; and £6175 for the ranks of Coronet, Lieutenant, Captain, Major, and Lieutenant Colonel], to be understood, are the simple regulation charges, the prices recognized and established by the rules of the service. In reality, however, the expense of the profession was far greater than even these figures represent, for, by the private arrangements prevailing in the different regiments, the price of each step was so enormously enhanced that the ultimate cost of a Lieutenant Colonel was about £14,000.

Without reading too much into the limited evidence available, it is clear that prospects for young Ensign Brown, newly-returned from India, without private means, were far from bright. The frequency of his leave-taking thus takes on an added significance for it took time and some care to find a prospective purchaser and to finalize the "private arrangements" which so often characterized the sale of a commission.

After the Eighth regiment moved from Gosport to Aldershot early in August 1861, Brown again proceeded on leave, this time for the full month of September.[29] Regimental records reveal that by then he was the senior Ensign in the regiment, a position that strongly suggests that others previously listed ahead of him either purchased promotion or sold their commissions and returned to civilian life. Significantly, at the end of September 1861 Brown's name disappears from regimental records. In its place a new name, J. B. Sterling, appears, followed by the terse notation "Ensign vice Brown Retired 5 Nov. [sic] 1861."[30]

Interestingly enough the purchaser, Sterling, spent little or no time with the Eighth. In December 1861 he transferred to a more fashionable and exclusive unit, the Coldstream Guards.[31] As for Kootenai, pay records for the period July 1–September 30 which were made up at the regimental depot at Templemore, County Tipperary, Ireland, reveal that he was listed as being transferred to that point for the interval September 6-30.[32] The entry suggests strongly that it was from there that Brown concluded the final severance arrangements which terminated his career in the British Army. From the standpoint of family and friends, the depot at Templemore was a sensible choice for doing so. Only a few miles north of Clonmel, its proximity to familiar ground was reassuring and reduced travel time as well as any other expenses connected with release to a minimum.

While we will never know with certainty what prompted Brown to sell his commission, his subsequent actions reveal his motives with a measure of clarity. Army Service abroad obviously did not quench his desire for further adventure. Lack of opportunity coupled with the dream of further excitement and the acquisition of untold riches provided the spur to action which resulted in the dramatic decision to emigrate to the goldfields of British Columbia. Whatever personal incentive Brown had for lingering in Ireland dissipated when, on January 31, 1862, Bridget Sophia, the dominant force in his life, died. Sometime during her last days, for the records are not specific, he left the British Isles "for the Panama Isthmus," never to return.[33]

Chapter 3

In Search of the Golden Rainbow

Brown was 22 when he "left England for the Panama Isthmus ...with a friend named Vowell."[1] Neither the choice of destinations or the selection of a travelling companion were accidental. Since the first discoveries of gold on the Fraser River the British Isles were thrilled by the possibility of a major strike in that westernmost region of British North America, a strike comparable in richness and excitement to that of the California discovery a decade earlier. Attention focussed upon the area while interest rose steadily, inflated by glowing tales, most of them written by individuals who themselves had never left the British Isles, of riches easily available to those willing to seek them out. Kinahan Cornwallis, for example, in a book entitled *The New El Dorado* published in 1858, told his readers that "all nations had been awakened to the knowledge of another El Dorado, outvying all besides."[2] In a particularly dramatic passage, Cornwallis unashamedly pitched his appeal to the downtrodden and exploited workers of the new industrial society, to:

> ...men who have been groping in the hazy squalor or poverty for years in this country, and might remain so forever, may at once take a plunge into the arena of wealth and all its attendant glory by embarking for the golden shores of our dazzling El Dorado.[3]

One can imagine the impact of such stirring appeals upon a young man such as Brown, newly-returned from India, faced with the frustrations of a career in the army limited because he lacked money, or the alternative prospects of making his way in civilian life in an Ireland not yet recovered from the famine years, or in Victorian England then rounding into full imperial glory. As the young subaltern settled into Gosport with the Eighth regiment, news of the gold discoveries on the northwestern area of North America were amplified by newspaper accounts of spectacular strikes at Antler Creek, and at Rock Creek in the Boundary country.[4] Elaborate and far-fetched schemes and organizations such as the British Columbia

Overland Transit Company were put forward or formed to transport men, machinery, and goods to the diggings.

Even the Bishops of London and Oxford met to look into the necessity of populating the new colony of British Columbia (proclaimed in 1858) with reliable people. From their talks emerged the British Columbia Emigration Society headed by Baroness Burdett-Coutts, and the ultimate despatch of some sixty women to take up posts as domestic servants. In such a climate of prevailing opinion the sale of an Ensign's commission and the booking of a quick passage to Panama, the first stage of the long journey to the Cariboo, was neither unusual nor unexpected.

Nor was Brown's partnership with Arthur Wellesley Vowell entirely surprising. The son of a prominent lawyer in Clonmel, Vowell served on garrison duty as an officer in the Irish Militia during the Indian Mutiny, retiring in 1860 as a senior Lieutenant. Since he was educated in "the grammar schools of Clonmel," and served in army depots in Ireland, Templemore probably among them, it is not amiss to suggest that he and Kootenai knew one another long before they linked fortunes and set course for British Columbia.[5]

The social set in which Bridget Sophia, her daughter Margaret and, while he was resident in Munroe House, James Montagu, moved was relatively small and in Clonmel must have brought families such as the Vowells and Browns into an awareness of one another, if not into direct contact. Again, it was not possible to be commissioned in the British Army unless one were a professed member of the Established Church. In Catholic Ireland Anglicans were a decided minority. The probability is that the two young officers from the same area were acquainted.

Although precise details of their journey to the Isthmus of Panama are lacking, in 1861-1862 there were many ways of getting across the Atlantic and the time of passage, compared with the voyage of the *Clara,* was relatively short. The Royal Mail Steam Packet Company ran a semi-monthly service between the British Isles, the West Indies, the Eastern coast of South America, and Aspinwall (Colon) on the Isthmus. Its fleet of 23 large steamships operated out of Southampton and other British ports and, as advertisements in the *British Colonist* (Victoria) claimed, afforded "speedy conveyance of Treasure, Goods and

Passengers to and from England to British Columbia and Vancouver Island in connection with the Pacific Mail Steamship Company's vessels and the Panama Railroad."[6]

If the company's modern vessels or the two "screw steamers" operated by Holts' Company out of Liverpool were too expensive for prospective gold seekers, the Panama Railway operated sailing vessels which ran on a monthly schedule between Liverpool and Aspinwall. With excitement and anticipation at a peak, with time an essential factor and with money on hand, we see Kootenai and his companion Vowell boarding one of the speedy steamships for the three-week voyage to the golden Isthmus.

From shipboard their first impression of the new world may well have been one of excitement, tempered by the impact of a landscape radically different from anything in the British Isles, or in the compass of Brown's experiences en route to and from India. From the sunlit sea of the Caribbean a wall of green mountains rises abruptly, towering over coral shores; a canopy of dense jungle steaming in the hot still air covers every vestige of land, while each intermittent breeze drifts the sweet smell of rotting vegetation across the water. This was the Darien coast first seen by the Spaniard Balboa, and this was the scene, scarcely altered, which met Brown and Vowell's eyes.

To Brown, Panama was "a queer place," one that impressed itself vividly upon his memory:

> I thought I knew something about hot countries – I had recently lived in India – but the heat in Panama was different to that in India. When rain fell on our hands or face it was almost hot enough to scald.... We found white men keeping stores at Panama and Colon the two terminals of the railway. The soldiers were a queer-looking lot, dressed in khaki with bare feet. The natives seemed to fish for a living and for recreation they gambled and promoted cockfighting. I have travelled a good deal in my day but a more miserable crowd of people it has never been my misfortune to behold.[7]

Brown's impressions certainly are borne out by other travellers. W. Champness, who traversed the same route to the Cariboo in the spring of 1862, describes conditions of life on the Isthmus in strikingly similar terms:

> On landing at Aspinwall our first impressions of the Isthmus were not very agreeable; as we found the temperature there intensely hot, the skies overclouded, and a close, damp, sickly feeling pervaded the atmosphere. We did not make any stay here but at once proceeded across the Isthmus by rail to

Panama.... Even a delay of a few hours, amid the hot and almost steaming morasses and jungles of the district, often produced long continuing or fatal illnesses.[8]

While every prudent traveller left the Isthmus as quickly as possible, Brown and Vowell were not so lucky. According to Kootenai, an accident to the steamer on which they were scheduled to sail to San Francisco forced them to stay over and to endure the harsh climate and high prices. Rather than sit around in Panama, the western terminal of the railway, and endure the stench and squalor of the town, the two young men seized the opportunity to explore the Chagres River by boat. Their initiative not only enabled them to fish and shoot – they bagged one alligator, according to Brown – but miraculously, to escape serious illness. "Panama Fever" and cholera were the most frequent afflictions, with the latter exacting a particularly heavy toll of those who ventured into the region. In the particular cases of Brown and Vowell, robust health and youthful desire for new experiences were unquestionably responsible for their physical well-being. The rigours of an outdoor life chosen by the young men were, as Champness suggests, less dangerous than staying in the settled areas:

A very unmistakable proof of the indolence of the population hereabouts is furnished by their gross inattention to the simplest sanitary measures. The dead bodies of their numerous mules are allowed to decay in the most offensive proximity to human dwellings and thoroughfares.[9]

Probably, too, a hunting-fishing trip along the Chagres was cheaper than the cost of living in the two terminal cities on the peninsula. In 1861–1862 there were at least a dozen hotels providing varied accommodation and daily rates varying from one to four dollars. It was sound practice as F. N. Otis, the historian of the Panama railroad noted, "to have terms understood well beforehand since the hotels normally did little business except on the arrival of the passenger steamers."[10] The traveller thus ran the additional hazard of being exploited by rapacious hostellers who were prepared to take advantage of any opportunity that became available.

Apart from the high cost of living and the discomforts of an enforced stay on the Isthmus, Brown and Vowell found transportation between Colon and Panama expensive and frustrating. Kootenai complained that although "the distance was not very great...travel was very slow. It took us four hours to go twenty-two miles.[11]' The railway engines burned wood, while the combination of weather and jungle growth made repair and maintenance a continuous problem.[12] The fare for the total rail distance of 47 miles – $25.00 per passenger with baggage not exceeding 50 pounds, with an additional charge of 10 cents for every additional pound – often made travel a costly necessity.

Even with their prudent withdrawal from the urban centres of the Isthmus, Brown and Vowell spent more in reaching San Francisco than they anticipated. The price of passage from Panama to San Francisco ranged from $140.00 for first-class accommodation to $52.00 for steerage. In early 1862, the two adventurers boarded one of the Pacific Mail Steamship Company's four vessels, *Golden Age, Golden Gate, St. Louis, or Sonora,* which ran regularly between Panama and San Francisco, two of some 15,000 to 20,000 persons annually attracted to the Pacific coast from all parts of Europe and North America. They thus became part of the stream of travellers whose characters varied as widely as their dreams:

> The fact that the steamers afforded the quickest and easiest means of travel to California and, of course, the gold fields of B.C. meant that persons of substance – officials and distinguished travellers – as well as many others went over this route. This was increasingly true after the pioneer years, when ships and Isthmian connections were improved to give satisfactory service.... Judges and financiers, generals and naval officers, gamblers and women of bad character travelled by way of the Isthmus because it was the obvious way to go to the persons who could afford it.[13]

Whether Brown and Vowell could afford it is a moot point. The unexpected delay on arrival in the Isthmus certainly cost them time and money and, in the end, interrupted their progression to the goldfields. Brown described their experiences in brief but telling terms:

> We landed at San Francisco in the early part of '62, and my friend Vowell and myself drove a team hauling goods from the old wharf up town.... The old wharf was built of piles and timbers with plank floorings and it was so full of holes that you had to be an experienced "skinner"...to keep your team from getting their legs broken. That was my first experience with horses, and I had a bad time of it. I didn't like it a bit but I was broke when I landed in San Francisco and had to do something. My friend was not a skinner either, so we only stayed till we had a little stake and "vamoosed" for the north. [14]

Until they "vamoosed," the two inexperienced skinners whipped and cursed their horses over the piles that projected nearly a quarter of a mile over the beach, carting their loads into the lower part of the city. It was the toughest part of the town, the area that attracted and housed the roughest of the transient population. There were frequent deaths, according to Champness, "from unwary persons falling or being thrust, at night, into the water, through some of the large openings occurring at intervals in the supermarine streets."[15] Many murders, he added, "have thus taken place."[16] The work was hard, prices were high, "much in excess of those...in Europe or the Atlantic States," and there was always the lure of the gaming tables, saloons and brothels, all of which flourished in abundance.[17]

Once Brown and Vowell saved their small stake, they probably boarded one of the three Oregon and California Steamship Company vessels, *Sierra Nevada, Cortez, or Columbia,* for the regularly scheduled run to Victoria. The vessels ran on a trimonthly schedule, and cost of passage ranged from a high of $50.00 for first-class accommodation, to $25.00 for steerage. The journey was comparatively short, four days under good conditions, 10 days at worst. It was also quite straightforward. Most travellers who boarded the vessels at San Francisco say little about the voyage. The prospect of journey's end must have been uppermost in their minds, and the aura of excitement tended to blot out minor complaints or discomforts. Few men, Brown and Vowell amongst them, at that stage of their quest were aware of the distance or hardships that still lay between them and the gold-bearing creeks of Cariboo. A small handbook produced in 1862, the year that Brown and Vowell reached Victoria, pinpoints the lack of hard information which characterized the rush:

> At the time of the first Fraser River rush from San Francisco in 1858...men who had undergone all classes of hardships in pursuit of gold in this country [ie. California], were surprised when at Victoria, they were as far from the mines as when they left San Francisco....[18]

Accordingly, and significantly, the authors of the handbook prudently suggested that "the outlay necessary to enable [a prospective miner] to go and return in case of failure...ought not be less than $300.00 and that used with great care...."[19]

Vowell noted that he and Brown reached Victoria in February 1862. That month, according to *The British Colonist,* five vessels, of which three were schooners and two steamships, docked in Esquimalt harbour. Few details of those who arrived

Above: James Douglas, governor of the Crown Colonies of Vancouver Island and British Columbia, referred to by Kootenai Brown as the "...head bamboo chief." At top right is Brown's partner, Arthur W. Vowell.

Victoria in the early 1860s. The rocks at bottom right were part of street work done by convicts while wearing two, three-foot-long leg irons which weighed 14 pounds and were shackled to their ankles.

by schooner are recorded, although the passenger list of one, the *Tolo*, was printed. One Brown, no other details, is included in the list of travellers which disembarked from the steamer *Brother Jonathan*, which docked on February 28, but Vowell's name is conspicuously absent.[20]

When Brown and Vowell reached Victoria it was a small rough-hewn settlement clinging to the southern tip of the Saanich Peninsula on Vancouver Island. Feverish building operations were in evidence everywhere, and it is estimated that in the year in which the two young Irishmen arrived some 1,500 "substantial structures" were standing on land which two years earlier had been covered by virgin forest. By 1863 the population "had increased to 6,000, and that not counting the large number of miners who yearly wintered there."[21] Kootenai's recollections of the town reflect its rude frontier condition and simultaneously reveal that for him the long journey to reach what was merely a jumping-off point for the goldfields had been a costly one:

Victoria in 1862 had no idea of ever becoming a capital of anything. It was just one of those little places. Any prairie town in Alberta [Brown was speaking just before the start of the first World War] is as big as Victoria was then.... Only an occasional boat landed at Victoria and it carried adventurers looking for various forms of excitement on the Pacific.... Chopping poles in the vicinity of Victoria kept me afloat during my short stay of one winter. The most interesting man there I remember was Governor Douglas [then Governor of Vancouver Island and the mainland colony of British Columbia] of the Hudson's Bay Company, who was head bamboo chief.[22]

By "chopping poles" Brown replenished his pocket-book, worked up a grub-stake, and together with Vowell "in early summer of that year...went to the Cariboo lured there by the gold excitement."[23] They were by no means the only ones to set out for the diggings:

During the spring of 1862, 4,000 miners pushed up the Douglas Road and Fraser River trail to Cariboo and 1,000 travelled the old brigade route through the Okanagan Valley to Alexandria. Most of them were on their way to Williams Creek.[24]

While Brown and Vowell had no real way of knowing that so many others who shared their dreams of quick riches would also share the rigours of the trail, they went forward hopefully, secure in the knowledge that they were at last approaching the destination for which they had set course so many months before.

42

Chapter 4

The Goldfields of Cariboo

By the time Brown and Vowell crossed the Strait of Georgia and began the arduous trek into "the sea of Mountains" that is British Columbia, great changes were transforming the interior. In May 1862 Governor Douglas, the great "bamboo chief," ordered the Royal Engineers to begin work on the most difficult stretch of the Cariboo Road, a six-mile section from Yale toward Boston Bar and nine miles from Cook's Ferry or Spences Bridge along the Thompson River.

Construction of the remainder of the great wagon road, 18 feet in width and covering a distance of 400 miles, was contracted out to civilians who were paid in cash, bonds, or were given the right to charge tolls over those portions of the route for which they were responsible.[1] Against this background of rapid construction and magnificent engineering, Brown and Vowell, together with a host of unnamed others intent upon the same purpose, made their way to the goldfields as quickly as resources, stamina and luck permitted.

In many respects the initial phase of their journey, the stretch from Victoria to New Westminster, then a small town consisting of "one long broad street," wooden houses and an assortment of tents, was the easiest. It took only one day and, according to Fery and Wight's handbook, cost five dollars. If prospective miners wished, they could go all the way from Victoria to Cayoosh Flat by a combination of boat and stage following the route from New Westminster to Port Douglas, then Pemberton, Lillooet, Anderson and Seaton Lakes, for a cost of $21.75.[2] In theory, the journey took little more than a week to eight days; in practice, the schedule was rarely kept and the cost of maintenance en route rose accordingly.

An alternative route "of the most rugged and precipitous nature" followed the direct line of the Fraser River by way of Hope, Yale, Lytton, and Fort Berens. However, only the hardiest and steel nerved chose to follow the trail beyond Yale as it

Discovery of gold on Williams Creek, above, created the rush which attracted Brown and Vowell to the Cariboo through 400 miles of wilderness. The creek yielded over $1,000 a foot.

The famous photo below, taken on August 20, 1863, by C. Fulton shows the Cameron claim on Williams Creek. It yielded some $1 million in gold, equivalent to about $30 million today. Sitting with the gold pan on his knees is John A. "Cariboo" Cameron whose share was estimated at $300,000. He nevertheless died a pauper and is buried overlooking the creek that was so bountiful to him.

wound its way along the precipitous cliff face high above the swiftly-flowing Fraser. Most travellers preferred instead to follow the alternative route of lakes, rivers, and portages to the west. Whatever choice Brown and Vowell made, however, they still were obliged to contend with the physical hardships which characterized the journey: changeable mountain weather, mosquitoes and flies, food of variable quality, and the inevitable competition with other rough and ready men who shared the road and sought whatever shelter or accommodation happened to be available. Champness, who travelled to the Cariboo at approximately the same time as Brown and Vowell, portrays the prevailing conditions, making it clear in his conclusion that the interior of British Columbia was no place for weaklings:

> Of all our colonies there is none where physical strength, patience and good temper are more essentially indispensable than here. It is utterly useless for persons of weak constitution or feeble powers of endurance to attempt the expedition to the up-country mines of Cariboo and the Creeks.[3]

Champness, in his account of his journey to the Cariboo, echoed a general feeling of disillusionment which so many hopefuls felt, and which was as much a part of the Cariboo experience as the excitement generated by the gold rush:

> We had constantly to experience the utter fallaciousness of certain writers who have sent glowing reports of this land and its advantages.... We met numbers of strong and active men who would have gladly given their hard labour even for their food, without any other remuneration; but their services found no employ. And it is a fact that we saw a crowd of men standing around a butcher's slaughter house waiting for the offal of a bullock to be thrown amongst them. This they seized like a pack of hounds.[4]

As it transpired, such warnings did little to impede the influx of men and women to the region.

Brown's and Vowell's experiences in the Cariboo certainly paralleled those of the majority who found their way to the gold-diggings. Like the others they, too, travelled hopefully, arrived, then came away with little but their belongings and memories. Vowell was the first to give up:

> His mining experience was not profitable from a financial point of view and he returned to the coast. He came to Victoria where he lived until 1864, when he joined the Civil Service....[5]

With Vowell's return to the gentler climate of Victoria, the partnership which brought them so far, ended. While Vowell subsequently went on to a distinguished but orthodox career that included such senior posts as Gold Commissioner in the Kootenays and Superintendent of Indian Affairs for British Columbia, Kootenai remained at the diggings before experiencing further adventures on the western plains.[6] As he himself put it: "...I have always had a roving disposition and since '62 I have seen most of western America and in its roughest state."[7] By the time Vowell headed back to the coast, the Cariboo was changing perceptibly. Mining became a costly affair, very different in scope and scale from that which marked the start of the gold rush a year or two earlier:

> Around Billy Barker's shaft below Richfield Canyon, miners were excavating holes and tunnels and erecting water-wheels, twenty feet in diameter, to work pumps. The hills were becoming denuded of trees and an ugly little village, perched high on logs, was beginning to take shape. In actual fact, three towns strung for five miles along Williams Creek were emerging: Richfield above the Canyon, Barkerville below the Canyon and Camerontown, where in December 1862 "Cariboo" Cameron struck gravel so rich that twelve one-gallon kegs yielded $155.[8]

It was in this setting that Brown spent the next two years.

As winter suspended all operations but those in the deepest diggings, the five communities – including Van Winkle and Lightning – took on an increasing air of permanency. Weather and lean pickings tended to weed out the flotsam and less reliable elements amongst the miners, and forced those who chose to remain to improve their quarters. Out of the original 4,000 to 6,000 who reached the diggings in the summer of 1862, it is estimated that five or six hundred remained in or around Williams Lake. Despite isolation, the men wintering in their moss-chinked, mud-roofed huts equipped with large fireplaces enjoyed a rude sort of social life and spent their time mostly in conversation and cards:

> Judge Begbie noted that the miners who had taken up residence in the shanties along the gulches and the creeks were of a different type: it appeared to him, he wrote, judging from the men whom he met in Cariboo, "as though every good family of the east and of Great Britain had sent the best son they possessed for the development of the gold mines of Cariboo."[9]

Without the capital necessary to continue the costly business of deep digging, the coming of cold weather forced Kootenai to seek a different way to make a living:

> My first winter in Cariboo I went in with a fellow on a trapping venture. We made about $3000 in about three months trapping marten. This gave me

46

my start in mining and I made a good many times that much and lost it in the next year.[10]

Just how Brown lost his money he never said. The cost of mining operations and commodities were certainly factors. During the summer of 1862, for example, *The British Colonist*, July 22, 1862, reported that shovels and axes sold for $10.00; coffee fetched $1.50 per pound; flour retailed at $70.00 per hundredweight; and whisky, the standard antidote for sickness, injury and despair, brought $12.00 to $18.00 per gallon, quality and strength unknown. With the advent of winter transportation costs rose, commodities grew scarcer and prices in the winter settlement around Williams Lake rose proportionately. Apart from the high prices for commodities or necessities, there were other ways of losing money. The temptations of gambling and strong drink were ever present, but at least one saloon in Williams Lake provided an additional innocuous attraction in the form of billiards at a dollar a game. *The British Colonist*, September 10, 1862, offers another possibility, and simultaneously reveals the wide social variations characteristic of a wide open frontier community:

> The prostitutes on the creek – nine in number – put on great airs. They dress in male attire and swagger through the saloons and mining camps with cigars or huge quids of tobacco in their mouths, cursing and swearing and looking like anything but the angels in petticoats heaven intended they should be. Each has a revolver or bowie knife attached to her waist, and it is quite a common occurrence to see one or more women dressed in male attire playing poker in the saloons, or drinking whisky at the bars. They are a degrading set, and all good men in the vicinity wish them hundreds of miles away.

While life in Cariboo was hard and uncertain in its rewards, the very nature of the society which flowered in that remote vastness created conditions which spawned trouble. The prospect of easy money attracted men, and as *The British Colonist* so pointedly observed, women of dubious character, with the result that brawls, robberies and even killings were not infrequent. The murders on July 26, 1862, of three men, Charles Rouchier, H. Lewin and David Sokolosky, Jews whose names Kootenai couldn't remember, who were carrying between $10,000 and $12,000 in gold between them, suggests the dangers that lurked everywhere.

At the end of the 1862 season Brown, like many other fledgling miners, sought more permanent quarters for the winter layover period and for that reason went to Williams Lake. In October he witnessed his first frontier-style shooting fray:

I was at Williams Lake House for the night and there was a big crowd. As usual a monte game was in progress, but because it was a slack season in mining the stakes were small. Gilchrist, a professional gambler, was dealing Spanish Monte. Now to make this story clear, I'll have to go back to San Francisco. It appears that some years before this night...Gilchrist had a dispute in a card game in Frisco with another man whose name I cannot recall. The two pulled guns but were separated by friends. They, however, vowed that if they ever met again they would kill on sight.

While Gilchrist was playing inside the saloon at Williams Lake House, his enemy from San Francisco rode into camp. A man who knew them both said to the newcomer: "your old enemy is inside dealing Monte."

After the stranger had put his horse away he came into where the game was in progress, but Gilchrist did not notice him as he was "keeping" the game. The visitor approached the table and threw down a twenty dollar gold piece on a card. This was rather in excess of the amounts that were being played that night so Gilchrist looked up to see who had plunked down the gold. Instantly, both pistols were pulled. The newcomer missed and somebody threw up Gilchrist's arm, and his bullet missed the man he intended it for, but flew across the room and struck a young Englishman right in the forehead, killing him dead.

Most of us, when the shooting had begun, made for the doors and windows, and the room was partially cleared. When we saw the young fellow fall we rushed back. The trouble maker from 'Frisco managed to get his horse and got away, and we never saw him again. Gilchrist, the man whose shot found a victim in the Englishman, came back with his six shooter in his hand."[11]

The case came before Judge Matthew Baillie Begbie, that stern unbending man whose chancery court terrified the miners, at Williams Lake towards the end of October. By then, Kootenai was far from the scene of the shooting, preparing for the winter's work of trapping. In recalling the event, Brown evokes something of the atmosphere that electrified the crowd in the saloon and, in the process, reveals a facet of his own personality. Judge Begbie's report to the Colonial Secretary buttresses Kootenai's observations providing, simultaneously, the contrast of a contemporary record as well as a portrait of the social conditions prevailing in that outlying region of the colony:

The only 2 serious offences which may be considered as of a normal nature were, in the one case wholly, in the other principally through the exertions of the people apart from the police, brought to formal trial, and in both cases the criminals were sentenced to penal servitude for life. The first of these was the case of Gilchrist who in an affray in a drinking saloon at Williams Lake (believed to have been got up with the view of shooting an old adversary of Gilchrist's) shot an inoffensive bystander named Pearce through the brain. The whole story was, as alleged, one of the ghastly parodies by which in California it is too often attempted to turn the administration of justice into a horrible farce.

Gilchrist, having an old grudge against a man named Turner, and having threatened to shoot him "on sight," raised a pretended dispute with an Irishman, which soon attained the necessary degree of violence to make it quite natural in Gilchrist to draw his revolver. "Friends" of course threw themselves on Gilchrist so as to divert the pistol from the Irishman – but instead of hitting Turner, the bullet lodged in the brain of Pearce. This would have been of course "death by misadventure" in California – in England, Gilchrist would probably have been hung – in British Columbia it is not perhaps an altogether unsatisfactory result that Gilchrist was convicted of manslaughter and sentenced to Penal servitude for life, while "his friends" (who are well known to the police and to me) have left the colony and are not, I think, likely to return. It is very satisfactory to state that Gilchrist was seized and detained in custody until my arrival in Williams Lake entirely by the inhabitants themselves.[12]

Certainly British standards of justice prevailed, and certainly the remainder of Brown's time in Cariboo could scarcely have been more exciting.

For the next year and a half, trapping and mining fully occupied Kootenai. He toiled long hard hours in the midst of the great lonely splendours of mountains and rivers, making his way through the winter stillness, or playing cards, indulging in horseplay with friends and spending money in crowded saloons. By his own admission his efforts did not result in a spectacular strike or riches that may have been the stuff of dreams in far-off England and Ireland:

I had no money when I went into Cariboo and I had none when I came out in 1864, but I had a little fortune for awhile in between. Like thousands of other miners I made and lost a fortune in two years. When I left Williams Creek I had fifty cents in my pocket; my clothes were in rags; I had no shirt and no socks, but I had a pair of good boots. When I got to Boston Bar, a little village on the Fraser River, I still had fifty cents in my pocket.[13]

Being broke is an unsettling experience at the best of times and Brown had no choice but to accept whatever employment was available. Accordingly, he looked for a job, and soon found work transporting provisions and tools for the gold-mining camp in Cariboo by boat and raft as far up the Fraser River as water conditions permitted:

It was no easy job, but, while it took a good man to do it, no man wanted to do it unless he was broke and down on his luck. From Boston Bar up river for twenty-five miles was a mad channel of white water. Huge canoes made of cedar logs, carrying five tons of cargo...had to be cordelled – that is hauled with a rope by the crew on shore – all the way. It took four days to make the twenty-five miles up stream from Boston Bar to Kanaka Bar....

We were paid $6 a day and board on the boats on the Fraser River, but the work was no sinecure. Sometimes the boat would stick and we would have to take the cargo ashore and "pack" it with hand straps a couple of miles or more over the sides of mountains impassable to horses and wagons. [14]

Such heavy, dangerous work could only be an interim measure borne out of necessity. As soon as he recouped himself beyond the level of "a coat, braces, pants, boots and hat," he turned to something more compatible.[15] As he himself put it:

After my experiences on the Fraser River I was made a constable at Wild Horse Creek (now Fort Steele) and in that capacity I saw some unusual things.[16]

Wild Horse Creek – it was first called Stud Horse Creek but the name was soon changed – a stream flowing into Kootenay River about fifty miles north of the International Boundary, was on everyone's tongue as news of a new gold strike spread through the colony in 1864. By the end of the summer, almost a thousand men were in the area exploiting the shallow diggings. Most of the population in the Kootenays were Americans who had come from the mines at Boise, a rough mobile crowd of men prepared to move to a new strike with a minimum of formality or notice. The Wild Horse diggings created new problems for the Colony of British Columbia – those of maintaining law and order and administration in the area, and providing a communications link that would enable merchants in Victoria and New Westminster to establish trade and commercial connections with the Kootenay communities.

In order to assess the situation, Arthur N. Birch, the Colonial Secretary, travelled the 500 miles of rugged trails from Hope to Fisherville, the main settlement in the strike area, in the autumn of 1864, and reported that over 700 men were living in a small town which sported three restaurants, several stores, a large brewery, saloons and the usual characteristics of a recently-established mining camp.[17] Although Carmichael Haynes arrived as Gold Commissioner in August charged with maintaining law and order, "the wild boys" were difficult to control and the Kootenay district, to all intents and purposes, was an American enclave within British territory. Such conditions, in fact, were the basis of Peter O'Reilly's transfer from Cariboo to

A collection of buildings which appeared around the rich claim of a miner called Billy Barker, inset, was named Barkerville in his honor. It was claimed to be "The largest community north of San Francisco," but in 1868 burned down. It was rebuilt, although its golden sun, like that of Billy Barker who died a pauper, had set.

　　Barkerville became almost a ghost town, but the B.C. Government began an ongoing restoration program and today the community attracts tens of thousands of visitors a year. The building at the end of the street is St. Saviour's Church, completed in 1870 and still in use.

the Kootenay as Gold Commissioner in the spring of 1865, and for Brown's appointment as Constable. Brown's appointment was made in either February or March 1865.

In a letter from Judge W. G. Cox dated Richfield, March 27, 1865, there is reference to an earlier communication dated February 8 from Birch, the Colonial Secretary, dealing with an appointment to an unspecified post in the Kootenay district. Cox, in his reply states, "Mr. Brown having private business of importance to transact at New Westminster, will proceed at once to that place and report himself to you."[18] An item in *The British Columbian*, April 13, 1865, brings Brown into sharper focus:

> From Mr. Brown, of the Police Department, who left Williams Creek on the 30th of March ult. we have obtained the following items. The weather on the creek was warm and pleasant during the day with keen frosts at night.... Provisions were dear and scarce. Flour was $.75, and other articles in proportion.

There are no further indications in official or public sources about the kind of business Brown had to transact in New Westminster, how long he remained in the comparative comfort of that community, or the nature of his interview with the Colonial Secretary, Arthur Birch. It is clear, however, that the post provided Brown with the certainty of employment at an annual stipend of £300 [about $1,500]per annum, and an opportunity to see for himself if there were any possibilities of striking it rich. Although the dream of doing so had faded in the cold realities of Cariboo experience, it nevertheless remained alive, nurtured by each new rumour and the perennial call of the unknown.

In New Westminster, Kootenai was inducted into the Colony's Civil Service and then set out for the gold diggings at Wild Horse Creek, following the standard trail through Princeton, Similkameen, Osoyoos Lake, Rock Creek, and Kettle River, and then over what subsequently became part of the Dewdney Trail; that is, up Boundary Creek to Grand Forks, past Christina Lake to the headwaters of Sheep Creek, across to the Columbia near what is now the city of Trail, down the Columbia to Fort Shepherd and, finally, by way of Moyie and Cranbrook to Wild Horse Creek.

The time on the trail naturally varied depending upon the season, but *The British Columbian*, July 15, 1865, notes that a William Read, bearing government dispatches, left Wild Horse on June 21 and reached the capital of New Westminster in 15 days. The route runs through spectacular country ranging from the heavily treed mountain slopes of the coastal mountains to the majestic valley of the Columbia and the drier heights of the Kootenay country. For a young man like Brown, in the prime of health and moved by nature, it was a welcome antidote to his failure in Cariboo and the hard work of freighting on the Fraser. Although the journey into the interior was arduous it provided, in a sense, a peaceful interlude before the responsibilities and dangers of a peace officer thrust themselves upon Brown. They were not long in coming.

Soon after Kootenai arrived at the diggings, he was obliged to carry out a difficult and potentially dangerous assignment. His recollection of the incident which took place in June 1865, is accurate and couched in characteristic language and style:

Three men came into Wild Horse and succeeded in passing several thousand dollars worth of bogus gold dust. It was an amalgam composed of 75 per cent copper, 5 per cent lead and 20 per cent gold. It was a very good imitation....

Well, these three fellows – Kirby, Conklin and a third whose name I forgot...these three brought in the amalgam, bought goods and paid for them with it. They were pointed out to me at once and I marked them as suspicious-looking characters. When it was discovered that a lot of bogus nuggets were in circulation on the creek, I went to arrest the three strangers. They were living in a one-roomed cabin and I knocked at the door. Getting no reply, I burst open the door and Kirby grabbed for his gun. I had him covered and I called out to him: "Throw up your hands or I'll make a lead mine of your carcass."

While I was getting Kirby out of the cabin, the other two escaped. After putting my prisoner under lock and key, I organized a posse and we were not long in locating Conklin and his pal, both of whom were also put behind bars. Just after this happened and before the prisoners could be brought to trial, I...left Wild Horse Creek. My successor, whom I recommended to Judge Cox as a suitable man for the job, had a streak of bad luck with the three men I left him in the jail.

Among the pieces of good advice I offered the young fellow [Brown was not yet 26 himself] was never to allow more than one prisoner out at a time and never, on any account, to turn his back on a prisoner. I regret to say that one morning he thoughtlessly disregarded this advice and let all three out at a time to wash for breakfast. He turned his back for a moment when Conklin "put the mug on him" (threw his arm under his chin and held his head back) then gagged and tied him. Then they took his horse and what money he had, his clothes and his gun and made a clean get away. The jail was in a lonely part of the creek and their escape was not known till the butcher called for the meat order. He knocked at the door but got no response. Returning with a blacksmith, the lock was pried off and on entering they found the constable bound and gagged and locked in a cell, but the cells of the prisoners were empty. A search party was organized but no trace of the desperadoes was ever found.[19]

The official account of the attempt to pass counterfeit gold and subsequent developments is dry and sparse. Peter O'Reilly, writing to the Colonial Secretary at the end of June, informed Birch about the arrest with minimum elaboration:

I have the honor to report for the information of His Excellency the Governor Frederick Seymour, that I have this day committed for trial at the next assizes to be held at Kootenay, three prisoners "Jos. Conklin," "Wm. Kirby," and "Ozias Harvey," the first for importing into the colony, and having in his possession a quantity of counterfeit gold dust amounting to several hundred dollars, purporting to be from "Boise," and the two last for circulating the same. All three are men of notorious character from the adjoining Territory.[20]

Roughly a fortnight after the three counterfeiters were committed for trial, Brown, the chief architect in their arrest, resigned from his post as Magistrate's Constable. His letter to the Gold Commissioner, O'Reilly, dated Wild Horse Creek, July 15, 1865, was brief and to the point:

In consequence of the good reduction of pay which has lately taken place in the Police Service and finding it impossible to live at the present rate of wages, I beg that you will accept this, my resignation, of my situation as Constable.[21]

Brown's resignation from the Colonial Civil Service, along with that of the Customs Clerk, a man named Young, was forwarded to New Westminster on July 24. Acknowledgment by the Colonial Secretary's office, however, was not made until September 11. The immediate cause of Kootenai's retirement is clear. The reduction in pay to which he so pointedly referred was part of an economy drive undertaken by the Colony's government, and indeed O'Reilly, at the end of the year, spoke of dispensing with the services of five constables, thus saving British Columbia an annual expenditure of £1,500 [about $7,000].[22] Certainly, on the basis of prevailing prices for food and equipment Brown's action is understandable.

Most supplies came from the United States, being packed into the gold diggings from Lewiston, Walla Walla, Wallabula, and Umatilla Landing, often at a cost of 20 to 24 cents per pound. Beef was even driven all the way from Salt Lake City. On the whole, the general run of prices was lower than those which prevailed in Cariboo during the two years Brown spent there and, unlike the northern diggings, food was comparatively plentiful. At the end of May 1865, flour sold at forty-five cents per pound, bacon fetched seventy-five cents, beans fifty cents, sugar seventy-five cents, dried apples sixty cents, tobacco $2.50, liquor twelve to fifteen dollars a gallon, gumboots ten to twelve dollars and candles seventy-five cents.

Two other motives for Brown's resignation exist. The bubble of confidence which marked the rush to Wild Horse Creek was pricked as the shallow diggings were exhausted, and as the news of an allegedly more fabulous field on Canyon Creek near the Big Bend of the Columbia River filtered through the community. As a result, the drift from Wild Horse began in the dead of winter and it was not unusual to see miners, snowshoes on their feet and packs on their backs, heading for the new site two hundred miles to the north.

The exodus was well in train when Brown reached the Kootenays and, while he had prudently staked a claim near the mouth of the creek, he realized that the reason for the movement and the general unsettlement it created was due to the simple fact that the mining operations on the Wild Horse, Findlay, and Fisher Creeks had become deep diggings too expensive to be operated by individuals. At the same time, with the prospect of a drastic reduction in salary and with the cost of living rising, he may well have tried to escape the scissors effect of such conditions by returning to the uncertainties of mining.

There was always the possibility that fortune would smile, and that he would become the Billy Barker of the Kootenay strike. Accordingly, after his resignation Brown began working claims along Wild Horse Creek. By then Big Bend commanded the Colony's attention, and provided hopefuls with an "all-absorbing theme."

While Brown resumed prospecting, the Gold Commissioner, Peter O'Reilly, reported in mid-August to New Westminster "the prisoner 0. Harvey, who was sometime since committed for trial charged with passing spurious dust, escaped from gaol on the night of the 15th instant.[24] Although not recaptured immediately Harvey, one of the men taken into custody by Brown, was eventually retaken and imprisoned in the isolated jailhouse from which he made his escape. Less than a month later, he and the other two men rounded up by Brown, before the latter's resignation, escaped and successfully evaded capture.

O'Reilly reported the incident to the capital immediately in a letter dated September 13, 1865:

...On Sunday the 10th instant the three prisoners, Wm. Kirby, Ozias Harvey, and Jos. Conklin, who were in custody charged with passing bogus gold dust, affected their escape from the gaol through the most culpable negligence on the part of Constable Lean who was the officer in charge at the time.

I regret that all our efforts to recapture them have been insufficient and I have little doubt that immediately on quitting gaol, they were provided with horses wherewith to effect a speedy flight across the line.[25]

The report ended with a terse and pregnant sentence: "Herewith I beg to forward the resignation of Constable Lean."[26] Obviously Constable Lean, "the young fellow" to whom Kootenai offered the sound advice of never allowing more than one prisoner out of the cells at any one time, failed to put it into practice.

With the attempt to pass counterfeit bullion drifting to its sorry conclusion and the end of the summer fast approaching, Brown, too, began to wind up his affairs at Wild Horse. The manner of concluding his business typified the place, the time, and certainly the man, while his account of the episode sums it up with pungent brevity:

I had been placer mining in the Cariboo district of British Columbia for two years and came down to Wild Horse Creek, where with four others I staked a claim near the mouth of the creek. It was not "panning" very well, so we sold out to a company of Chinamen for one hundred dollars apiece and one horse. We took twenty-five chips apiece and gambled for the horse – and I won.[27]

The Chinese to whom Kootenai and his partners passed on their claims were labourers who reached the Kootenay district while working on the Dewdney Trail. Many remained in the Wild Horse area and persisted in working the shallow diggings with limited success, while other men such as Brown, or the American miners from Boise, headed to more promising areas.

With their claim successfully sold, with official responsibilities sloughed off, Brown and his partners headed into the unknown, lured by the possibility of better luck in a new site, and inevitably, fresh adventures:

Having disposed of our holdings on the creeks, the five of us packed through the South Kootenai Pass and soon after started for Edmonton, where we heard they were mining placer gold on the Saskatchewan River. We had no very clear knowledge of where Edmonton was, and there was no one to tell us.[28]

For Brown it was the end of an exciting, varied, and precarious existence – that period in his life spent in the hurly-burly of turbulent mining camps nestled precariously amidst the grandeur of magnificent mountain scenery.

When, on the strength of rumour, he and his companions crossed over the great divide into the Flathead country of what is now Montana, Brown exchanged the limitations imposed by pick, shovel and mountains for the mobility demanded by the prairies, and for a life that was even more hazardous. The contrast is exemplified by the landscape through which the five men passed.

Debouching from the mountains, they were thrust into the great rolling plain of Western Canada which flattens and merges into the horizon, a merciless land that imposes its own conditions on all who venture upon it. Kootenai's break with mountains and lakes, however, was not permanent. Eventually, although he loved the variations of the great lone land, Brown compromised by settling in the shadow of the Rockies. When he ultimately returned to Wild Horse many years later it was for a very different purpose, and under very different circumstances.

Chapter 5

Pony Express Rider

When Brown and his unnamed companions pierced the mountain barrier of the Rockies and looked out from the eastern entrance of the South Kootenay Pass across the vast expanse of British North America, the plains were still wild and unpeopled. Between the mountains and the Red River occasional trading posts, maintained by the Hudson's Bay Company, provided fixed navigation points and contact with the settled world of eastern Canada and Europe. Otherwise, across the southern reaches of the empty land adjoining the United States border ranged the Blackfoot, Blood, Peigan, Sarcees, the plains Assiniboines, Cree and Sioux Indians, Métis and French half-breeds, following the ebb and flow of vast buffalo herds or, in the decade preceding Brown's arrival, occasional expeditions such as the one led by Captain John Palliser.

Indeed, until the Palliser expedition of 1857-1860, the majority of fur traders and travellers who had penetrated into the area followed the traditional route along the North Saskatchewan River through country that is vastly different from the treeless landscape to the south. By travelling east through the mountains from Wild Horse Creek instead of heading north to the new gold diggings on the Big Bend of the Columbia River, or returning to New Westminster or Victoria, Brown and his partners proved themselves to be unusual men. Although they were by no means the first white men to cross the relatively flat, dry Tobacco Plains, brown as its very name suggests, and to pass through the Flathead River country with its beautiful valley surrounded by mountains, they were certainly in 1865 among a small handful to accomplish the feat:

> Other white men had probably crossed the [Kootenay] pass before, men like the Canadians Hugh Munroe and Picard; some half-breeds had certainly, in 1865, done so, including the group of returning emigrants led by Whitford, whom Palliser had met at Fort Ellice, but [Lieutenant Thomas] Blakiston was equally certainly the first white man whose crossing [in August 1858] was put on public record.[1]

Apart from such isolated ventures by white men, the Kootenay Indians crossed the mountains every summer to hunt buffalo, returning with enough meat and hides to exchange for blankets, tobacco, knives, and other necessities at a small trading post on the Kootenay River – Fort Kootenay – maintained by Hudson's Bay Company men who came there each winter. The Indians followed the easier, less steep South Kootenay route over the divide, so that the trail was fairly well marked.

In addition, the Kootenays, as Lieutenant Blakiston in his report noted, were an open, hospitable people willing to act as guides or to provide information.[2] Moreover, since they were also horsemen it is possible that Brown, whose nickname was derived from this unusual tribe, may well have obtained mounts and additional supplies for the journey across. The route followed by Brown's party therefore must have been fairly straightforward to follow and reasonably easy to negotiate, for they had no difficulty in reaching the eastern slopes of the Rockies.

After the parched dryness of the Tobacco Plains and the close fastness of the mountain pass, their first glimpse of the comparatively green eastern countryside was a breathtaking, unforgettable moment:

Emerging from the South Kootenay Pass we hit the foothills near the mouth of Pass Creek and climbed to the top of one of the lower mountains. The prairie as far as we could see east, north and west was one living mass of buffalo. Thousands of head there were, far thicker than ever range cattle grazed the bunch grass of the foothills. We killed a three-year-old bull just at the entrance of the pass. None of our party up to this time had ever seen a buffalo.

I had three horses. I was riding one and had the other two "packed." Each one of the others had a horse and between them two pack horses. As we rode through the mass of buffalo, the great beasts just moved off slowly. We made a lane of only about one hundred yards and they paid little attention. When we fired on them they would run off a few hundred yards and begin grazing again. We only shot for what meat we needed and we packed this on our already heavily packed horses.[3]

The continuation of mountains, lakes and prairie, merging as they do in the southwesterly portion of Alberta, and the great mass of buffalo, made a lasting impression upon Brown:

I recall my first impression of Kootenay Lakes, now known as Waterton Lakes.... Coming down from the mountain, where we got our first glimpse of the buffalo, we soon reached the prairie shore of a large lake at the further side of which a mountain rose to a sofa-like peak among the clouds. This mountain was afterwards called Sofa Mountain and is so named on the topographic maps of that region of the Rockies.[4]

The beauty of the scenery, with the red and green argillites streaking Sofa and the other peaks mirrored in the long narrow channels of the two Waterton Lakes, is as unforgettable now as it was on that autumn day when Brown first came through the South Kootenay pass. It impressed itself upon Blakiston seven years earlier. Himself an ornithologist, he promptly and without hesitation named the lakes after Charles Waterton, that eccentric English ornithologist, the first man in the British Isles to establish a bird sanctuary on his Yorkshire estate.

Once launched upon the prairies with horses, supplies, rifles and ammunition it was easy enough to travel across the vast expanse. There were numerous hazards of course, some a natural part of the country such as weather and wild life, some introduced by the intrusion of man:

Around Seven Persons Creek we found hundreds of rattlesnakes and were not anxious to camp there very long. We saw very few coyotes on the open prairie, but hundreds of wolves ran the country in bands.... A few coyotes were encountered in badlands, coulees and foothills where they are found today [ie. circa. 1914-1916]. At the time of which I speak, there roamed all along the south branch of the Saskatchewan River hundreds of grizzly bear, small grizzlies, but grizzlies just the same. Buffalo, mired in the quicksands when fording the stream became their victims.[5]

From the moment the travellers reached the plain they knew that they were in hostile Indian territory. Whether they got their information from the Kootenays, or from traders en route it is impossible to say. Brown does not reveal his source; the important point is that he and his companions were well aware of the dangers they faced:

It was Blackfoot territory then and we knew it and were watching for them.[6]

The encounter was not long in coming:

My first conflict with Indians was at Seven Persons Creek, near what is now Medicine Hat. With me were the three pals [it is difficult to explain the difference in numbers Brown lists here, except possibly to put it down to a lapse in memory caused by old age] with whom I left Wild Horse Creek. We were looking for an encounter with the Blackfeet because we were in their territory. We were travelling in a north-easterly direction, believing that we were on our way to gold fields in the vicinity of Edmonton. At a clump of cottonwood trees we stopped to eat. As we were eating we were suddenly surprised by a flight of arrows...and we knew that our first "war party" had begun. The

60

arrows used by the Blackfeet were of chokecherry wood with a point of flint or obsidian of different colors. I remember finding one on the top of Sheep Mountain years after. It had a point of moss agate and I presented it to Lord Lathom on the occasion of one of his visits to the mountains of Southern Alberta.

We thought our time had come. The Indians had no firearms but they were all young bucks, thirty-two of them, no old men or war-women – all young warriors – a war party, out for anything they got (presumably a wandering band of Crees), perhaps a white miner making his way across the continent to Wild Horse Creek. We got up and started shooting at anything we could see. We had not much cover as the Indians had driven us away from the cottonwoods, many of which were two feet in diameter. If the Indians had had guns they would have killed all four of us. But we had the shelter of some brush and killed two Indians before they tired of shooting arrows and wandered off.

It was at this time that I received an arrow in my back close to my kidneys. It was a miracle I was not killed. I thought my time had come, but I pulled it out – an arrow head two and a half inches long and the head was out of sight. The jagged edges caught the flesh as I pulled it out and gave me great pain. I had a bottle of turpentine and, opening up the wound, one of my companions inserted the neck of the bottle and when I bent over, about half a pint ran into the opening made by the arrowhead. This was all the doctoring I ever got and in a few days I was well again.

We were using old muzzle-loaders with balls and caps and we carried bullets in our pockets and in our mouths. Two Indians fell victims to our intermittent fire and the rest, after about twenty minutes' fighting, rode to the [south] Saskatchewan River and, jumping their horses into the stream, swam them across, taking one of my horses and one other with them. The Indians... all rode bareback and guided their ponies by rawhide halters with one strap tied through the animals' mouths. They never waited to pick up the bodies of their fallen comrades.

That was the last I saw of Seven Persons Creek till 1885, when, as chief of scouts in the Rocky Mountain Rangers, I went with several rangers to the scene of our encounter. This was twenty years later, but we found two Indian skulls and extracted five bullets out of the cotton-woods on the creek bank.[7]

It was a dramatic introduction to the prairies, and foreshadowed further adventures that were in store for Brown.

While the skirmish with the Indian band pointed up one of the continuing dangers travellers crossing the prairies constantly faced, it also divided the party. Tensions which usually dissipate quickly, indeed almost automatically in settled social conditions, tend to come to the surface when men are bound together by enforced isolation and they crystallized after the redskin's departure. Brown summed up the particular circumstances which applied to himself and his companions in that autumn of 1865 with characteristic directness:

I was very angry that all the others had advised following the directions we did to get to Edmonton. I was for heading closer to the mountains. We had a row over this.... I charged the other three with being responsible for getting us into the fight with the Indians, for the loss of my own and another's horse, and for the wound in my back, which since the application of the turpentine had become very painful.

One squabble resulted in a split-up there and then. The other three said, "We're going on to Edmonton," and they crossed the river where the Indians crossed. They each had a horse. The poor fellow whose horse was taken by the Indians was afoot. I was sorry for him. I had two horses, and the thing I supposed I should have done was to give him one. But I had all my earthly belongings packed on that horse, which consisted mostly of ammunition for hunting. Anyway I didn't give him the horse. I suppose, if I had, he would have forded the river and gone off Edmonton bound, with the other three.

So we got together and decided that we would follow down the course of the Saskatchewan River. I reasoned that it must flow into the Hudson's Bay or the Atlantic Ocean and that it would eventually bring us to the fringe of civilization, probably to Fort Garry, of which place we had heard at Wild Horse Creek.[8]

One would expect that two men, thrown together by circumstances as hazardous as those in which Brown and his horseless companion found themselves, would tend to remain together. Instead, they separated, each prepared to take the chance of surviving weather, starvation, hostile Indians or accident, alone. Whether they were so violently disposed towards each other that emotion totally obliterated reason remains a mystery, for Brown, in his laconic summary of the event, gives no explanation for their action.

The intimation is that the separation was voluntary and amicable. Certainly, at least one possibility cannot be discounted. Rather than walk across the plain, probably because it would not be possible to ride the other horse and still carry all or most of the supplies on hand, the other man preferred to take his chances following the South Saskatchewan on the theory that any settlement in the region would be located along or near the river. In addition, the possibilities of survival through the availability of shelter and by fishing were probably higher in the river valley. Transportation was the major problem and the solution arrived at by the two men was novel, if not completely efficient:

I made a bull-boat for my horseless friend. This was very simply done. The bull-boat was the only watercraft used by Indians in the very early days on

When Brown and his companions crossed the prairie in 1865 it was still a dangerous land. The Blackfoot, opposite, especially resented the whites. Had the warriors who attacked Brown been equipped with rifles, the white men would have ended up scalped and left on the prairie like the Crow Indians below. Instead, they escaped, although Brown was wounded by an arrow.

the plains of Western Canada. There was so little need to navigate any water that plain Indians never became expert canoe men. They devised makeshift watercraft that would enable them to cross streams or make short journeys by water. The bull-boat was the only thing used at that time. The frame, about six feet in diameter, and as near a circle as can be made, is of willow saplings bent and twined in the shape of a basket about eighteen inches deep; over this is stretched a green buffalo hide, fastened by strips of skin at the top and the whole is allowed to dry. The bull-boat cannot be paddled in the usual way. The occupant must sit in front with equal weight behind and pull the craft along with his paddle. It is never used against the current.... The boat must be taken out of the water several times a day and dried. If this is not done water will soak through, fill the craft and all will go to the bottom. Sometimes the bull-boat was made very large, taking three or four buffalo skins. It would then hold three persons and carry enough provisions for several days.

I had no trouble killing a buffalo for the boat I made for my companion, and putting in what meat it would hold, I pushed him off in it for – well, I don't know where. I thought I might run across him at Fort Garry, for the river flowed in that direction, but I was not sure.[9]

Where Brown learned about bull-boats, or how he knew about them in 1865, he does not say. His description, however, is full and accurate, and is similar to the observations by Major General Philippe de Trobriand when he came to the Dakota Territory in 1867.[10] It is possible, indeed likely, that Brown and his friend had heard about bull-boats from other travellers, or read about them, and it is equally possible that Brown may have seen something similar during his sojourn in India.

Then again, the two men may have applied their talents and devised the boat, making use of materials easily available. In any case, we see the two men parting company on the river's shore, one putting his trust in a frail conveyance and the stream's current, the other making his way across the prairie on horseback, leading a second animal burdened down with packs of supplies. Neither knew whether he would ever see the other again, or where exactly they were headed. Fort Garry was a name and little more.

As both men drifted northeast, one in his makeshift bull-boat, the other with his two horses following the general direction of the river, the countryside through which they passed changed slowly but perceptibly. Gradually the buffalo grass of the prairie gave way to the wooded countryside of the northland. It was in the parkland that Brown made his first contact with a settled community which provided him with shelter, companionship, and taught him a way of life that made his adaptation to the plains so manifestly successful:

> I remember my first sight of Duck Lake. My determination to follow the Saskatchewan River brought me to this French half-breed settlement in the early fall, and I accepted their invitation to spend the winter there. I found about fifty families in the settlement who came from Fort Garry. They were hunters and moved from place to place in the hunting season, stopping wherever it was convenient. In winter they made Duck Lake their home and built rude houses out of the small timber from the river bottoms.... There was not a man in the settlement who could speak English. Fortunately I could speak good French and I soon picked up the Cree Indian language.[11]

It was Brown's first encounter with the Métis, those unique people of the plains, and once made, the connection was never broken. A naturally gay, open-handed and happy people, as all travellers who met them remarked, they were resourceful masters of their element. They observed the landscape in all its minute details, and their endurance in travel, as the Earl of Southesk testifies, was astounding. Brown was fortunate in spending the coldest of the winter months in the warmth and cheerfulness of the Duck Lake community. The Métis way of life was in its last period of unfettered freedom. Even then the imminence of the forces that threatened to submerge them, the transformation of an empty prairie into a province, the establishment of courts, systems of education, the sale of real estate, and the relentless advance of the prairie schooners bringing ever increasing numbers of enterprising settlers were closer than the Métis cared to admit.

The settlement at Duck Lake which Brown saw was already the retreat of those hunters from the Red River who were unequal or unwilling to compete in the new conditions foreshadowed by growing opposition in the Red River Settlement and, in Canada, to the Hudson's Bay Company rule in the Northwest Territories. After Confederation and the shock of Louis Riel's first rebellion, the sociological pressures upon the Métis increased inexorably, and their withdrawal to the regions of Duck Lake and Prince Albert took on an air of sullen aloofness streaked with bitterness. Whether Brown was aware of any feeling at Duck Lake is doubtful. His stay was relatively brief, and his recollections centre upon two minor episodes.

The first reminiscence has a happy ending and is touched with a measure of humour:

Shortly after I arrived at Duck Lake, a half-breed came out to where I was "still hunting" one day and said. "Mr. Goldtooth has just come to the settlement and asked if you were here. He wants to see you." I had no idea who this man might be, but I rode into camp with the half-breed and he took me to "Mr. Goldtooth".

The man I had made the bull-boat for at Seven Persons Creek had a big gold tooth right in front of his mouth and it was his arrival the half-breed was announcing.[12]

The reunion must have been a moment of great relief to both men. From that instant, it was clear that their stay in Duck Lake would be limited. In recognizing that truth, Brown during the winter months made a sleigh, and in the early spring hitched his two horses to the conveyance and set course for old Fort Garry. This time he and "Goldtooth" travelled together, their route taking them through White Mud River and Portage la Prairie. As Brown later said: "it took six weeks' steady driving and we were afraid the snow would leave us with our runners on bare ground.[13] Kootenai's stay at Fort Garry was brief, "only about a week." There the two companions parted company and Brown began a short, and for him, a rather inglorious career:

"Goldtooth" had had enough of the west and returned to Eastern Canada, but I went to Portage la Prairie and began trading with the Indians. I got supplies from Charles House, an American trader.... I traded between Portage la Prairie and White Mud River, twenty miles west of Portage la Prairie, mostly with Chippewas and Crees, who were in small scattered camps trapping [musk] rats, mink, foxes, coyotes and wolves. This was the summer and winter of '66 and '67.

My trade was mostly in clothing and whisky, but I had blankets, thread, beads, tea, sugar and a few odds and ends, but my big money was made in whisky, which I sold for thirty dollars a gallon. In Indian camps the very dogs got drunk and it was not very pleasant being around when a whole camp got drunk.... At White Mud River there was an Anglican mission in charge of a half-breed clergyman. A trader named Fry, an old English half-breed, Willox Spence, and an old American, Andrew Jackson, were dickering with the Indians and catching furs and fish. It was only a short distance to Lake Manitoba and they fished in the lake in the summer time....

I had no permanent living place at White Mud River and was hardly in the same house two nights in succession. I sold my horses while in these camps and bought dogs.[14]

Selling spirits to the Indians cannot be considered a credit to Brown, but it should be remembered that the Hudson's Bay Company's fur trading monopoly was only then being challenged once more by independent traders, the majority of them

Americans, and that whisky was a quick and sure commodity to divert business from the Company's post near what is now Portage la Prairie. Whatever may be said in favour of Kootenai, and little can be said on his behalf for this particular period of his life, he was certainly not the first to begin trafficking in liquor in the district, and that his resources after the long trip from Wild Horse Creek must have been depleted to the point where the temptation to make quick returns was overriding. The very brief duration of his stay at Fort Garry suggests that he was little able to afford the price of staying in a settled community, and that he returned to the open spaces of the countryside where fish and game were still relatively plentiful and easy to obtain.

It was at the very start of his trading career that Brown became involved in an episode that resulted in the deaths of two men, one white, one red. The background to the affair has been recorded with some precision by the pioneer Portage la Prairie clergyman, A. C. Garrioch, "who for a third of a century travelled over this country by Red River cart and dug-out, and fared sumptuously on buffalo, pemmican and other foodstuffs of that period."[15] Garrioch attributes the trouble to the influx of new settlers into Portage since its founding in 1853:

> ...but as the population increased and became more mixed especially mixed with whiskey – then some of the Indians were bad, and the same with the old timers and the Ontarians and the Americans, and the badness in the community was more than it could handle, and deeds of violence and murder began to be perpetrated....[16]

According to Garrioch, "two hundred gallons of whiskey" were the root cause of the trouble:

> The whiskey formed part of a trading outfit brought in on wagons by three Americans, Bob O'Lone, Jim Clewett and Bill Sammon, who traded in Portage la Prairie during the winter 1865-66.... The writer [Garrioch] remembered seeing them at Church at least once. They did not seem any worse that Sunday than any other mortals.... Sammon, who was an ex-sergeant of the U.S. army [sic] seemed to be a very nice young man....
>
> All appeared to be going well enough with them until May 28th, 1866, when there occurred a row between them and the Salteaux. The Indians of course were blamed for starting the trouble, especially Kwingwahaka, the Wolverine, who was a notorious rascal. It appears that the Americans had secreted their whisky in an out-building only a few yards distant from the dwelling house and store, and that when things began to look threatening, Jim Clewett moved in there to guard it. An Indian who professed to be anxious to assist him in protecting the stuff was also allowed to enter; but shortly after-

wards attacked him with a knife and stabbed him in the side. Fortunately, the knife struck a rib and being deflected made only a surface wound. In the excitement that followed Bill Sammon and Kwingwahaka came into conflict, one on each side of the outhouse door, and as soon as the door was slightly ajar, the latter thrust the barrel of his gun into the opening, and when Sammon caught hold of it, he pulled the trigger, sending a ball into his chest that came out at his side and lodged in his arm. Kwingwahaka then fled....

Before Bob O'Lone succeeded in disentangling himself from the Indians, he had to make lively use of a repeating rifle.... In this row there was a death on each side. During a lull in the fighting an Indian approached the trader's quarters.... As he neared the house, the crack of a rifle was heard, and he was seen to stagger and hurriedly retrace his steps, and as he was in the act of climbing a fence he fell over dead.... It is, however, to be regretted that poor Sammon could not have been given a better fighting chance for his life. He dreaded the journey to Fort Garry by wagon; and no one was much surprised to learn that he died soon after arriving there.[17]

Garrioch, in his humanity, commented that perhaps Sammon "was taken because he was the best prepared to die." It was into this turbulent scene that Brown strayed, fresh from his winter stay at Duck Lake, and only recently arrived from his week at Fort Garry.

Kootenai's remembrance of Portage and the particular affray described by Garrioch, even after almost half a century, is laced with vivid detail and feeling that is unusual if not extraordinary in its own way. Even taking into account the fallibility of memory or, as one writer so poetically put it, the consideration that "distance lends enchantment to the scene," Brown's description, including its touches of a dialogue, is that of a participant:

I was in the habit of taking furs to Portage la Prairie to John Gibbons, who ran a store there. When I arrived on this occasion there were about thirty Red Lake Indians from Minnesota. I could speak their language and Johnnie persuaded me to stay around for the day. In the store there was a cousin of Gibbons, Bob Olone [sic] and Billy Salmon [sic]. The store was out of Portage about two miles in the direction of the Hudson's Bay store. In those days all traders sold rum and whisky to natives.... On this day [Brown did not, unlike Garrioch, specify the day] the red men had run out of fur before their thirst for whisky had been quenched. They had been bringing in rats, otter, beaver, lynx, fox, but the supply had been exhausted. Chief Starving Wolf [presumably the same Indian that Garrioch referred to as the Wolverine] had come in for a free drink. By this time they were all very drunk and I didn't like to give them any-more. So I said to him: "My friend, you know I am not a man of two tongues. I'll give you one drink and that's the last you'll get". So he drank his drink and away out of the door he went. It happened that we had two puncheons of rum, which being too large to go through the door, we had put into the storehouse just fifty yards behind the store. After the Indians had gone out, Johnnie

Gibbons said to an old fellow, Jimmy Clewitt, who was hanging round the store: "Go out into the storehouse and bring in a gallon for the house. It's a long time between drinks."

A moment after Clewitt had gone out, I looked out of the window and saw Chief Starving Wolf jump through the door after him, carrying a gun in his hand. I yelled to Olone [sic]. Instantly we heard the report of a gun and saw Clewitt running for his life for the store. We also saw the Indian emerge from the store with a large copper pot which we assumed was full of rum, and so it was. Clewitt made the house, and falling into the porch, groaned: "I'm done for."

In the meantime, although we didn't know it, it appears that Billy Salmon [sic], the young clerk, was afraid that something would befall old Clewett and followed him out to the storehouse. They were both there when the shot was fired. Salmon also was able to make the porch and rolled over the top of Clewitt, yelling that he was shot.

The Indians immediately began peppering away at the store from their hiding place behind the storehouse. Odd bullets came through the chink and there was rattling and clashing of all sorts of stuff on the shelves of the store. We three survivors, Gibbons, Olone and myself grabbed Hawkins muzzle loaders, and whenever the leg or wing of an Indian appeared around the corner he was nailed. Even Clewitt, whom we expected was dead, jumped up and, grabbing a rifle, began peppering away through a window. After several rounds had been fired, an Indian jumped out from behind the storehouse, probably to get a good aim, and Clewitt and myself both shot him. Another Red Laker ran out to pull in his body, but while getting over a fence he was shot in the leg and fled, dragging the broken member after him.

About this time Olone shouted that we were almost out of ammunition. Had this become exhausted we were goners, for nothing else would have kept twenty-eight Red Lake Indians from entering the store and murdering every last one of us. The nearest house was that of De Marias, a French half-breed. So Olone, gun in hand, gave a yell and started as fast as he could out of the front door and away for help. He made good time and brought back about twenty half-breeds and whites. When the Red Lakers saw reinforcements coming they ran off....

I have said that everyone of us got drunk, but not till we had looked after Clewitt and Salmon [sic]. Clewitt, we found, had not been shot but stabbed. He carried the knife between his ribs from the storehouse to the porch, pulling it out when he got up to use the rifle.... Poor Salmon was not so fortunate. He had two balls in his body, we knew not where. A doctor had just come to Fort Garry, so we made Billy as comfortable as possible in a light wagon belonging to John McLean and started for the fort. Fearful that we might be ambushed by Indians, Gibbons and Co. hired an escort of six mounted men and we drove by easy stages to the doctor. He [Salmon] was given every attention...but at the end [of ten days]...we had to bury him at what was called "the new church", down the river from the settlement about four or five miles.[18]

The points of overlap in the two accounts, excluding minor variations in spelling, are striking. Garrioch, for example, notes the name John McLean in connection with the incident, and has much to say about the Demarais family, Charles, the family head, and his son Francis.[19] Again, he pinpoints the action of Bob O'Lone who "succeeded in disentangling himself from the Indians" by keeping his legs apart in Irish or American style, leaping from side to side, occasionally raising his rifle to "let fly in the direction of the enemy."[20] The fact that Garrioch has not recorded Brown's presence during the shooting is not surprising. As he notes, the action caused much controversy amongst the small knot of settlers then in the area, and accounts of what actually took place differed widely.

Again, Brown at the time was a newcomer to the district, and according to his own memory of the fracas, happened only by chance to be in the store the day it took place. As a newcomer, as a trader who trafficked in spirits, he was lumped in with the "Yankee Boys," who were thoroughly disapproved of by the Garrioch and other pioneer families in the Portage area. For Brown that encounter with Indians inflamed by drink proved to be the highlight of his trading days, a narrow escape that called for an uninhibited celebration.

Soon, however, he was drawn into a very different kind of occupation. Indeed, unknown to Brown, the shooting at the Portage trading post was prophetic of the risks he was constantly required to run.

We know little about Brown's life during his remaining days as a trader. There are, however, brief tantalizing glimpses of his activities, including visits to Fort Garry, a small place then as he observed.[21] He mentions a man named Mulligan who ran a boarding house and Beaucamp, a saloon keeper:

I sat for a tintype photo at Fort Garry and was told it was the first ever taken at the Fort. The man with the camera was a Swede named Olson, from St. Paul.... I was only in Fort Garry a short time, but while there a fellow came in looking [for riders] for a pony express route in Dakota territory. He took two or three of us to Fort Totten and I began riding from this place to Knife River, a tributary of the Missouri where Theodore Roosevelt afterwards established a cattle ranch.[22]

Thus, from a casual encounter Brown was launched into a new and exciting life.

The company for which Brown worked when he first crossed into the Dakota Territory in the early summer of 1867, and which he never named in any accounts, was a typical fron-

This 1870 photo of Brown is the first commercial photo taken at Fort Garry – today's Winnipeg.

tier enterprise, bold in concept and a failure in practice. The same year that Brown was hired, 1867, Charles A. Ruffee of Minneapolis secured a government contract to operate a pony express between Fort Abercrombie on the Red River and Fort Benton in the Montana Territory.[23] The projected mail route ran from Abercrombie to Fort Ransom, then along the Cheyenne River and across to Fort Totten, west from that post by way of the Mouse River to Fort Buford, along the Missouri to Fort Peck, up the Milk River to Boulder Creek, and finally, in a direct line to Fort Benton.

Ruffee planned to establish camps or stations at intervals of approximately 50 miles, with two men stationed at each point. These were to carry the United States Army mail bags to and from neighbouring stations and, in the process, serve the chain of new posts that were being established through the two Territories. Fort Stevenson, for example, was only established in June 1867, while construction of Fort Totten began in July.[24]

Brown was thus, unwittingly almost, thrust into the vanguard of the pioneers who were starting to push their way westward after the end of the American Civil War, and who saw the new Army establishments intended to protect communications between Minnesota and Western Montana being built. At first it was thought, optimistically, that Ruffee's company could carry mail on a thrice-weekly schedule, but the plan proved to be absurdly impractical.

The chief reason was that the staging stations could not be maintained, for the men either deserted their posts or were killed, beaten or threatened by marauding bands of Sioux Indians. As a result, the company never succeeded in getting the mail carried further than Fort Totten, which was still under construction, and the enterprise failed financially during the winter of 1867-68.[25] Brown's analysis of Ruffee's failure corroborates contemporary evidence; his experience with the company in fact made the failure a very personal remembrance:

> There must have been sixty or seventy riders on the route which [theoretically, for Brown probably never knew the exact details] extended from St. Paul right to Helens [sic], Montana. There were station keepers every fifty or sixty miles. They ran bigger risks than we did, although they were not paid any more money. Indians always knew where to find them. Most of the station-keepers were eventually killed and the company lost hundreds of horses, killed and stolen by the Indians. Their enormous losses finally led the company into bankruptcy and they still owe me $400 today.[26]

Brown was not the only Company employee to lose his pay. General Philippe de Trobriand, the United States Army Commander in the Dakota Territory, notes in his journal March 6, 1868, the experience of a Mexican rider called Joe the Spaniard:

> For seven months he has been in the employ of the mail contractor, Ruffee, and during these seven months has not received a cent of his wages, and like others, never hopes to get a penny of it.[27]

Brown had other reasons for remembering his unpaid services with Major Ruffee's mail company. Sometime during the autumn of 1867 he was captured and briefly held by a band of Sioux. The Indians looked upon the coming of the United States Army with apprehension, and expressed their feelings initially by disrupting Ruffee's mail runs as a warning that more serious consequences would follow if the service was continued. De Trobriand briefly mentions Brown's brush with the Sioux in connection with the capture of another mail carrier, Gardepie, a French Métis from the Red River colony:

> Gardepie himself came from [Fort] Berthold, bringing the packet of letters for Fort Stevenson in order to tell me about the incidents of his trip. Like Brown, one of the carriers who preceded him, he was captured by hostile

Indians one day's travel on this side of the Yellowstone [river].... Most of the savages were rather drunk, which proves that a half-breed trader was there with a supply of Indian whiskey (alcohol cut with water) and ammunition. They told Gardepie again that they were determined to intercept all mail from Fort Buford and to kill all American carriers. Don't complain, the Chief told him, and consider yourself lucky that your life was spared. You are allowed to go because we all know you, but don't come back again or you will be treated like an American. For what difference is there between you and the Long Knives if you carry their messages and if you are paid by them for services. Do you know what you are doing? It is not our life that you are working for; it is our death, the destruction of the redskins, of our warriors, of our women, and of our children. Wherever the white men establish themselves, the buffalo go, and when the buffalo are gone, the red hunters of the prairie must die of hunger.[28]

The warning was unmistakable, the dangers evident. To demonstrate that they were serious, the Sioux in the Dakota Territory that winter translated their threats into action, threatening, beating, and killing Ruffee's employees and shattering the communications link between Army posts. As a result of their efforts, Ruffee's Company went bankrupt.

With the final suspension of company operations, the United States Army was forced to establish its own mail service. No attempt was made to duplicate Ruffee's venture. Instead, each commanding officer of an Army establishment was given the responsibility of maintaining communications between his own and neighbouring posts. Since soldiers could not be used to carry out the mail runs because of their inexperience in the country, it became necessary, and, under the circumstances proved sensible, for each post commander to employ at least some of the most experienced and trustworthy men that had been in Ruffee's company.

Although the majority of the most experienced men were Métis, most either did not want to continue in the face of Indian opposition, or were not considered reliable by the Army selectors. Preference was given to whites who were expert horsemen, knew the country, and had an acquaintance with the languages spoken by the plains tribes. Brown, stranded and, like Joe the Spaniard, unpaid by Ruffee, was one of those recruited. On April 20, 1868, at Fort Stevenson, he was taken on strength as a civilian "tripper" at "a salary of $50.00 per month and ration."[29] His brief encounter with the Sioux only a few months before, which he never mentioned to his amanuensis, now faded into the background of minor experience, overshadowed by the adventures that were to follow.

Chapter 6

Facing Torture by the Sioux

When Brown was taken on strength as a mail carrier, Fort Stevenson was still unfinished; a strange collection of incompleted adobe brick buildings, a temporary palisade erected as "a means of inspiring the officers' wives with a sense of constant security," a double corral for cattle and horses, and a steam powered sawmill.[1] Located on the edge of the Missouri – the Big Muddy – that miscellany of buildings and the small garrison had resumed construction after a cold hard winter. Brown, of course, as a former employee of Ruffee's pony express company, was familiar with the area, and saw the post spring up from the time it was first a temporary camp located "on an elevated plateau forty or fifty feet above the water."[2]

He was co-opted into the service of the United States Army at a critical time when the growing hostility of the Indians and the pressures created by the establishment of the new western territories, Colorado, Dakota, and Montana, impinged directly upon the force. In the years immediately following the Civil War the new territories attracted thousands of discharged soldiers from both the Union and Confederate armies. Railway building, gold and silver to be mined in the Montana hills, free land for settlers, quick returns from the ready sale of buffalo robes and furs, money for selling firewood to the steamboats plying the Missouri from St. Louis to Fort Benton, attracted the adventurous and, inevitably, the most turbulent.

In part, the central government was to blame for the unsettled nature of frontier society. Immediately following the Civil War the State Department, which was responsible for the territories until 1873, paid little attention to problems developing in the new regions. To the post Civil War governments the newly created western regions provided welcome new sources of patronage in the form of territorial offices, army camps, land offices, post offices and Indian agencies. The important point from Washington's standpoint was that the western regions had to be cleared of Indians, and the lands surveyed, sectioned, and sold to the waves of migrating settlers beginning to surge beyond the Mississippi. The United States Army thus became an important factor in the process of opening up the American West.

In the Dakota territory, its importance was enhanced by the presence of the Sioux which, despite the ravages of smallpox, were steadily increasing in numbers. Their mounting belligerency, coupled with their strategic position in the imperfectly known bad lands between the North Platte and the Upper Missouri Rivers on the flank of the rapidly advancing emigrants, made them a distinct threat to western settlement.[3]

The most troublesome of the Sioux, as Brown discovered while in the employ of Major Ruffee, formed what has become known as the Teton division, a loose confederation of seven tribes, one of which was the Hunkpapa, led by Sitting Bull. It was in the heart of Sitting Bull's territory that the civilian mail carriers were to operate.

At the same time, it was to this difficult country that the United States Army posted officers and men who had never experienced frontier life. Major General Philippe Régis de Trobriand, a Frenchman who had fought with distinction on the Union side, typified such appointments. While on leave in France he was given command of three posts in the Dakota Territory: Fort Buford, located at the junction of the Missouri and Yellowstone Rivers; Fort Totten on Devil's Lake; and Fort Stevenson on the Missouri some 15 miles below Fort Berthold.[5] All were established following General Alfred H. Terry's reconnaissance trip through the area in the spring of 1867. Significantly, all were situated in the heart of the buffalo's northern range which, equally, was the home of the Sioux.

Fortunately, de Trobriand was an able, sensitive man. When he arrived in Fort Stevenson on August 19, 1867, after more than a month of continuous travel from France, the three posts under his command were still in the early phases of construction.[6] To his surprise the majority of the civilian construction workers, some 40 out of a total population of 260, were French Canadian Métis:[7]

There are many French-Canadians here. The traders at Berthold are French with the exception of one. Their people are all of French-Canadian origin. French is their language. The interpreters speak it much better than they do English. The contractor and almost all the carpenters and masons are either French or Canadians. The half-breeds are all sons of Canadian fathers. My native tongue will certainly be of great help to me here.[8]

As a civilian mail carrier Brown was thrown into the milieu of the mixed bloods, renewing, as a result, the contact he first made during his journey to Red River in the winter of 1865-1866. It was an event of considerable personal significance.

Because it was located on the Missouri and therefore easily supplied, Fort Stevenson became the entrepôt for equipment and material required for the construction and maintenance of Fort Totten located 120 miles northeast on the edge of Devil's Lake, the largest body of water in North Dakota. Between the two posts lay an empty brooding land. De Trobriand, recording his impressions on arrival at Fort Stevenson, catches something of the spirit of the plains that receded and merged into the horizon:

> The countryside is vast, and one has an unobstructed view of it. It is composed of an immense, long plateau, bordered on the north by a chain of irregular hills and on the south by the river which runs from east to west. In its windings, the river leaves uncovered on one side or the other huge sand points or alluvial lands covered with osiers, brush, or wood of full-grown trees. These trees are the only ones visible on the horizon, with the exception of one.... But on the chain of hills to the north and on the high and sharp cliffs which border the right bank of the river to the south, nothing can be seen but some brush growing in the hollows of the land. The rest is a carpet of smooth grass. The plateau stretches out uniformly to the east and west for great distances until it finally merges with the sky.... There is nothing especially picturesque about all this. The character of the countryside is completely desert-like; space and solitude.[9]

Space and solitude, however, were not the only characteristics of the landscape. The emptiness, together with the elements, were constant hazards; the capricious hostility of the Sioux was another matter. Brown, by accepting the appointment of mail carrier, was destined to experience both.

If Brown's experiences with Ruffee's company hadn't succeeded in impressing him with the dangers implicit in his new job, Special Order number 51 should have done so. Signed on April 20, 1868, by de Trobriand, it specifically authorized the acting Post Quartermaster at Fort Stevenson to "employ two (2) suitable mail carriers to replace those lately killed by hostile Sioux between this post and Fort Totten, D.T."[10] The salary was "$50.00 per month and ration."[11]

Brown, together with the two others taken on strength at the same time, were not only replacements for carriers lost while on duty. Specifically, because of their knowledge of the land and the habits of the Sioux, they were to replace Métis carriers who had been hired when the Army first took over the mail run. By Army standards the Métis were undesirable employees because, as Quartermasters soon learned, when the buffalo season arrived they were unable to resist the lure of the hunt and simply left whatever they were doing.

If Brown and the other new carriers were not fully aware of the hazards of their employment, the point was soon driven home. Less than a month after they were entered on the Army payroll two men, Charles MacDonald and Joe Hamlin, both of mixed blood, were killed by the Sioux near what was then called Strawberry Lake. Their bodies were never found but, ironically, it was Brown and J. Martin, another mail carrier, who in their own moment of danger were able to confirm the murders.

The enmity of the Sioux in the Fort Stevenson-Fort Totten area was particularly fierce because the route between the two posts passed through territory that was of special significance to the Indians. John Henry Taylor, who lived in the Dakota Territory from 1867 until after its division and statehood in 1889, pinpoints the reason for the Sioux hostility:

The country through which the trail is located is a high treeless plain. Within forty miles of the banks of the Missouri the trail crosses over the Dog Den range [the chain of hills to the north noted by de Trobriand in his journal], a spur of the Coteau du Prairie, the great divide or grass covered mountains that cross the two Dakotas beginning in the Bijou Hills in South Dakota, extending northwest until lost in the surface depressions of the lower Saskatchewan valley. The Dog Den had long been a sacred ground and place of mystery to the Indian tribes who had lived within the northern buffalo range....

Over among the deep ravines and canons [sic, canyons] on the north side where the mysterious ghost dogs snarled and growled at the cavern's mouth that led deep down through earthy crust to that underground land with ever-green pastures, but whose crowded conditions led the beasts [i.e. buffalo] to seek outlet to the wide land above when the drowsy watch dogs snored in rest-less sleep, and thus the Great Spirit sent forth the fattened herds from the grassy sides of the Dog Den range that the Avicarces [a branch of the Sioux federation] might live in plenty and be glad.

Around these elevated plains of the Dog Den country the buffalo contin-ued in large numbers until about the year 1868, when they disappeared....[12]

Into this region of Indian legend and reverence, Brown and the other carriers entered at their own risk.

The resentment and bitterness towards the advancing wave of soldiers and settlers felt by the Sioux centered upon the mail carriers because they were vulnerable to attack, and because the half-breeds initially employed in that capacity were regarded by the Indians as traitors. De Trobriand relates the experiences of Gardepie, a Red River Métis who fell into the hands of the Sioux in December 1867 while carrying dispatches between Fort Buford and Fort Stevenson. The encounter, which served as a blunt warning to the Army of how strongly their presence was resented, also was responsible for the reluctance of mixed bloods to accept the responsibility of carrying the mails:

> They [the Sioux] told Gardepie again that they were determined to inter-cept all mail from Fort Buford and to kill the American carriers. [13]

Gardepie was also told not to return or he, too, would be treated like an American. [14]

A hard winter did nothing to diminish the Sioux's bitterness. Indeed, the disappearance of two carriers, Charley MacDonald and Joe Hamlin, who left Fort Stevenson on the morning of May 15, 1868, with mail destined for Fort Totten, dramatically stressed the point. Because MacDonald and Hamlin failed to return, Brown and a Sioux half breed, Joe Martin (also employed as post interpreter), were sent to Fort Totten with dispatches and other mail on May 23.

Normally, the trip took the better part of three days of steady riding. Compelled by that feeling of urgency which stemmed from the disappearance of the other carriers, Brown and Martin pushed their horses to the limit. Late in the afternoon of the first day they arrived at Strawberry Lake, over thirty miles from Fort Stevenson, bent on reaching a shelter located near the water. It was a miserable day, cloudy with heavy intermittent showers.

As the two men neared their destination, they cautiously scanned the countryside before proceeding into the ravines and coulees which characterized the terrain of the Dog Den hills. When they reached the bottom of one of the depressions and were most vulnerable to observation and attack, a band of Sioux in the classic fashion of a western movie, burst down upon them.

As de Trobriand noted, no terrain could be better laid out for ambushes:

Dog Den is called by the Indians The Mountain Which Looks (La Montagne qui Regarde) a name which is much more exact and with a much more real meaning.... It is a height composed of a collection of rather abrupt hills, separated by deep ravines well covered with trees, or by narrow winding gorges filled with rocks. This height rises alone in the middle of a vast plain. From the top, there is an unobstructed view for a considerable distance in all directions...so the raiding Indians, in search of evil deeds to do, make it their rendezvous.[15]

In a moment, as Brown vividly recalled many years later, he and his companion were swept up by the Sioux, their lives dependent upon the whims of excited young braves.

The situation and the setting were unforgettable, and imprinted themselves upon Brown's memory:

We were within half a mile of Strawberry Lake and it was about seven o'clock in the evening of the twenty fourth of May, the Queen's birthday. I have good reason to remember the date. We jumped off our horses and crept up to the top of the hill to take a good look for Indians.... Getting on our horses again we rode down to cross this coulee and to get to the camping grounds by the lake. Just as we went down the steep bank, the Indians charged on us yelling out, "Don't shoot, don't be fools, we're friends...."

In the dash they made at us Sitting Bull was leading, riding a fine big grey horse.... In the melee that followed, Lady Jane Grey, our pack mule, broke away and started for Fort Stevenson as fast as she could travel, but the Sioux took after her, soon captured her and appropriated everything in our pack....

Sitting Bull ordered us to get off our horses and when we did he had us stripped as naked as the day we were born. They took everything, dispatches, mail, guns, horses, clothes.... Some of the young bucks began yelling "Kash-ga, Kash-ga", meaning kill them, kill them. Sitting Bull raised his hand and shouted, "Don't be in a hurry, we'll make a fire and have some fun with them." We understood every word they said, of course, and we knew that Sitting Bull meant some playful mode of torture that the Sioux often inflicted on their captives. It might have been sticking pieces of pine pitch or other inflammable dry wood all over the victim's bare body and setting them afire.

But someone called out, "come over here, we'll have a little talk." So we went over to the edge of the coulee...and sat down in a circle. My companion who was a Santee Sioux half-breed said to Sitting Bull in Sioux, "what is the matter with your people? Why do they rob us and talk bad to us. I am a Sioux half-breed, one of your own people. This man with me is a Sioux half-breed too. Why do you want to kill us?"

To this Sitting Bull replied, "I see you are Sioux, but your companion here (pointing his finger at me) looks like a white man." Then turning to me he said, "this true that you are a half-breed?"

In those days I wore my hair frontier style, about twenty inches long....

To Sitting Bull's questions I answered in Sioux, "My father was a white man and my mother a Santee Sioux woman."

"Well," he said, "your skin is very white and your eyes are blue, but it may be that you are a half-breed. You talk good Sioux. Why do you help our enemies, the isa thonga?" (meaning the long-knives, the Sioux term for American). I said, "we are poor and just come down from the prairies, and as we were passing Fort Stevenson the soldiers gave us some letters to carry for one trip."

It was now getting dark and a dispute arose over the disposition of our two horses, Lady Jane Grey, the stuff in the pack on her back, and our personal belongings. To settle the matter, Sitting Bull called his warriors in a council about forty yards from the fire around which we were huddled bare naked. This was on the very edge of the coulee leading into Strawberry Lake. I said to Joe, "Lie down and let us roll into the coulee and they will never miss us."

"We'll be killed sure," said Joe, "but we had better be shot than burned alive."

I was watching the council circle carefully and as soon as I saw their eyes off us I nudged Joe with my elbow and whispered, "roll, roll." We rolled about a hundred feet into the coulee and down we sprinted for our lives, bare feet, bare naked as the day we were born, right into the lake.

It was quite dark by this time and as Strawberry Lake was covered all about the edges with cat tails and other weeds that could easily hide a man, we were safe for a time at least, but we didn't know for how long. We were standing in water up to our necks, with Indians running up and down the shore firing at random into the weeds.... It was blowing a regular hurricane and pouring down torrents of rain and this is probably what saved us. Failing to locate us in the lake they conceived an idea that we had run down the road. Anyway, they left us, but we stood in the water for another half hour. Finally, half dead with cold, we stole quietly out in the pitch darkness and scrambling up the bank took to our heels, but not along the travelled road. We kept away from that. After we got away a couple of miles we stopped to get our breath and Joe said, "We're safe now, we will travel the road again." So away we went in the darkness toward Fort Stevenson with not as much on our bodies as Adam and Eve in the garden.

The sun shone on us next day and millions of mosquitoes seemed to find out that two naked human beings were available for food. They fairly swarmed upon us and there was not a spot on our bodies as large as a pinhead that they had not bitten.

We arrived at Fort Stevenson early in the afternoon. Our travel was slow during the night but when daylight came and we got our bearings we made good time.... There was bastions on the fort and one of the sentries saw us coming. He reported to the Sergeant of the guard, and he in turn reported to the officer of the day that two Indians were approaching the Fort bare naked. The guard was sent out to capture us but when the Sergeant saw who we were he ran to meet us with "what's up? what's up?" I replied, "Oh, nothing much. The Sioux have your mail, horses, and our clothes, and came very near getting us. We have walked from Strawberry Lake." [16]

While serving as dispatch rider for the U.S. Army, in May 1868 Brown and a companion were captured by Sioux Chief Sitting Bull, opposite, but escaped while the Indians were deciding how to torture them. Eight years later at Little Bighorn, Sitting Bull's warriors killed General George Armstrong Custer and all 210 of his men, including Custer's brother, brother-in-law and nephew. After wiping out the soldiers, Sitting Bull and his people fled to Canada.

Sioux Indians on the prairie in the early 1870s. Although their tents are still genuine, their clothes reflect the white man's influence.

According to Brown, the two men, their feet bleeding and their bodies covered with insect bites, were immediately paraded before de Trobriand so that "the old Frenchman" could observe their condition for himself:

He asked us how it happened and, as we related the incidents, he used very unparliamentary language most of which was directed against the United States Government for allowing such hostiles to be alive. One of the things I remember him saying was, "They should be wiped off the face of the earth." There was a decanter of whisky beside him and pouring out three glasses we all had a drink. In fact, we had several drinks, and because we had not eaten since noon the day before, the whisky went to our heads and I suggested to the General that we should go to our quarters before we said or did anything foolish. We were both in such a state that we didn't care whether we ever got anything to eat or wear. The General agreed and we were taken to our quarters, fed, clothed, and our bodies and feet doctored and we were soon asleep. Neither of us were conscious again until next morning.[17]

While Brown's recollection of de Trobriand's "unparliamentary language" and his observation of the whisky decanter on the desk are the authentic touches of the event and his reaction, it is the comment attributed to the Frenchman which stands out. It suggests that de Trobriand, a literary man brought up in the romantic climate of opinion created by the philosophers and writers of France, through observation and contact with the Indians, abandoned Rousseau's popular concept that man was most noble in his natural state. Whether he held that view with the same degree of fervour as did other less sophisticated spirits on the frontier is not revealed in his writings.

Brown's graphic account of his adventure with Sitting Bull and the angry young men of the Hunkpapa band, recalled during World War I, contrasts sharply with the contemporary report recorded by de Trobriand at Fort Stevenson on May 26, 1868:

The day before yesterday, Sunday [24 May], two of our carriers left with the weeks mail to meet those from Totten halfway. They were Brown, an Irishman recently enlisted in government service, and Martin, a half-breed employed since last year. Both knew the country well, spoke Sioux fluently. Toward evening of the first day, they were approaching Clear Lake when they noticed something that looked like buffalo to them. In reality, it was Indians, who, in order not to betray themselves, lay on the necks of their horses, which made them look like the animal for which they wanted to be mistaken. So our men went on their way, while the Hunkpapahs set an ambush for them. Arriving at a narrow ravine through which they had to pass, the carriers suddenly found themselves surrounded by Sioux coming in on them from all sides crying, "Don't shoot! We are Medicine Bear's men (an allied chief). We are friends." And the first ones exchanged handshakes with Joe Martin, who was nearest to them. Brown's horse took fright and ran away, and some young men ran to bring it back. The pack mule with the despatch pouch and supplies galloped off in an opposite direction, his speed accelerated by fear. When Martin was so surrounded that he could not defend himself, an Indian slapped his hand on the withers of his horse, uttering a cry of triumph, the meaning of which the prisoner could not mistake. He felt that he was doomed. He was immediately stripped of everything, weapons, equipment and clothes. His horse had been taken from him first. Brown was brought back and promptly suffered the same fate. He had been brought back by an enemy riding the well known horse of Charley MacDonald, which set him thinking. When they were in just their boots and drawers, the chief gave Martin an old overcoat to cover himself (for it had poured all day, and was still raining), and he easily recognized it as Joe Hamlin's. The overcoat was pierced by two bullet holes in the chest and two rents in the back. The chief asked the prisoners who they were and what they were doing on the prairie. They answered that they were half-breeds from the Red River and that they were going to St. Joseph to hunt.

Their chief then told them that his men had killed two men and a soldier a few days before; our two carriers and a man from the convoy commanded by Lt. Smith. "I would not have had the two men from the Red River killed," said the chief, "but the young men killed them before they found out who they were "I am the one who killed one of them," said one of the savages, coming forward armed with MacDonald's sixteen-shot carbine (Henry system). "I shot an arrow through his body; he fell from his horse and I finished him off on the ground with a revolver." Then the two prisoners noticed that the chief was wearing MacDonald's watch chain and recognized several pieces of his clothing and Joe Hamlin's on the backs of the Indians. "Let's kill them," several of them were saying. "Why waste time talking? Let's do to them what we did to the others." At that the chief took the prisoners aside and said to them: "The young men are saying evil things and are ready to do an evil deed. Take advantage of the night that is coming and run away quickly before it's too late." He did not have to tell our men twice, and, half naked, they hurried off. Instead of following the direction they had first taken, they ran to hide in the marshy underbrush, making a circle calculated to throw them off pursuit.

It was well for them that they did. The chief had given them life only because he did not yet know that they were carriers. As I have said before, the mule carrying the dispatches had run away. It took some time to capture it, and, those who did feasted on the supplies they found in the saddlebags. When they came back bringing the animal and the packet of dispatches, our men had already left. They [i.e. the Indians] took up their trail intending undoubtedly to put them to death; but night had come on, or at least dusk was falling, and they were unable to find them.

They [Brown and Martin] wandered around part of the night, and at daybreak found themselves still in sight of the enemy. By sneaking in ravines and hiding themselves as well as they could, they hurried away in the direction of Stevenson, where, completely worn out, not having had a mouthful to eat since the morning of the day before yesterday, they arrived today at sunset with no further misfortune.[18]

Compared with Brown's and de Trobriand's accounts of the Sitting Bull incident, the *Annual Report on Military Affairs in the Department of Dakota* submitted by Major General Alfred H. Terry merely summed up the affair in one line, noting incorrectly that it occurred on May 25.[19]

Whatever the true details of Brown's brush with Sitting Bull, it is clear that he and Martin were exceedingly fortunate to have escaped with their lives. The authorities in the Dakota and Montana Territories considered the Sioux chieftain to be one of the most dangerous of the Indian leaders, and for that reason put a price on his head. A contemporary description by de Trobriand paints a detailed picture of the Bull:

> He is a man about forty years old, medium height, and somewhat inclined to be fat, a very rare thing among the Indians. He is vigorous, and wears his hair cut at the base of his neck; that is, short for a Sioux. His fierceness is masked by a good-natured manner and a conversation abounding in good humour. To judge by appearances one would believe him to be the most harmless of the redskins. In reality, he is a ferocious beast who seems to be laughing when he is showing his teeth. When he passed by near Fort Berthold, he told some Rees [Arikara Indians] that he was going to establish himself for a time on the route from Stevenson to Totten, because many people passed there, whites and soldiers, and that he would stay there as long as he could find evil deeds to do.... He seems to like to talk, for the little time that our carriers spent with his people, he entertained them with his exploits and plans.... His business, he says, is to kill whites, and he will kill them as long as he and his band last.[20]

The presence of Sitting Bull's band for a time disrupted communications, but the delay was only temporary. Eventually, in the wake of a general peace in the area negotiated in the summer of 1868, which gave the Sioux that part of Dakota which lay west of the Missouri, the horses, mules, and harness taken from the murdered mail carriers were recovered. In the same way, "part of the papers stolen by Sitting Bull from the mail carried by Brown and Martin" were returned to the Army authorities.[21] Eventually too, even the Sharp's rifle belonging to Martin was recovered in the wake of the peace treaty.[22]

To those on the frontier the cessation of hostilities seemed, at best, a temporary condition. The subsequent massacre in June 1876 of General George Custer and his men by the Sioux on the Little Big Horn River certainly appeared to confirm the sceptics' worst fears. Yet that bloody event symbolized the Indians' desperate awareness that the white man's advance was inexorable and that extermination of the buffalo was at hand. After the massacre, Sitting Bull led his people across the 49th parallel to the Canadian Northwest Territory. In that respect, Sitting Bull's withdrawal from a time of trouble paralleled a similar course of action taken by Brown when he too reached a point of crisis in his life a year later.

Immediately following the Strawberry Lake encounter with Sitting Bull and his impetuous young braves, Brown withdrew from the operational hazards of carrying dispatches to the more sedate role of a storekeeper at Fort Stevenson. The change, presumably, resulted from the need to recuperate from his ordeal with the Hunkpapas, and because men with any degree of experience and education were required to keep track of supplies during the summer season when shipping on the Missouri was in full spate.

Rather ironically, his pay was increased to $75.00 per month, but the increase did not assume significance in terms of danger until the autumn, when Brown once more resumed his duties as scout, guide, and mail carrier.[23] Indeed, from November 1868 until June 19, 1869, Brown was in charge of mail carriers and scouts operating out of Fort Stevenson.[24] During that time no men were lost while on duty runs. On the other hand, all the mail carriers constantly faced the unpredictable and often bitter winter weather. As Brown discovered, the danger of death on the prairie was ever present and took many forms.

With the approach of winter, preparations to maintain communications between the Army posts in the Dakota Territory began. Brown, naturally, was involved and once he was put in charge of the mail carriers his responsibilities increased accordingly. One result was that he was thrown into an even closer contact with the Métis people, for it was from their ranks that men skilled in the handling of dogs and sleds were recruited. De Trobriand notes in his journal that the sled dogs and their drivers arrived in Fort Stevenson on September 19, 1868:

> The latter are half-breeds of a Canadian father and an Indian mother. They are young and vigorous; the Indian type is notably dominant in them: dark eyes, long, dark, straight, stiff hair the color of burnt earth. From their father they get a heavier build and dark sparse mustaches.... The breed of dogs used to drag the sleds is tall on its legs, very close coupled, covered with thick hair, half dog and half wolf in appearance.[25]

Men and dogs could go up to 50 miles daily on the trail, but during the trips between Stevenson and Totten they were not expected to do more than 35 to 40 miles per day. Even that reduced distance, however, was formidable enough over rough terrain during inclement weather.

Instead of using a toboggan-like sled normally employed by the Métis, the United States Army substituted a vehicle of its own design. Here is de Trobriand's description of the Army's more commodious and more perfected form of the sled:

...it has the exact form of a shoe whose sole, flat and extended out behind, replaces the heel. The driver, wrapped in buffalo skin, gets on. His legs and the lower part of his body are doubly protected from the cold, and if all the load of the sled cannot be put in the shoe, there is no difficulty fastening it on back. This extremely light sled is made of buffalo skin stretched over a light frame, like the bull boats.[26]

Such was the equipment used by Brown and his half-breed companions on the Stevenson-Totten trail during the winter of 1868-1869.

The trail itself during the winter months put a premium on the durability of equipment and the stamina of men and dogs. Certainly de Trobriand's journal makes it clear that carrying dispatches for the United States Army during the winter was no sinecure. Delays and difficulties were commonplace:

Between Stevenson and Totten...there are five stations or cabins where our men can at least find shelter every night. At the halfway station, (the third), they ought to have met the carrier from Totten the evening of the third day; that is, the twenty-second [of December 1868], and be back here the evening of the twenty-fifth.... If they fail to arrive tomorrow, our new carrier will leave the day after tomorrow before we receive the letters and papers that the carrier sent out the twentieth ought to have brought us. This is the benevolence of a winter in Dakota.[27]

The shelters noted by de Trobriand were vital components in the winter mail runs, and Brown, as the chief carrier, was intimately acquainted with them. Indeed, he supervised construction of the shelters in November before the cold weather really set in.

The men take with them all necessary materials: the cabins are built of slabs under the direction of Brown.[28]

Completion of the shelters by mid-November signalled two things: the impending arrival of winter and the withdrawal of the Sioux as a direct threat to the mail carriers.[29] The Indians, through long experience, knew that winters on the prairies were treacherous, and they only ventured from their camps if it were necessary to do so. Thus while the danger from the Sioux diminished, that posed by the weather increased, as Brown soon discovered.

Brown's encounter with the elements, an experience which he never forgot, began ominously enough early in March 1869. He was persuaded to act as guide for two men: Richer, the head carpenter at Fort Stevenson, who was called home to Canada because of family business, and Voyles, an ex-Sergeant quartermaster in the United States Army. Actually, the two men, in company with a Captain Clarke who was going on three months leave, had set out from Fort Stevenson for Fort Totten on the morning of March 5.

They left in a dry storm from the northwest with the temperature at zero Fahrenheit, conditions that prompted de Trobriand to comment that they must have the devil in them to travel in such weather when they weren't forced to do so.[30] The next day the travellers returned "in a pitiful condition; noses and ears frozen, numb and crippled, a lame horse."[31] On the seventh of March 1869 the weather cleared; at the same time the temperature dropped considerably and de Trobriand recorded a reading of 18 degrees below zero (Fahrenheit) in the morning. Despite the extreme cold and their earlier experience the party of travellers insisted upon starting out once again, this time with Brown in command.

His "detailed account of the circumstances attending the unfortunate expedition" speaks for itself:

> The party arrived at the Big Hollow mail station 33 miles from Fort Totten on the 12th. This day I was attacked with snow blindness but had no fears as up to here the trail showed faintly. On the morning of the 13th we set out intending to make to Crow Island Mail Station 15 miles from Totten. The morning was fine but about 8 a.m. the wind and drift rose obscuring all the butes from view. After making 7 miles to the Coulee called the 1st Crossing of the Cheyenne, the trail was lost, but as the sun shone brightly and the wind blew steadily from the W.N.W. I had no fear but that I could keep the proper direction. 4 miles further on I recognized and crossed the 22 mile coulee. From here the snow was deep from 1 1/2 to 2 ft. all over. We made about 4 miles, yet I then thought we ought to be within 3 miles of the station, when suddenly the wind rose with great violence, bringing a snow storm. This was at about 4.30 p.m. such a fearful storm I have scarcely ever seen. From behind the sleighs the horses could scarcely be seen and it was only by shouting loudly we could make one another hear.

As travelling was now impossible, I directed a snowhouse to be made. We were unable to do so properly from the violence of the wind and drift. However, we all got in and covered with a piece of canvas which I fortunately had brought with me. Here we passed the night suffering from want of space and cold. I had hoped for a fine morning but, alas, the drift still continued and it was intensely cold, with a strong wind blowing from the N.W. The sun shone clearly and though snowblind I trusted to keep to the direction and that some of our party might be able to see the timber. On emerging from the snow house all our clothes were stiff with snow water and were at once frozen solid to us. I continued to make a small fire with a portion of one of the sleighs, I froze my left hand in doing so.

From the great depth of the snow, travelling with the sleighs was considered too slow. It was proposed for the present to abandon them and each taking a horse, to try to get to the timber on the bluffs toward the big lake which I rightly judged was not more than 5 miles off and in the same direction I had been all along keeping. I requested all the party to try to keep together and make as much haste as possible. Pt. Shank who had the black horse, and myself then took the lead, followed by Msrs. Richer, Voyles & Bittner. After we had proceeded about 2 miles in this way, the wind and drift still increasing, we perceived our companions lagged behind very much. I strove to encourage them, and said that Shank and myself would push on quickly and if we struck timber would make a fire at once and that they could easily follow our track. To this all assented. We pushed on for two or three miles further, when seeing no sign of timber, Shank began to despair. I felt sure we were close to timber but yielded to the persuasions of Shank to return to the sleighs. We retraced our steps and soon met Mr. Richer. I explained to him that failing to find timber we had concluded to return to the sleighs to burn one up and to try to stay by it till it burned. To this he assented. I then enquired for Messrs. Voyles & Bittner. He informed me that not withstanding his urgent entreaties they had left him, Voyles declaring that he believed the timber lay to the south, and that it was now everyone for himself. As we retraced our steps Shank fell behind but as we imagined he was close behind on our track we paid not much attention, till we had gone about a mile when we stopped for him to come up. He came not however, and to look for him, or wait longer, would be perhaps death to ourselves, we kept on, and soon reached the sleighs. Here we remained for 3 days and nights not being able to travel, the weather still being intolerable.

We endured the greatest misery, the cold being intense. At last on the 4th morning, my eyes continuing bad, we retraced our steps to the Big Hollow mail station. On Friday the 19th the lake mail arrived, and on its return on Monday 22nd we set out and reached Fort Totten the same day. I related the circumstances to General [J. N. G.] Whistler, who dispatched parties in search of the missing men.... I am myself under medical treatment and am unable to return at present on horseback. My hand is well but my left foot is, though improving, far from well yet.[32]

How close Brown and Richer came to perishing during the blizzard is confirmed by de Trobriand in his journal entry of March 22, 1869:

...Richer and Brown, were found by the mail carriers, and they were half dead with cold and hunger, arms and legs frozen, etc.... As for the other three, they disappeared,...and we do not know, or know all too well, what has become of them, for they had left their buffalo robes and blankets in the sled, and did not have anything with which to make a fire. Unless a miracle happens, they are dead.[33]

But miracles during western blizzards rarely occur, and the three men, as de Trobriand surmised, died. Two of them, Shank and Bittner, eventually were found, one of them only three miles from Fort Totten, the other eight.[34] The body of Voyles was never found. Ironically, amongst Bittner's papers were found a forged discharge certificate and various other falsified papers, including letters ostensibly signed by the post commander at Fort Stevenson, General de Trobriand. Possession of the forgeries and the intention of putting them to quick and profitable use may well have been responsible for the desire of Bittner to get away from Fort Stevenson and the Dakota Territory as soon as possible, and to take chances with the unpredictable spring weather. Instead of profit he reaped only death for himself and his companions.

For his part Brown, in his report to de Trobriand, was anxious to have the authorities absolve him of any blame for the incident:

...from this statement, together with the certificate...from Mr. Ritcher it will be seen that I am as Guide of the party altogether free of any blame which might attach itself to me. I can only add that I have done my best that owing only to snow blindness and storm I in the first place went a little out of the course and still had all taken my repeated advice all might have been saved.[35]

His account was accepted, and he continued as chief carrier at Fort Stevenson until the expiration of the mail contract on June 19, 1869. By then the United States Army felt it had accumulated enough experience to handle communications between Fort Stevenson and Fort Totten. With the expiration of the contract, Brown transferred to Fort Buford, the most westerly of the chain of Army establishments in Dakota Territory. There, on August 17, 1869, he contracted with the Acting Assistant Quartermaster of the 13th Infantry to operate a military express between Buford and Totten by way of Fort Stevenson.[36] Under the agreement the express was to run twice each way every month for eight months, and for the service Brown was to receive the sum of $200.00 per month. It was the beginning of a new, and for Brown, significant period in his life.

Chapter 7

Buffalo Hunting With The Métis

In itself, Brown's transfer to Fort Buford was neither unusual nor unexpected. It simply reflected that the centre of mail carrying operations was shifting westward, paralleling the forward thrust of the United States Army and the consolidation of the area protected by Forts Stevenson and Totten. The removal to Buford was itself only a matter of two or three days ride on horseback, certainly not a major effort for an experienced plainsman such as Brown. Once transferred to his new operational base Brown immediately resumed the mail runs. The initial trip east was normal, if indeed, any trip through Indian territory over insect-infested plains during hot summer days could ever be considered normal.

The Buford post returns for August show that Brown duly made one trip and received half a month's pay.[1] However, while at Fort Totten, the terminal end of the route, Brown, because of his knowledge of the surrounding territory, was selected by the Deputy Quartermaster of the United States Army, Brigadier General Samuel B. Holabird, to guide a party commanded by Major General W. S. Hancock on a tour of the region north and west of the post. The reconnaissance, which extended west as far as the Mouse River, lasted a month, and Brown received $160.00 for his services.[2] During his absence hired men, half-breeds in all probability, operated the regular mail run for which he had contracted.

For Brown the unexpected departure from normal routine was of particular significance. Towards the end of the tour, Hancock's party paused for a time at Pembina, then a tiny cluster of log cabins in the Dakota Territory just below the 49th parallel. Its main significance was its strategic position along the main overland route between the Red River settlements and St. Paul. Along that route creaked and squealed the Red River carts, scarring the land with deep ruts as they carried their loads of buffalo hides for the markets of the east. Pembina also had the dis-

90

tinction of being acknowledged (tacitly at least) as the Métis capital of the Red River Settlements if, indeed, a capital can be claimed by a people who shunned settlements.

How long Major General Hancock's party remained at or near Pembina is not clear. For Brown, however, the pause was sufficiently long to enable him to marry a young Métis girl, Olive Lyonnais. According to parish records the ceremony took place in St. Joseph's Church on September 26, 1869. It was performed by Joseph le Block, O.M.I., and witnessed by Joseph Lyonnais, the bride's father, and a young Irishman, Thomas Cavanagh.[3]

The union was not an unusual one. Casual or temporary arrangements between white men and Métis or Indian women were commonplace. De Trobriand, who touched upon the matter in his observations of plains life, describes the conditions which prevailed with characteristic penetration:

> There are no white women at Berthold, or in any other non-military post in the country. Here every white man takes an Indian wife with whom he lives and who keeps his house and bears him children. These children almost never speak any language but that of the mother, and stay in the tribe if the father leaves the country, which is rare.... These children are better cared for than many, the girls especially, who dress like their mothers in Indian garments as they do in our regions.... It is notable that the French language is a good deal more common among them in these parts than English, which is the result of a great infusion of Canadian blood in the tribes.[4]

Under the circumstances, what is surprising is the number of marriages that were permanent and based upon genuine affection. Such was Brown's marriage, though his references to the union tend to be brusque in the most Victorian sense:

> I had been married while in Dakota to a girl of eighteen years named Olivia D'Lonais, who lived in Pembina. I was thirty-two [in reality, 30, according to official records] years old at the time of our marriage.[5]

Under the circumstances Brown's marriage to Olivia, as he was disposed to call her, was not in the least extraordinary. Since she was also beautiful, according to Marie Rose Smith, the quick courtship ending in marriage seemed appropriate.[6]

Many other travellers found that the mixed-blood women, uncommonly pretty and provocative, proved to be gay companions as well as devoted wives and mothers. More than most men, Kootenai had close and direct contacts with the Métis almost from the time he had debouched from the mountains unto the plains. Their spontaneous gaiety, love of adventure in the open and a desire to be free of the restrictions implicit in settlement, paralleled his own eclectic personality. Moreover, life in the Métis camps bridged the gap between his experiences in society in England and Ireland, and the solitary life of the Cariboo miner and the mail carrier which had been his for the better part of a decade. Some of the same feeling was caught by de Trobriand when he was newly arrived in the American West:

> I think of the Parisian life I left two months ago today [August 11, 1868] and look around me at natural life in its most simple unrestrained form. Here there are no laws, no taxes, no rules - nothing but space and freedom. And this brings me to remark that civilization and freedom must go together. What are the results when they are separated? Collective degradation or individual abasement.[7]

To Brown, a pretty young wife, a connection with a Metis community, seemed at the time at least, to be a happy compromise with civilization.

After the marriage, Kootenai and his bride returned to Fort Totten, settling there instead of Fort Buford. Since Totten was the mail run's eastern terminal it did not much matter where Brown, as the contractor, settled. At the same time, the post was the closest United States Army establishment to Pembina and his bride's family. The couple remained at Fort Totten for the next two years, until August 1871. Both are listed among the post's population of 246 in the returns of the 1870 United States Census.[8]

Brown's marriage and move to Fort Totten in 1869 coincided with growing unrest in the Red River Settlement. Indeed, it was in the latter part of the summer of 1869 that the Métis took the first steps to organize their opposition to the transfer of the Red River to the Dominion of Canada. By October, as Kootenai and his Olivia were repairing to Fort Totten, the small secret gatherings in the Red River had begun to swell into large assemblies that were resolved to prevent the entry of any Canadian official until half-breed rights were guaranteed. In the background, Louis Riel was beginning to assume leadership of a people who were prepared for fiery speeches and radical action.

Undoubtedly, Brown with his close Métis connections must have been aware of the smoldering discontent within the Red River Settlement. Whether he condoned the challenge to Ottawa's authority is not known, for Brown never revealed his feelings about the first Red River rebellion. On the other hand, it is equally certain that Brown, despite suggestions by John Henry Taylor who lived in the Dakota Territory from 1867 until the area received statehood in 1889, was never approached by Riel to raise a force for the Provisional Government:

> With the wafting breeze that brought the first news of the Red River rebellion over to the Upper Missouri country, came also the rumor that John George Brown of Fort Stevenson was commissioned to raise a force of hardy frontiersmen and come over to General Riel's assistance.
>
> Brown was an Irishman, married to a Cree half-breed woman, and it is said he had formerly been an officer in the British army. At the time of receiving his commission from the insurgent leader, he was post interpreter at Fort Stevenson.[9]

More likely Brown, throughout the period of crisis in the Red River Settlement, was more concerned with the constant threats of thunderstorms, prairie fires, blistering heat, swarms of mosquitoes and, above all, interception by the Sioux. That the mail operations proceeded satisfactorily is confirmed when the Army command in the Dakota Territory renewed Brown's contract at the start of the new fiscal year on July 1, 1870, and raised his compensation to $300.00 per month. By then the rebellion to the north had all but petered out. Nevertheless, a certain amount of tension, amplified by rumour and speculation, continued throughout the Upper Missouri country. John Henry Taylor recalls that:

> An organization for the help of the half-breeds' Republic was attempted at points along the Missouri, but the vacillating conduct of the leaders in Manitoba weakened the resolutions of those beyond the borders, who wished them ready success. A "medicine lodge" for Riel's cause had been formed at the Tough Timber [a stand of timber on the Missouri bend between Fort Rice and Fort Stevenson near the present town of Hancock], where the long nights and isolation, demanded a stimulant for mental action.[10]

Such an organization was never a serious factor in the Red River rebellion. It was, indeed, more the product of fertile imaginations, a point borne out by Taylor's list of principals in the Tough Timber group: Wheeler, the Deitrich brothers, Flopping Bill, and Taylor himself.[11] As the last notes of the insurrection were dying away Brown, far from being involved with politics north of the border, was much more concerned with the problems of operating his mail service.

Although his stipend for the service had risen considerably, the higher rate of pay also reflected the increase in volume of mail carried between posts. The result was that Brown, as the contractor, had to hire additional men in order to fulfill his agreement, and reliable experienced men were distinctly limited in numbers and hard to find. One despatch from the post commander at Fort Totten, Major J. E. Yard of the 20th Infantry, touches upon some of the difficulties Brown had to contend with:

I have the honour to report [to the Assistant Adjutant General of the Department of Dakota at St. Paul] the burning of a mail station together with the United States Mail at Sulphur Springs, about 15 miles east of Fort Stevenson D.T. I was informed by the half-breed carriers employed by the contractor Mr. G. J. [sic] Brown that it was fired by Indians. A party of Indians arrived at this post yesterday [May 16, 1871] from the Missouri who were camped three miles from the station and saw the fire and who say that no Indians but themselves were near the station. From what I can learn I feel confident the loss is due to the carelessness and neglect of the half-breed mail carriers themselves.[12]

Although Yard's despatch raises the question of who should be believed, it also touches squarely upon the matter of the Métis character. The half-breeds' unwillingness to accept responsibility and to maintain consistent moral discipline was well known. Periods of sound service were all too often followed by long drinking bouts and exhausting dancing parties. Soon after the establishment of Fort Totten, the Adjutant of the post wrote to the Assistant Adjutant General for the Department of Dakota about the Métis:

Most of the Half Breeds have families, they are mostly transient, seeking employment where they can get it until the Buffalo season, when they are off.[13]

Brown, of course, was aware of the Métis attitude of mind. He employed them because they were the only experienced plainsmen on hand, and because of his direct connection with the Métis community through his wife, Olive, and her family.

Apart from a short interval of three months – April 1 to June 30, 1871 – when he was employed as guide and post interpreter at Fort Stevenson, and for which he was paid an extra $100 per month, Brown remained at Fort Totten until his mail contract with the United States Army expired. At the end of August 1871 he and Olive left Totten for Fort Stevenson.

Once moved he did not take up formal employment with the United States Army immediately. Presumably he had enough money to purchase basic supplies; perhaps he joined his Métis in-laws for the autumn buffalo hunt. At the end of November, however, the Post Returns show that Brown and another man, James Richmond, were employed by the Acting Assistant Quartermaster 17th Infantry, to guide another officer, First Lieutenant George Acheson of the Seventh Infantry, from Fort Stevenson to Fort Totten for the sum of $30.00. The choice of Brown and Richmond for such a job was understandable, though it had to be justified to the Officer Commanding the Department of Dakota. Major R. E. Crofton, the post commander who authorized their employment wrote:

> Application having been made to me for an escort, I arranged with Messrs. Brown and Richmond, the most competent guides at hand, to conduct the party to Fort Totten, feeling that the severity of the weather would imperil the lives of the men composing the escort across the plains at that season without such assistance.[14]

Early in the next year, on February 29, 1872, the same officer signed Special Order No. 22, which placed Brown once more upon the United States payroll. He was employed as interpreter and guide at Fort Stevenson at the rate of $100.00 per month, replacing the previous incumbent, a Métis named Pierre Beauchamp.[15] The reduction in pay, which at first glance seems considerable, was simply due to the fact that Brown did not have to hire assistants as he had to do when he contracted the mail between Forts Buford and Totten.

At that, his rate of pay was substantially higher than that of other civilian employees. Carpenters at Fort Stevenson in 1873 received $75.00 per month, blacksmiths $100.00, while labourers, artificers and storekeepers received 20 cents per day plus their keep.[16] Similar rates prevailed during the period at Fort Buford to the West.[17] For Brown, the post of guide-interpreter had two advantages: it was not seasonal as were the jobs of the building trades, labourers, and teamsters; and, more important, it kept him outdoors leading the life he loved.

Until Brown was struck from the Army payroll on June 9, 1874, his period of service at Fort Stevenson was uneventful. During that time the country was pacified and conditions of life in the Dakota Territory were gradually transformed as settlers and survey parties followed in the Army's wake. In addition, the combination of the Sioux Treaties signed in 1868 and the shift of buffalo further to the West into Montana Territory had reduced the level of danger on the trails considerably. At the same time, service on the prairies was no longer a novelty to the United States Army. Also, with increased experience and knowledge the great empty land was not regarded with the same degree of apprehension that it was in the years immediately following the Civil War. Nevertheless, experience still counted, and on many occasions was a vital necessity.

One such occasion occurred in the summer of 1873 when Brown was detailed to lead an armed escort of the Sixth Infantry in search of "Mr. Winnie's wagon train," a section of the United States Northern Boundary Survey whose whereabouts north and west of Fort Stevenson was unknown.[18] The search party was away for twenty days, and contact with the survey party must have been re-established for there is no other mention of the expedition in the Post Returns. During Brown's absence, his duties as interpreter were taken over by James Vicker on authority from headquarters in St. Paul.[19]

The fact that Brown's duties were taken over so easily by another individual, while seemingly unimportant at the time, soon took on another perspective. By 1874, Fort Stevenson and the territory immediately surrounding it were in the backwash of frontier activity. Army posts further to the West were at the vanguard of westward expansion, and the demands of ranchers and traders in Montana Territory for action against the marauding Sioux and unsettled Blackfoot confederation were becoming increasingly vociferous. The Northern Boundary Survey, too, was almost at the end of its work with the mountains, the terminus of its commission, almost in sight.

As a result of these circumstances, the need for experienced scouts, translators, and mail carriers in the Dakota Territory diminished steadily, and in March 1874 Brown found himself the victim of advancing civilization. His pay that month was reduced by half, a change that he resented and deplored. Seething with indignation because he "refused to work for such a mere pittance," he left the employ of the United States Army on June 9, 1874.[20] Instead of seeking work further west, or settling down to ranching or farming, Kootenai, like his Métis employees, went buffalo hunting:

> When I left the government work, I came back with my wife and one small child (a daughter) to Canada, and joined a camp of half-breeds.[21]

It was the beginning of a brief but colourful and exciting period in his life.

Brown's decision to leave the employ of the United States Army early in the summer was not a hasty one. A certain amount of time was required to join Olive's family and to become integrated into the life of the Métis band before the autumn buffalo hunt.

J. W. Taylor, the United States Consul at Winnipeg and a shrewd observer of the plains people, pinpointed the essential nature of the hunts:

> It is the custom of the French population to proceed to the adjacent buffalo plains, under strict military discipline, for an October hunt.[22]

Writing to the Secretary of State, Hamilton Fish, early in 1870, Taylor noted the military nature of the Métis organization which made it easy for various bands to take possession of Fort Garry and other points in the Red River Settlement. The same point is made by the historian of the Red River rebellion, G. F. G. Stanley. Nevertheless, even without co-ordination, organization, and sound leadership, the Métis constituted a formidable fighting potential. By the time Brown and his wife joined the Métis, however, the first Riel rebellion was over, and the people of the Red River were facing a new problem — that of maintaining contact with buffalo herds that were diminishing in numbers and steadily retreating westwards. G. F. G. Stanley delineates the problem admirably:

> For many years the Métis had set out from the Red River valley upon their great hunts over the western prairies, but the gradual withdrawal of the buffalo further and further from the eastern plains made these long journeys unprofitable. The Red River Métis were then faced with two alternatives, to follow the wild animals westwards, or to settle down to a life of agriculture. The Métis had a horror of sedentary existence. The chase to them was a necessity as well as a pleasure, and many, choosing the easier road, followed the well-defined buffalo trails into the interior.[23]

Brown, although not a half-breed, was one of those who chose the easier solution.

The band that he and Olive joined epitomizes the last phase of the buffalo hunts. Its operational area centered upon the region delineated by the Milk and the Saskatchewan Rivers, and in the three years that Brown and his family spent with the Métis people, the camp wintered twice on the Milk River and once upon the Marias in United States territory. The 49th parallel, despite the work of the Northern Boundary Survey Commissions, held little meaning for the Métis, and they crossed it frequently and at will in following the great herds.

Thus in the autumn of 1874 we see Brown then in the prime of life, indistinguishable from his companions, the dark-skinned brightly dressed half-breeds, hunting the buffalo, the "crooked-back oxen" of the prairies. In the process he enjoyed moments of great excitement, many thrilling sights, and the conviviality of a happy, hospitable people. It was a way of life which was to end with unexpected and dramatic suddenness. Brown's descriptions of the chase and the life he led during those carefree times, although recalled when he was an old man, not only catch much of the pungent flavour of the camps, but square in essential details with the careful researches of scholars. G. F. G. Stanley delineates the organization which characterized a Métis camp with spare precision:

> These hunting expeditions were seldom disordered, isolated efforts. The Métis gathered in large bands under command of chosen leaders and self-imposed regulations. Early in their history they learned that only by union could they cope with hostile bands of marauding Indians. Experience and necessity had evolved a loose code of rules and restrictions which, tightened by the bonds of tradition, governed the conduct of the hunt.[24]

When the half-breeds gathered to prepare for the hunts, which were usually held twice a year in June and September or October, the occasions afforded opportunities to carry out social, political, and business affairs. Acquaintances were renewed, important questions discussed, agreements reached and transactions concluded. Once the hunt got under way, the organization of the camp which governed the daily lives of all its members began to manifest itself:

> The organization of the half-breed hunting camp was very complete. Every season at an appointed time a chief hunter was appointed by a vote of all full-grown men. This officer acted as mayor, magistrate, priest, camp manager, and general overseer. We very seldom had the same chief two years band running, but I remember a hunter named Alexander Wilkie who was elected

two consecutive years. He had very little Indian blood in him, but any one with the least trace of Indian in him was termed a half-breed.

Every evening regular in summer during the hunting season when weather permitted, all full grown males of the camp gathered in a huge circle, squatted on the ground with the chief hunter in view of all. This gathering, too, was opened by prayer by the chief. The events of the day were talked over. If there were any disputes they were referred to the chief and settled by him there and then. His word was law but if he were in doubt he frequently asked for a vote of the circle. Plans for the next day would be decided on and the number of buffalo killed estimated. The chief could always read and write and it was his business to go to each man and say "So-and-so, how many did you kill?" The hunter would say three or five or seven or whatever the number happened to be and the chief went on from man to man. Now and then he would come to a breed who would lower his head and answer "none." This would nearly always call out a laugh from the circle and the hunter would begin to make excuses, but they would laugh just the same. French half-breeds are great jokers, so are Indians in their own way.[25]

Once the move to the hunting area began, discipline, organization and humour, as Brown makes clear, were essential:

When the hunting season opened everybody – men, women, and children left the wintering places in carts, wagons, and some even with the old travois. We took all our belongings which sometimes did not mean much, but we took them anyhow. After we had travelled out of range of winter quarters in which we had killed off all buffalo, scouts were sent ahead on horseback to find where the buffalo were in numbers sufficient to move the whole camp. Sometimes these scouts would have to travel a hundred miles before returning to report that it was worth while making camp. Often it would be several days before we would make our first stop, but after that we would not need to travel so far. You understand that a little hunting was done all winter and because of this buffalo did not live in large numbers near the camp.

When the scouts returned they would meet the camp which had been following them up, and when near the point where the buffalo were found in numbers, all the riders – between one hundred and fifty and three hundred in number – would range themselves abreast to give every man a fair chance. With the captain of the hunt about the centre of the line and about three horse lengths ahead, we would advance at a slow walk toward the buffalo who would huddle together and show signs of alarm and finally break into a fast walk. The leader of the hunt would yell "Trot". About this time we would be three hundred yards from the herd. They would shortly break into a slow gallop and the chief hunter would give his final command "Equa, Equa," meaning, "Now, Now," and every one of the long line of hunters would spur their runners into a gallop at full speed. From this time on it is every man for himself. Those who had the fastest horses got their pick of the herd. Sometimes a hunter on a very fast horse would have three, or as many as five, buffalo shot before the main body of the hunters got up. A great deal depended on the horse he was riding. Some of them were the best race horses that could be bought on the prairie. Some hunters in a drive of this kind would kill as many as ten buffalo and the whole camp would probably total one thousand head.

It was some experience for a new hunter – dust flying, horns clashing, buffalo bellowing, men yelling, and all going at top speed. The buffalo dare not stop as the rest of the herd would trample over them. There was hardly ever a drive in which someone was not hurt. It rarely ever happened that a hunter was shot, but sometimes he would be knocked off his horse and another rider would run over him. We had to be very careful and, at the same time, we had only a few minutes to do our execution. And we had to remember the buffalo we killed, for each hunter had to skin and transport his own game. In time of scarcity when there was only a small amount of food in the camp, as sometimes happened in later years, a general drive would be ordered by the captain when everything killed was "Minis-a-wak" (common property).[26]

Under the best of conditions and with good equipment such concerted action would be difficult. With comparatively inefficient weapons the work of the hunter was compounded, and his skill put to the premium test. As Brown recalls, much of the equipment used by the Métis hunters bordered on the primitive:

In those days most of us had saddles – I suppose three quarters of us had – but not the stock saddles used in the west today... [most] were what we call pad saddles. They were made of buffalo hide and usually stuffed with antelope hair. They were light, only weighing a couple of pounds. The stirrups were made of wood cut from the timbers in the river bottoms and the stirrup straps were made of two-ply of good six-year-old buffalo, about the only use we had for a six-year-old bull. We used loose ammunition, black powder and ball and cap. We carried the bullets in our pockets, and for immediate use in our mouths. The powder we had in a horn and it was poured haphazard into the barrel and a ball rolled in. Sometimes we overloaded and every season there would be two or three hands blown off or a few fingers mutilated by guns exploding.[27]

Obviously it required much skill to use weapons effectively from horseback during the high excitement of the chase. Brown, unlike most of his half-breed companions, was better equipped, an advantage which stemmed from his comparative affluence and the need to get the best possible weapons available while he was carrying the mail for the United States Army. He mentions using a Hawkins rifle, a weapon considerably superior to the ball and powder antiques used by so many of the Métis.

Contrary to most generalizations, the Métis were not wanton wasteful killers. Here is Brown's account of the hazards involved in the chase and his description of the work that followed a successful hunt:

100

In running buffalo a hunter with a good horse would kill only prime animals. No calves or yearlings were ever killed – nothing but full grown, three, four, five, and six years old. Buffalo live, barring accidents, to about the same age as domestic cattle. We always preferred front quarters of a buffalo because they were fatter and as we boiled our meat in summer, front quarters made the best food. Of course, it was a rule in all half-breed hunting camps that every part of every animal must be used unless it was diseased. Mange was the principal disease, but we frequently found buffalo with lump jaw and occasionally with wounds inflicted in drives or by the arrows of roaming bands of Indians. These diseased or maimed animals were only killed by accident.

The run of the herd would average about one mile. Some of the slow or long-winded horses might run a couple of miles but most of the killing was done in five hundred yards. It was just a miniature battle but the killed were always of the fleeing army of buffalo. A hunter would occasionally be hurt. I remember once breaking my shoulder blade. I had killed six buffalo in a drive, which should have been amply sufficient for the day, but I was riding a fast horse and was too greedy and rode into a bunch ahead of the slow animals that had got behind. A number of buffalo crowded into my horse and he stumbled and fell. I got free of the stirrups and I don't know how many animals ran over me. When I was picked up by the other hunters I was unconscious, and when I was taken back to camp in a meat cart it was found that my shoulder bone was broken. I was laid up for a week but was not able to hunt for the remainder of the season.

As soon as the drive was over, the women with the children and old men followed on with the carts to carry the meat back to camp. Immediately after the hunter has stopped shooting, he turns back to find the buffalo he has killed. Dropping his bridle rein, his horse feeds about while he cuts up his game. It is all done with a knife – skinning and quartering, and never an axe used. Each hunter must look after the animals he has killed and his woman is on hand to haul it away with a cart. The drive begins as early as possible in the morning. This gives plenty of time to dress the killing and get it to camp before dark at night. A cow and a half was considered a good load for a cart, which of course, was hauled by only one horse. It was the hardest kind of work, skinning and cutting up buffalo in the boiling sun of a midsummer day, and we were always glad when the carts came back for another load as our women always brought a keg of water. We were always very thirsty. The dead buffalo were as-thack-a-kay (placed on their backs with their heads tucked under their shoulders ready for skinning). It took only a few minutes to skin one. The carving was not done close to the hide because of the danger of cutting the hide. This was particularly so in the winter when the hides were sometimes used for robes or other purposes. After the hide was taken off the flesh was scraped with a "Mick-a-Quaw," (a macking iron), which was an arrangement with teeth that scraped off the meat or "mick" next to the hide.

The hides of buffalo over four years of age were rarely ever used because it was heavy and coarse. If we wanted a prime hide we went out and killed a two-year-old cow buffalo. Old bull hides were used for lariat or lass ropes and, in later years when we killed for robes of commerce, only three-year-old animals were slaughtered. In summer the hides of bulls were always left on the prairie with the entrails. I suppose I have seen thousands of buffalo hides left to rot on the plains. There was no demand for them, no use for them. The hair was short in summer and we could not use them in our houses or huts and there was no market for them then. I wish I had a few thousand of them now.

As a general rule no hunting was done for two or three days at least, and sometimes ten days after a drive. If the buffalo were still in the vicinity in which the first drive took place, the camp remained stationary and another drive was made usually in two or three days, or before they wandered too far away. But if the first drive resulted in the usual slaughter of buffalo, it took a week to get the meat disposed of. The morning after the drive the women started cutting up the buffalo quarters and making dried meat and pemmican. No meat ever spoiled. It was sliced up as quickly as possible and sun dried and if kept from damp, dried meat or pemmican would keep for a thousand years. I suppose our drives in the good hunting season would average one a week but all depended on the buffalo. Sometimes they wandered a long way off and sometimes other hunters came in and disturbed them.[28]

Such was the usual order and pattern of activity in a Métis camp during the hunting season.

While the stimulus of the chase and the hard work which followed the kills were dominant aspects of a Métis camp, they were by no means the only or the most significant features of the halfbreed communities. Virtually all who travelled through the Red River Settlements or who, like Brown, accompanied the people into the field during the buffalo hunting season, were struck by the deeply religious nature of the Métis colonies. J. W. Taylor observed that "probably no similar population in the world are better provided with religious and educational institutions."[29] G. F. G. Stanley also has drawn attention to the religious nature of Métis life:

As a rule these [hunting] expeditions were accompanied by a missionary priest, who, with his portable altar, daily celebrated mass in his tent, taught the children their catechism, visited the sick and injured, and formed the nucleus of a fervent, though nomadic parish.[30]

Even if a priest did not accompany an expedition or attach himself to a half-breed band, the same religious fervor prevailed as Brown himself experienced:

The half-breed hunting camp was a religious and law-abiding institution. I have never been a very religious man any time in my life but I think I was brought into closer touch with religion in the years of my buffalo hunting with French half-breeds than at any other time in my life. It was not my religion though. I was born into the English church and have since embraced theosophy, but I never lived with a people more deeply religious than those French half-breeds of the early hunting days on the plains of Western Canada. Before every buffalo drive, when we got saddled and ready to ride after the herd, the long line of hunters dismounted, and having crossed themselves, knelt on the prairie while the chief hunter made a short prayer. In it he called upon the Almighty to give success to the hunt, to prevent accidents, and to give us food for our wives and little ones. It was an extempore prayer not found in any prayer book and it varied in words and length every hunt. The French half-breeds were Roman Catholics, of course, and I was the only man in the camp who did not cross himself very devoutly before meals. There was mass every Sunday conducted by the chief hunter.

Sunday was always a day of rest in the half-breed camp. No hunting nor any kind of work was done on that day. It was quieter by far than any western village on a Sunday in these times. There was a fine of $10 for any man who would shoot a gun on this day of the week. I usually went with my wife to mass as it was one of the rules of the camp that everybody should attend. But one Sunday I was at home alone and looking out across the camp I spied a fine antelope feeding on the hill. The temptation to shoot was very strong because it was a rare thing for an antelope to come near our winter village. So taking up my gun, I stole around the hill, and when I got a good position I let-her-go and dropped the animal in her tracks. The report of the gun was heard by the worshippers at mass and in the middle of the service two "sa-mag-inis-uck" (camp soldiers or police), were sent out to arrest the hunter. Next day I was hailed before the chief hunter and fined $10, which I had to pay, dead sure. There was no such thing as money in camp – not a red cent; everything was trade or barter. I paid in skins or meat or something, I don't remember what. Oh, no. You couldn't shoot on Sunday in a French half-breed buffalo hunting camp, and I don't think I ever did such a thing again.[31]

The humorous episode of the Sunday shot told, with such relish by Kootenai, not only delineates the reverence with which the Métis observed the Sabbath; it also reveals Kootenai's humour, a trait which, according to those who knew him, he never lost.

Apart from the constant hazards of the hunt as pointed up by Brown's own experiences, and the usual conditions of illness, flies, mosquitoes, prairie fires, and cloud-bursts, the Métis hunting camps also had to contend with the dangers posed by Indians or by the buffalo, the very beasts they were pursuing. Even when Brown and his wife joined their half-breed band, late though it was in terms of the buffalo hunts, the danger from hostile Indians was not overlooked:

The Blackfeet were scattered over the prairie in the territory where we hunted and every night we made a coral of our carts and kept our horses inside this coral. Two or three men stood guard from dark to daylight to warn the camp should any attack by Indians take place. Ours was a large camp and we were never troubled because the Blackfeet were afraid to attack us. Our guns were far superior to theirs; in fact, they did not begin to use guns for many years after their use in the hunting camps. They were afraid of them. All young men of the camp had to take their turns as soldiers or policemen, keeping order in the camp, but mostly guarding the camp day and night from possible attack from hostile Indians. At night they patrolled with loaded guns. The tents and lodges of the camp were in the circle made by placing the shafts of one cart on the tail-board of another. One would be surprised today at the immense circle the camp carts would make. There were many carts used for hauling wood as the camp moved from place to place. These remained stationary while the drive was on and while the pemmican was being made and if the carts used for hauling meat were used during the day they were placed in position before the horses were unhitched at night.[32]

While the danger of attack posed by Indians was a constant feature of Métis life, there were others that were not so readily anticipated or countered:

Our camp had quite an experience once. It happened on a Sunday morning and I was the only sinner not at mass. It was near what afterwards became Fort Steele in the Cypress Hills and I was nursing a broken shoulder blade. Our camp consisted of about one hundred and fifty lodges and our carts had all been packed for moving on Monday for a new drive and to make a new camp. I was lying in a tent when I heard a great rumbling noise. I knew at once what it was but could not understand why a herd of buffalo should be stampeding into our camp. They were coming pell-mell and to try to head them off I ran out with a Hawkin's rifle and resting the barrel on one of the carts I shot with one hand. I had only time for two shots when the whole herd came careering into the camp. Nearly half the tents were upset and many of them torn to ribbons. If it had happened at any other time but during mass when everyone was away from their tents, who knows how many would have been killed. As it was, only two dogs fell victims of the stampede. But carts were overturned and many shafts and wheels broken. They went right through the camp leaving a trail of destruction in their wake. Behind them were a party of white hunters who, when they saw what they had done, rode off at a full gallop and we never saw them again.[33]

During the winter, the order and pattern of daily existence in a Métis settlement differed radically from that of a mobile tent colony following in the wake of the great buffalo herds. When the vice of winter tightened upon the prairies, the half-breed families who did not return to their homes in the Red River Settlement were forced to seek provisional quarters:

Their winter camps were chosen with care. They had to be near a wood for building purposes and fuel, close to a stream or river, and not too far from the favorite haunts of the buffalo for the next spring's hunt. The construction of log huts gave the camps an air of solidity and permanency, which indicated the possibilities of a definite settlement. Winter after winter the Métis returned to the same districts and gradually, through the efforts of missionaries and the diminution of the chase, these became the sites of permanent villages. The most important of these hunting communities were to be found between the lower reaches of the North and South Saskatchewan Rivers near Duck Lake and Fort Carlton, and in the Qu'Appelle valley.[34]

Brown graphically describes the log cabins and the community life which the Métis led whenever winter overtook them:

These cabins had large fireplaces and, usually, puncheon floors. These were made by split logs from the river bottoms, smoothed with an axe on one side and the round side lay on the ground. The large chimneys were made of rocks picked up on the prairie and plastered with mud. As a matter of fact, the chimneys were mostly mud, but it is wonderful how they stood up. Of course, they were hardly ever used two winters in succession. The wood was put in them on end and was cut about five feet long. They gave out an immense heat even though half of it went up the chimney. It was a common thing at night to see flames seven and eight feet high shooting out of a score of chimneys in a half-breed camp. Cooking was done in this fireplace. There was no such thing as a stove for many a year after this time. We didn't even have candles for light. The fire usually gave all the light that was needed but this was sometimes helped out by bowls of grease in which were set twisted rags. In summer no lights were needed for we were in bed before dark and up at sunrise.

As a rule the village used for winter quarters was built in November or December and was deserted for tents about May. French half-breeds are very gay people and as there was not much to do in the long winter evenings, we had a dance nearly every evening. Sometimes this would be in a private house and friends and neighbors invited. Other times it would be held in a hall in the half-breed village always built for the purpose. In the camps where I was there would be about one hundred and fifty lodges or houses and averaging them at seven persons to a house there would be a total of about one thousand souls in a half-breed hunting camp.

One thousand people of nomadic proclivities would require a great many horses. We had between four and five thousand. Of course, we did not cut any hay for horses and they had never known what grain was. When we were through with them in the fall they were turned out to rustle for themselves and sometimes we never saw them until spring. The camp knew where they were, however, for there was always a chance of wandering bands of Indians picking them up and taking them off. We always lost horses this way every winter. These horses were used for carts which women and old men and children drove while the men hunted. You must remember that when we pulled stakes in May we took everything we could load up for we never knew for sure that we would ever see the village again. There would be between one hundred and fifty and three hundred buffalo hunters and each of these would have at least two buffalo runners, that, is fast horses for running down buffalo. I had three runners and two four-horse outfits besides; and I had the only light wagon [not a democrat] in camp. It was used by my wife and children [a second daughter was born to Brown while he and Olive were with the Metis] when changing camp and hunting.[35]

A camp of Métis hunters from Red River on their annual buffalo hunt. Sketched in 1853 by J.M. Stanley, this camp contained 824 Red River carts, 1,200 horses and 1,300 people.

The sketch below of Métis hunting buffalo was done in 1874 by Henri Julien. He was an artist who accompanied the North-West Mounted Police on their westward trek and made the only illustrated record. The Métis used all of the meat, a startling contrast to the whites who left the carcasses to rot when they virtually slaughtered into extinction some 60 million buffalo.

Such winter camps were distinct social institutions, each with an environment of its own, each a law unto itself.

To the Métis and the plains Indians the buffalo was the mainstay of their lives. The extent to which this was so has been reiterated countless times and Brown, too, stressed the point in his own distinctive way:

Buffalo meat was the staple food and ninety per cent of all the food eaten was either this meat dried and cooked in various ways or made into pemmican. Occasionally for a change we killed antelope, ducks, geese, and sage hens and in the fall the women and children picked wild turnips and berries of various kinds. Pemmican was all made in summer and used for food in winter or perhaps some of it sold to the few post stores along the frontier. It was from the flesh of bulls killed in August, September, October, and November and sometimes in May and the first week in June. No meat was killed in the rutting season which was June and July.

It was a rare sight in rutting season to look out at the great cloud of dust in every direction thrown up by the pawing and rolling of thousands of bulls in every large herd. All over the prairie today [i.e. circa 1914-1916] are to be found depressions, some now containing water, made by the feet of bull buffalo, the earth out of which was thrown into the air and carried off by the wind. They are known as wallows, and will stand out for many years to come as reminders of the "once mighty herds which shook the earth with trembling sound."

Buffalo were harmless to one on horseback. We rarely ever heard of a buffalo attacking a horse and rider unless severely wounded. They would not even attack a person on foot but would crowd around out of curiosity and the pedestrian was liable to be trampled down.... There were countless thousands of buffalo in those days, thicker than even range cattle were on any range on earth. I have stood on the top of the Cypress and Sweet Grass Hills in Alberta and Saskatchewan and, as far as I could see in all directions, was a living mass of buffalo.[36]

No one who had lived for as long as he had in such close proximity to the great shaggy beasts and in such intimacy with people who had interwoven their lives with the buffalo to the extent which the Métis had done could ever forget the sights, sounds, and smells of that experience. Yet, even as Brown was in the full throes of those days, game on the plains was becoming scarce. In 1870 the plains were covered, as Brown relates, with buffalo. The very next year Lieutenant Butler traversed the great lone land between the Red River and the Rockies without seeing a single beast.

It was an ominous portent of the dramatic suddenness with which the great herds disappeared. By 1878, according to

Norbert Welsh, one of the last of the white hunters, there were no buffalo in the Cypress Hills, and none between the Milk River and the Missouri, the area in which Kootenai hunted.[37] While F. G. Roe, in his definitive work on the buffalo, suggests that this was not literally correct for the Cypress Hills – Fort Walsh territory, it nevertheless "exhibits a sufficiently life-like picture of the advance of the final extermination, as it presented itself to an observer whose base was near Qu'Appelle, to the north-eastwards."[38]

With the advance of the railway and the coming of domestic cattle to replace the untamed "monarchs of the plains," the Métis and men such as Brown who had committed themselves to their way of life were forced to meet sociological problems of great magnitude. In his later years Brown was philosophical about the changes that were imposed by the slaughter of the buffalo:

> In the course of human events and in the march of civilization the buffalo had to go. We couldn't have settlers and buffalo.... I am sorry as a lover of sport that the buffalo had to go; sorry as a humanitarian that they are gone; but they had to go.[39]

At the time, however, Brown, after almost three years of communal life, left the shelter of the Métis community and took up wolfing, a tough, precarious business, but one which often yielded quick, substantial profits. As it turned out, his days with the halfbreed hunters were the most carefree and happiest in his long and varied life.

Chapter 8

"A Bloody Deed"

With the depletion of the buffalo becoming more evident daily, Brown's decision to change occupations, if running the buffalo could be termed an occupation, was understandable. The transition to wolfing entailed little capital outlay and yet still required Brown to utilize his skills as a plainsman. More important, the returns were high:

> We got $2.50 a piece for them [wolf hides].... We averaged about one thousand wolves in a winter and as we were living on buffalo meat which didn't cost us anything and using tents or cabins we built with our own hands, our only expense was the ammunition we used for killing buffalo and the strychnine for poisoning wolves.... We never wasted any ammunition on wolves. No one ever thought of shooting a wolf unless he should attack a colt or a calf or bother about the camp. "Wolfers" always used strychnine which we bought in bottles of one eighth ounce and for which we paid five and six dollars and often as high as eight dollars.[1]

Another reason Brown took up wolfing was that he didn't want to leave his family:

> In later years I trapped and poisoned wolves in the Sweet Grass Hills and took my wife and family [two girls by then] with me. One winter we lived in one of the cabins built while we were with the half-breeds hunting buffalo. Another winter we had only tents, but they had double tops and were well sheltered and we were very comfortable. When the buffalo were entirely gone, and game on the prairie became scarcer, the wolves became less and we got tired wandering around with our children, so we decided to squat somewhere. Our decision was not hard to reach. I had settled long years before that when the day for squatting came I would come back to this spot [Waterton Lakes] and so in 1877 I built a cabin between the Middle and Lower Lakes....[2]

The last sentence of Brown's reminiscences quoted above affords perhaps the most penetrating indication of his character and personality. In one easy transition he bridges the wolfing period of his life with its uncertainties and its domestic difficulties, and turns abruptly to the matter of settling down in his beloved Waterton Lakes. In fact, except to close friends, Brown maintained a discreet silence about all but the superficial aspects of this time in his life, betraying, in the process, a lifelong feeling of remorse and guilt. Indeed, it was through wolfing that Brown in 1877 went through one of the most dramatic and trying experiences in the whole of his adventurous life. But that will follow.

Although the taking of wolf skins constituted an easy transition from the life of a buffalo hunter in a Métis camp, it also had its own particular hazards. Most wolfers were rather rough rapacious men universally hated and despised by Indians and Métis alike. The reasons for the plains people's attitude is clear. Without exception the wolfers were white men, as Brown points out, the sort that the Indian and the half-breed blamed for their every misfortune:

> For the wolfing business we organized ourselves into small parties of four, six, or perhaps ten persons, but these were all white men. I was not associated with half-breeds after my experiences in the buffalo hunting camps. The most prominent wolfers during my time...were: Sol Abbot, Jimmy McDevitt, Van Hale, Bill Preston, and Chas. Duval.[3]

Then again the very methods they employed to obtain their skins constituted a hazard, particularly to the Indians. With the means at hand the procedure was simplicity itself:

> Our plan was to poison a whole animal at one time. This was done by "spread-eagling" the carcass, that is placing the dead buffalo on its back, skinning the legs on the inside and the belly down to the ground, then cutting the carcass open and removing the inside. Heart, lights and liver were put into a tub or large box of some sort. These were cut into small pieces and a bottle of strychnine scattered over them. The poison was thoroughly mixed with these small pieces and with them was rubbed into all parts of the carcass. The meat on the ribs was cut into strips which were left attached and the two got a good rubbing. There was a regular scale to determine the quantity of strychnine necessary for poisoning a carcass. It took four bottles for a full grown bull; two bottles for a two year old of any kind; and one for a calf if we happened to kill one which was not very often.
>
> After the carcass had been poisoned a flag, a red one if it was possible to get that colour, was placed over it till it had time to freeze solid. The object was to keep the wolves away till it was frozen. If this was not done, one or two or a half dozen wolves would eat the whole bait. A quarter or a half pound of meat (poisoned) was enough to kill a wolf and as strychnine was expensive we were careful not to waste any. It was a common thing to get twenty wolves dead the first morning after the poison had been put out. Instances had been known where fifty to eighty have been poisoned, and old Bill Martin who was my partner in the Sweet Grass Hills one winter tells me that once he got one hundred and twenty-five wolves in one week within two hundred yards of a big bull buffalo bait.[4]

Wolfing could be a very profitable business, but it was not always simple or as easy as memories recalled in the tranquillity of old age suggest. The dangers varied from those posed by severe winter weather to those of Indians, or the difficulties that sometimes arose in disposing of the winter's take. Feuding between wolfers and Indians was constant and bitter:

> Because the buffalo carcasses poisoned and left as bait by the wolfers killed the Indian's dogs and sometimes the Indians too, the tribesmen were continually at war with these hunters and their bodies often were found "so full of arrows they looked like porcupines." The wolfers, therefore, objected strenuously to the sale of magazine rifles and modern cartridges to Indians: not only did this speed up the killing of buffalo, making poisoned carcasses less inviting to wolves, but it also enabled the tribesmen to pick off wolves more swiftly and at longer range.[5]

Such differences, apparently, did not intrude into Kootenai Brown's experiences. On the other hand, he soon learned the hazards inherent in selling the winter's take of wolf pelts. The Montana Territory was still unsettled frontier country, a magnet for all manner of men bent on adventure or making quick money in quantity.

Each spring, with the opening of the navigation season on the Missouri, Fort Benton, the "Chicago of the Plains," became the hub of frantic commercial and trading activities. The wolfers – in company with gamblers, soldiers, North-West Mounted Policemen on duty or leave, including deserters from the Force, miners, speculators, missionaries – thronged into Benton to sell their winter's take of pelts at the spring sales. Inevitably, the final division of profits among the partners was the climax of the sale, and, after a winter of hardship, loneliness and varying fortune, friendships and business arrangements were often strained to the breaking point. Quarrels were common and these frequently ended in violence. The population of the Fort, which fluctuated violently at the best of times, increased tremendously each spring, and accommodation, hopeless to begin with, became totally inadequate. For this reason, Kootenai and Olive preferred to stay with the half-breeds who camped nearby while the final transactions were concluded.

The dangers of rifts developing under the prevailing hunting and marketing conditions applied, of course, as much to Brown as to anyone else in the wolfing game. In the spring of 1877 he came to Benton as usual with his companions to take

In 1874, when Brown joined the Métis on the plains the region was a lawless land where U.S. traders were wiping out the Indians with bullets and whiskey. They even had a series of forts. Whoop-Up, above, near today's Lethbridge was the largest, complete with its own cannon and flag. To bring law and order, in 1873 Ottawa formed the North-West Mounted Police. In an epic three-month journey in 1874 they trekked from Manitoba across 800 miles of prairie and established a police post called Fort Macleod. The Mounties quickly ended the liquor traffic.

Below: A North-West Mounted Police patrol in 1878. In 1905 the force became known as the Royal North-West Mounted Police and in 1920 as the Royal Canadian Mounted Police.

part in the annual sale, and to get his share of the anticipated profits.

Something however, went wrong, and he quarreled bitterly with one of the traders, Louis Ell, who was widely known at the Fort. Ell (or El) was also known throughout Montana Territory, and Charles Larpenteur, who traded on the Upper Missouri for forty years, recalls employing Ell at Fort Stewart, a post on the "Big Muddy" beyond Fort Buford.[6] In a moment of anger Brown's temper (for which he was noted in later years) was transmuted into savage, uncontrollable violence. The victim of his fury was Louis Ell. *The Fort Benton Record*, May 4, 1877, reported what followed under the dramatic caption "A Bloody Deed" and published two widely differing accounts:

One of the most brutal murders that has ever occurred in this Territory was perpetrated in the vicinity of the Teton river in the afternoon of Wednesday the 2nd inst. A Frenchman named Louis Ell, well known in this community, was butchered in a most brutal manner by a man named John Brown, formerly of Bismark, and for some time a resident of Missoula county. Ell had attached some furs belonging to Brown for a debt which the latter refused to pay. On the day following the seizure the two men met on a hill near the Government Coulee, where Brown plunged a sharp edged butcher knife into Ell's abdomen, and wrenching the weapon sideways almost severed the unfortunate man in two, killing him instantly. The murder was evidently premeditated, as Brown had his horse readily saddled, and the moment the bloody deed was done he mounted and started, it is supposed, for the boundary line.

Two lines further, under the single pregnant word "Later" the paper substantially revised its account, though the dramatic features of the encounter were not lost upon the writer. It was not, as first intimated, a simple premeditated matter with a clearly-defined motive:

The two men had been to the half-breed camp on the Teton, but were returning to Benton. Our informant was standing at the door of his tent when the men rode away together, and he heard one of them call the other a liar. He next saw them dismounted. Ell was on the ground and Brown was in the act of drawing the knife from his body. The wounded man got upon his feet and came toward the half-breed camp followed by Brown, who no doubt intended to finish his victim. The half-breed, our informant, attempted to interfere but Brown flourished his knife and told him to keep off or he would serve him the same. The half-breed then went to his tent for a weapon, and returning met Brown at the door of the tent. A tussle ensued, in which Brown was knocked down, and the knife with which he stabbed Ell fell on the ground and was picked up by the half-breed before the murderer could recover it. Brown, however, managed to reach his horse, and make his escape. Ell died about fifteen minutes after reaching the tent.

The camp on the Teton River was approximately five miles from the town. As soon as news of the slaying reached Benton, Sheriff Rowe started in pursuit and, according to the paper "captured Brown at a point about seventy miles up the Marias river." Rowe had the double advantage of being able to stick to the most travelled route to the border, most of which Brown avoided, and of knowing the country intimately since he and Johnny Healy used to run consignments of whisky from Benton to Fort Whoop-Up, that notorious short-lived establishment in southern Alberta, during its hey-day before the arrival of the North-West Mounted Police. The details of the interception and final capture are not recorded by the Benton paper, and Brown, to the end of his days, rarely spoke about Ell or his brush with American frontier justice.

The *Benton Record*, however, took a keen interest in Brown once he was returned and safely locked up in the rather rude, ramshackle prison, itself a source of continual controversy in local county politics. Murder and capture of the killer was news even in that hard-bitten outpost, and the editor of the paper, like most newspaper men, made the most of the incident. Less than a week after he was lodged in prison the editor succinctly summed up Brown in these terms:

John Brown, the murderer of Louis Ell, is still confined in the Benton jail. He is intelligent and evidently a well-educated man, and is said to have been an officer in the English army. He is very much affected, but insists that the crime was committed in self-defense.

And little wonder that Brown was very much affected. Olive and two little girls were cause enough for concern, though the question of hardship was mitigated at least in part because they had reestablished themselves with the hospitable Métis and Olive could, if it came to the worst, rejoin her family. The other worry that beset Brown was the characteristic one on the frontier – what particular course in his case would justice follow. Ell was well known in Benton, and it was highly possible that his friends might band together and take the law into their own hands. The time of the year, a period of intense business activity, tended to act in Brown's favour and, more important, at the beginning of June Johnny Healy assumed office as sheriff. As long as he was sheriff the possibility of vigilante action in Choteau county was remote, but at the time of Brown's arrest Healy's abilities as a police officer were unknown.

Killing a man, whether by design or accident, has its personal repercussions. Brown, literate and sensitive in his own way, was tormented by the whole affair. The combination of worry about his family, the uncertainties of trial by judge and jury, and the debilitating effects of confinement, for he was always an active and lively man, ultimately drove him to desperate action. Escape was virtually impossible without external assistance, and any attempt would have been welcomed by Healy who was anxious to prove himself in his new job. On July 27, 1877, the *Record*, in its column Local News, reported:

> Brown, the prisoner confined in the Benton jail for the murder of Louis Ell, attempted suicide on Friday last [July 23, 1877], by stabbing himself with a dirk knife obtained, as it is supposed, from a fellow prisoner. When Sheriff Healy entered the jail with the prisoner's breakfast, Brown had on an overcoat, and was walking up and down the cell keeping his hand concealed behind him. His singular appearance and strange actions at once aroused the suspicions of the Sheriff, who drew a revolver and ordered the prisoner to throw up his hands, which he did, revealing a small dirk knife in his right hand. On searching the prisoner it was found that Brown had cut himself in the left breast causing a flesh wound from which he had been bleeding profusely. Dr. Turner considers the wound dangerous, and believes Brown to be insane.

Medical care proved successful and recovery followed, though surveillance and supervision increased accordingly. By autumn Brown was sufficiently fit to travel to the Territorial Capital to stand before a Territorial Grand Jury, and the move was duly reported in the Benton paper:

> Sheriff Healy left for Helena this morning [November 2, 1877], having in charge the prisoner Brown....

The journey itself took only two or three days and legal action followed speedily. Unfortunately, the details of the case, and the story heard by the Grand Jury are lost, perhaps forever. The press accounts are scarcely more illuminating. *The Helena Independent*, November 11, 1877, in its column devoted to Court Proceedings merely stated the bald facts of the case: "Territory vs. Brown; murder. Plea of not guilty. Trial for Monday, 12th." Two days later the word "Acquitted," followed by the single, fateful line, "The Jury in the case of John G. Brown, on trial for murder rendered a verdict of not guilty," appeared in the same paper. The same item, repeated verbatim, appeared three days later [November 16, 1877,] in the *Fort Benton Record*.

On the basis of the reports carried in the Territorial newspapers, Brown, it would seem, had faced a courtroom jury and had been acquitted. The accounts conjure up scenes of dramatic evidence, impassioned argument, and legal fencing. The case, however, was not quite so dramatic, although Brown must have considered it harrowing enough without the embellishment of courtroom histrionics. Grand Juries do not conduct trials in the courtroom sense; they only consider the nature and extent of the evidence available against an accused person and determine whether or not an indictment should be returned against the person. If an indictment is returned a trial is then held before a petit jury, and lawyers have the opportunity to display their talents in court. Since there is no record of an indictment being returned against Kootenai Brown, and since no case in which he was a principal is listed, the inevitable conclusion is that the Territorial Grand Jury declined to return an indictment against him.[7]

Too often, as the historian Hubert Howe Bancroft has pointed out, lawless hangings were carried out in the Western Territories before whatever legal justice existed in the region had an opportunity to act. The incidence of crime in Montana was much higher than in organized settled communities, while the Criminal Code for the Territory was vague in its wording and difficult to implement. Bancroft wrote in 1890:

> Under it nearly half of all the complaints tried resulted in acquittal, owing to the ambiguity of the language in which a crime was defined by the legislators.... It cannot be wondered at that there existed dissatisfaction with the courts, though they were not responsible for the defective statutes or that lynch-law so often hastened to remove criminals from their jurisdiction. The cause lay even deeper...in the great infusion of a reckless element which is strengthened by still larger numbers of careless and tolerant persons, whose experience of the freedom of the frontier had made them callous to the horrors of violated law, even when it brought them face to face with sudden death.[8]

Bancroft was not the first to note that people in frontier society tend to become indifferent to the sight of bloodshed and violence. William Perkins, who kept a journal for three years during his mid-century stay in California, made the same point.[9] A man drew his gun on the slightest pretext for a quarrel with the same readiness that he would resort to striking a blow with his fist in another country, or in the more settled Atlantic seaboard. Killings were commonplace on the frontier, and the degree of acquired callousness such that at least one observer has recorded the gunning down of a man in a barber's saloon did not even interupt the business of shaving.

Whether, in Brown's case, his release was the result of a consensus of "careless and tolerant persons" who made up the Territorial Grand Jury, or whether it was due to lack of evidence, we shall never know. What mattered was that he was given his freedom, and an opportunity to resume his life. Whatever he may have thought during the months of imprisonment we do not know for he rarely spoke frankly or freely about the encounter with Louis Ell or its aftermath. When he did, it was in confidence and then only to those whom he considered to be trustworthy friends. However, John Healy, the sheriff, who kept Brown in custody, suggests in a letter written in 1905 that he was, if anything, sympathetic towards Kootenai:

> I had an interesting adventure with him when I was sheriff. He was a "bad man" and I had him for some time for the killing of a celebrated hunter named Louis Ell.[10]

Without doubt the experience of imprisonment, arraignment and acquittal proved to be a great dividing line, a watershed, as it were, for Brown.

The impact upon him was permanent. W. McD. Tait, who spent much time with Brown in the last year or two of his life, records that towards the end of his time Kootenai told him that "the most wonderful words in the English language were 'Not Guilty'."[11] Whatever else Brown may have told about the affair is lost for Tait refused to discuss or write about it. Marie Rose Smith, who knew Brown from the days of the Second Riel Rebellion, records that Brown killed a man in Montana, and for that reason returned permanently to Canada. And that is the crux of the matter for it was the encounter with Ell and the experiences which followed that precipitated Kootenai's decision to return to the place of his dreams, the Waterton Lakes.

Chapter 9
Land of the Shining Mountains

When the Montana Territorial Grand Jury released Brown and he stepped from the room in which the hearing was held a free man, his life altered perceptibly. He turned his back, as it were, upon the thrusting turbulence of frontier society in the American West, put aside dreams and get-rich-quick schemes which had been a part of his life from the moment he left the British Isles and set course for the Cariboo goldfields.

Instead of returning to the Red River country or re-establishing himself with Olive's people, the Métis, Kootenai chose to remove his family and himself to that remote corner of the Northwest Territory in Canada where mountains and plain suddenly meet. There, just four or five miles north of the 49th parallel, in the glorious surroundings which the Indians call the land of the Shining Mountains, Brown in 1878 resumed a domestic life that was at once simple and lonely. It signified a withdrawal, a period of reassessment and calm before external pressures once more drew him into the turmoil of activity.

In those first few days following the jury hearing, however, we see him in reunion with Olive and his two daughters, perhaps at Helena, perhaps at Fort Benton, preparing to return to Canadian territory where British law and custom prevailed. Kootenai's choice of location, once he had decided to leave the Montana Territory and not to return to the same area in which Olive's family lived, deliberate yet sensible under the circumstances, is not difficult to explain. It stemmed from his attempted wild dash for the border immediatly after the quarrel with Louis Ell, and was confirmed during his confinement in the Fort Benton jailhouse:

> I had settled long years before that when the day for squatting came I would come back to this spot [Waterton Lakes]....[1]

The chastening experience of enforced confinement resurrected that intention while stories, backed by the growing volume of business easily observed by all persons in Benton, sharpened the desire. Traffic between Benton and Fort Macleod in Canadian territory, coupled with accounts about the effectiveness with which the North-West Mounted Police administered the area, particularly the way in which the Force shattered the whisky trade built up by independent traders backed by Benton merchants, were commonplace and tantalizing. The contrast with the violence in Montana Territory, and the unpredictability of territorial justice, was salutary.

Once preparations were complete, Brown and his young family set out on the slow journey by horseback and wagon, a trip punctuated by the normal hazards of travel over rough ground, variations in weather, insects, unexpected illness or accident. Their route brought them to the Whoop-Up Trail, by then deeply rutted by long heavily-laden bull trains which ran to Fort Macleod some 240 miles to the northwest. When Kootenai and Olive travelled over the trail, it was at its peak as one of the main supply routes in the American west:

...for a quarter of a century it was a main artery into the western plains, carrying thousands of tons of freight to government installations, North-west Mounted Police posts, United States Army camps, cattle ranches, and Indian reservations. Along its dusty tracks rode Indians searching for game or plunder, scarlet-jacketed Mounties seeking enemies of the Queen, blue-coated United States cavalrymen preserving order, greedy whisky traders seeking likely sites for their short-lived trading posts. In its boom years between 1874 and 1885, this trail carried one third of all the freight handled through Fort Benton and enriched Montana merchants with profits drained from Canada.[2]

Fort Benton, the point from which the Whoop-Up Trail originated, was the last hub of an overland transportation network which served the gold mining centres in the mountains to the west. Located at the head of navigation on the Missouri River, Fort Benton was a colourful cosmopolitan frontier town, the "Chicago of the Plains.":

Eastern pilgrims always watched with mingled emotions the motley crowds that greeted their boat as it nosed into the wharf, for there stood merchants in high-collared broadcloth coats, French-Canadian and Creole rivermen wearing bright-colored sashes, tough trappers and traders heavily armed and wearing buckskin, bull whackers and mule skinners in coarse, rough denim, and, in the background, red savages wearing leggings and blankets.... Through this inland port passed pious missionaries and hunted desperados, merchants and gamblers, American soldiers and British policemen, hopeful landseekers and speculators, miners, roustabouts, muleskinners, bull whackers, and cowboys.[3]

It was this society, as epitomized by Fort Benton, that Brown exchanged for the quieter reaches of what is now southern Alberta.

In terms of personal danger or any real modification to a way of life, the difference between Montana Territory and the Canadian northwest, particularly in the vicinity of the border, was only a matter of degree. The country, however, was changing rapidly as the number of newcomers increased. When Brown left for the Canadian northwest, a state of nervous suspense gripped the land for no one knew how the Blackfoot Indians, already restive under the new, strange restrictions of Treaty Number Seven, signed in September 1877, would react as the Territory developed. For those already in the Territory, and for newcomers such as Brown, Fort Macleod became a focal point of prime importance.

Precariously situated on an island in the Old Man River, constantly in danger of being flooded each spring by high water, the small stockaded strong-point represented authority and civilization. There, a handful of scarlet-coated Mounted Policemen, their bright uniforms contrasting with the monotonous drabness of the plains, their unbending dignity and calculated showmanship impressing whites and natives alike, successfully challenged the tradition of free-wheeling lawlessness which had developed in the American west. But while the para-military discipline of the Force established one datum, Fort Macleod as a supply base and communications centre was otherwise an outpost of American civilization.

United States firms whose names soon became familiar to all travellers passing through Fort Benton – I. G. Baker, T. C. Powers, Murphy Neeland and Company – dominated the economic life of the region, hauling and selling the commodities required by both Mounted Police and settlers. Until the penetration of the Canadian Pacific Railway into the Canadian northwest in 1884-1885, these American firms enjoyed a virtual monopoly in transport and supply, with the inevitable result that the range of goods was limited while prices remained consistently high. For a considerable time, too, an unofficial United States Post Office flourished in Fort Macleod, indicative of the extent of American influence there.

Fort Benton on the Missouri River five miles from where Brown murdered Louis Ell. The inset photo is of Sheriff John Healy who took Brown to Helena to stand trial. Healy was also one of the U.S. whiskey traders who built Fort Whoop-Up.

Fort Benton wasn't the West's healthiest town as the sign below on today's main street indicates. During the frontier era the local paper carried a news item that a horse thief had been caught and promptly hanged from a telegraph pole. The headline said simply, TELEGRAPHED HIM HOME.

THE BLOODIEST BLOCK IN THE WEST

"IT'S A TOUGH TOWN, WALK IN THE CENTER OF THE STREET AND KEEP YOUR MOUTH SHUT." GUNSLINGERS WALKED THIS STREET; FEW MADE A REPUTATION, MORE EARNED ETERNITY HERE THAN IN OTHER FABLED WESTERN TOWNS.

INDIANS WERE FAIR GAME. THEIR CORPSES DUMPED IN THE RIVER STARTED WAR AND MASSACRE. MOSE SOLOMON SALOON OWNER ELIMINATED 2 CUSTOMERS ON THE CORNER LOU MARSHALL ADDED HINCHLEY AND SEVERAL OTHERS GUNNED DOWN ON THIS STREET "WON'T BE MISSED"

POKER WAS PLAYED WITH 6-GUNS ATOP THE TABLE AND FEMALES FROM THE BROTHELS WERE AS TOUGH AS THE MEN. MADAME MUSTACHE BRANDISHED COLTS TO HALT THE LANDING OF A STEAMBOAT CARRYING SMALL-POX. SALOONS AND "HOUSES" STAYED OPEN ALL NIGHT. THIS BLOCK WAS LINED WITH SALOONS, CATHOUSES AND GAMBLING DENS—SO LAWLESS IT HAD TO BE CIRCLED BY A CAVALRY TROOP SO A U.S. MARSHAL COULD SERVE WARRANTS ON FIVE OF ITS RESIDENTS.

For Brown, Fort Macleod provided two essentials in his rehabilitation: contact with familiar social and military conditions, and information about developments in the region. It is not difficult to see him observing the Mounted Police, noting their turnout and drill, adding, in the process, new contacts with officers and men. It is equally easy to think of him circulating amongst the inhabitants in or around the Fort, having a drink in the saloon, talking over the latest news brought out from Benton, and assessing his own prospects.

During the course of such activities he met H. A. (Fred) Kanouse, one of the earliest arrivals in the area, and the first man to bring cattle to the Kootenay Lakes-Fort Macleod area.[4] Kanouse not only knew that region thoroughly, but had built a small cabin on the eastern shore of the Upper Kootenay Lake near, in fact, where Brown and his companions emerged from the mountains when they came out of Wild Horse Creek. There he grazed his cattle and sold goods to the Kootenay Indians during their annual hunting excursions to the plains. For Brown, such a location was ideal and the possibilities of earning a living sufficient. An arrangement mutually satisfactory to both men followed, and sometime during the late autumn or early winter of 1878, Brown installed Olive and his two daughters in the new but primitive quarters. For Brown, the move to the long lakes brought his wanderings to an end. No more was he destined to cross oceans and continents. His expeditions instead became those of a hunter in search of game, a guide for the vanguard of investors and travellers already starting to trickle into the country, and a scout whose talents and abilities could be called upon by the community in a time of emergency.

Although the cabin between the upper and lower Waterton Lakes where Brown squatted was isolated, earning a livelihood was not difficult. With fish and game plentiful in and around the lakes – the title bestowed by Lieutenant Thomas Blakiston did not come into common use until the formation of Waterton Lakes National Park in 1911 – with Fort Macleod within reasonable if not easy reach, Kootenai and Olive established a pattern of life that differed little from that which they led with the Métis. Only the mobility of the buffalo camps and the conviviality of winter settlements were missing.

While Olive cooked, looked after the children, sewed, or helped in the preparation of skins, Brown ranged over the mountainsides and prairie, rifle in hand. When he was not hunting, Kootenai ventured out on the lakes to set nets or tried his hand with fishing lines. Fish, the large succulent lake trout in particular, became the main staple in the household. Fish, too, were bartered for flour, sugar, tea and other necessaries, or sold by Brown whenever he travelled to Fort Macleod or visited neighbouring ranches:

I used to sell fish at Macleod. We caught them in the Waterton Lakes, and fished both winter and summer. I have seen me get $75.00 for my load of fish and we thought that a big price in those days.[5]

Also, once settled, Brown, in order to supplement his income, for the second time in his life became a trader:

I remember starting a store at Waterton Lakes on what afterwards became my first homestead.... In the store I had a partner, Fred Kanouse, a well-known character around Macleod and Pincher Creek. Fred and I had a stock valued at $4,000 and our customers were Indians, mostly Kootenais, Nez Perces, and Flatheads from the Flat-head Reservation in Montana. Customs regulations didn't bother them; we didn't know where the International line was in those days any more than the buffalo did. The Kootenai Indians were friendly with the Blackfeet, but beyond good-humored joking when they chanced to meet in our store, there was not much intermingling. If one got a chance to steal the others horses there was no hestitation on the part of either Kootenais or Blackfeet. No other tribe of Indians that I know of really liked the Blackfeet.

Well, we started this store in a little log shack on the Lower Waterton Lake and our supplies were all hauled from Fort Macleod by I. G. Baker bull team.... The Kootenais would bring furs out of the mountains and we would trade them dry goods and "wet goods" and provisions. We didn't sell much whiskey to the Indians although a good deal of it was consumed on the premises. To sell to the Indians was too risky a proposition though it yielded much profit. Our customers were all Indians and to let them get all the whiskey they wanted would mean a carousal in which they might burn up or carry away our stock.[6]

The intermittent periods of trading with the redskins not only yielded profit but also provided a contrast from the incessant but vital round of hunting or fishing, as well as opportunities for pleasure. At such times, Brown's instinct to take a chance – his Irish background perhaps – came to the fore:

Indians are naturally great gamblers and are very anxious to take part in all games of chance. Someone taught the Flatheads and Kootenais to play poker and this became their great pastime when they visited the store. It took a card shark to beat them. Kanouse was an expert poker-player so he attended to that part of the business. I was a footracer and a good shot and in competitions on the track and with the rifle I could always beat them. We had two good horses and in horse-racing we also got the best of them. In fact, we beat them at every turn.[7]

Although the two enterprising partners inevitably got the better of their native customers, their victories were not always well received by the losers. Many of the encounters, borderline in terms of honesty or intent, brought Brown and Kanouse to the verge of trouble, and they had to rectify Indian gambling losses to the point where the redskins were sufficiently mollified to return to their home territories without causing serious trouble.[8] While business lasted, the experiences were a colourful variation in Brown's life. Eventually, however, the influx of settlers, the establishment of large ranches and a more careful monitoring of Indian movements across the International boundary caused trade to dry up:

When the Indians began trading on their side of the line, business went bad with us and I sold my share out to Kanouse for $250. He continued in business a year after I left, when he moved to Macleod and took his stock with him. When I sold my interest in the business I built a log cabin in what was known, when a survey was made, as Section 31, Township 1, Range 29, West of the Fourth Meridian.[9]

With the dissolution of the partnership and Kanouse's departure to Fort Macleod, Kootenai's brief role as a merchant trader of the plains ended. With the disappearance of the Indians, who were the main customers, something of the excitement and social variation which marked their visits came to an end. Life for Kootenai and his family became a solitary existence characterized by an occasional visit from a Mounted Policeman on patrol, or, very infrequently, a trip to Fort Macleod.

Beyond the mountain valley and the lakes the country was changing rapidly. As the Mounted Police demonstrated that they were capable of maintaining law and order, as prohibition became the law of the land, the unruly elements in what is now southern Alberta retreated across the 49th parallel. In their place came the ranchers, many of them former members of the North-West Mounted Police. Brown saw the infant cattle industry from its earliest beginnings and knew most of the pioneer stockmen who established themselves in southern Alberta:

They all came after I did, but I was pretty well into the mountains...and did not come into contact with them except at the time of the annual roundup.

I believe Joe McFarlane, of the old Pioneer Ranch, was the first to start near Macleod.... In 1876, Lynch and Emerson brought out a bunch of heifers, which they sold to settlers coming into the country. Ed. Maunsell, whose cattle now [ie. circa 1916] range over his lease on the Peigan Indian Reserve, got his start out of the bunch brought in by Lynch and Emerson. Robert Patterson and Bob Whitney, on the Belly and Old Man Rivers, were in early, and both of them were formerly members of the Mounted Police.[10]

Soon the small establishments which occupied leaseholds in the country around Macleod were joined by large ranches, enterprises financed by monied men in eastern Canada or in England. Under the Dominion Lands Act of 1881, huge "spreads" of 100,000 acres could be established on 21-year leases at an annual rent of one cent per acre, with the leases not subject to cancellation.[11]

The combination of cheap grazing land, easily obtained, and unusual security of tenure attracted large-scale investment and the establishment of very large ranches. Many prominent people, including Senator M. M. Cochrane, the Allan family of Montreal, Lord Lathom and A. S. Hill from England, and Dr. McEachern, the Chief Veterinary Surgeon for the Canadian government, secured leases and stocked their holdings with good cattle. Brown certainly was aware of the new men and the new era their investments represented. His own recollections are limited but precise enough to give the developments a personal note of awareness:

Among the big ranches, the lead of the Cochrane Ranch Company was quickly followed by the North-West Ranching Company. They came in about 1882. Then I think the Waldrond was started by Dr. McEachern, of Montreal, with capital supplied by an Englishman, Sir John Waldrond. Around 1886, the Oxley came in. Their cattle ranged along the Kootenai and Old Man Rivers up to the Porcupine Hills west of Macleod.[12]

In the process of their establishment, Brown met the owners and principal men behind the great ranches, and the contacts sharpened his awareness of the magnitude of the holdings and their significance to the country.

While such sweeping economic changes were taking place, Brown was establishing himself as one of the fixtures in the Fort Macleod region. With the founding of a newspaper, the Fort Macleod *Gazette*, in 1882 by two former Mounted Policemen,

E. T. Saunders and C. E. D. Wood, we see Kootenai more sharply delineated against the background of beautiful scenery and a changing society.

Brown was one of many local people who were reported in the *Gazette*. The first of the items concerning him appeared in that paper on Saturday, September 23, 1882, under the caption "Kootenai Lakes." After writing enthusiastically about the many charms of the climate and scenery, the great numbers of bears, water fowl and fish, the excellent timber in great abundance and the relatively mild temperature corroborated by a thermometer used in the winter of 1881 and later tested by Dr. Dawson of the Canadian Geological Survey, the editors reported:

> The only settlers in this vicinity are Messrs. H. A. Kanouse and J. G. Brown. The former generally lives in Macleod and the latter resides in his place on the Kootenai Lakes. He follows the varied occupation of ranching, hunting, guiding tourists; being well acquainted with the numerous passes of the mountains and an old successful hunter himself, we consider Mr. Brown fully capable of rendering great assistance to any persons requiring his services.... Mr. Kanouse's house is situated on the first lake.... There is a boat on the lake and horses can be procured from the guide, Mr. Brown. For trolling and fly-fishing there is abundant tackle and all the necessary requisites, and parties visiting his place are always sure of their fish as Mr. Brown can catch them where all others fail.

In another column the editor casually stated that "we are indebted to Mr. J. G. Brown for the main points in our article on the Kootenai Lakes and vicinity." Clearly, Brown had wasted little time in publicizing the lakes he loved so well, and his newly acquired profession of guide. At a time when the west was still a vast empty expanse, when the Canadian Pacific Railway was looked upon with scepticism and derision, and tourism as an integral and major sector of a national economy was undreamed of, Brown shrewdly and farsightedly had pointed to the order of things to come. And he continued to press the claims of the lakes and mountains consistently and persistently, serving the cause of conservation in his own inimitable manner to his very end.

Brown's claims for his lake, and his abilities as a fisherman even as reflected by the *Gazette's* ebullient editors (with some prompting), were soon verified. In the spring of 1883, this brief item appeared in the paper:

> Mr. J. G. Brown, of Kootenay Lakes, brought to town on Saturday last a trout weighing thirty pounds, which he caught in one of the lakes. Some peo-

ple may think this is a fishy story, but we have seen the trout and can vouch for its truth.

A similar item in the April 4, 1883, issue reported that Brown had killed the first goose at the Lake on the second of March, and that green grass four inches high was already in evidence. The item, in addition to mentioning that Brown had brought "some fine white fish to town," also indicated that the lakes were free of ice, an abnormally early clearance even for that portion of the chinook country. Kootenai had indeed taken his place as a colourful and accepted member of the community.

By the middle of that year, the changes implicit in Brown's new occupation of guide were evident on a much larger scale. The progress of the Canadian Pacific Railway in laying down track had not only subdued a great deal of scepticism about the northwest's economic potential, but also underlined the point by carrying more and more interested travellers to the west. Many of those reaching the end of track continued their journeys by horse, and it was from this vanguard that Brown's services were required with increasing frequency. His intimate knowledge of the region west of Fort Macleod and his ability as a packer, already well known to local residents, were soon advertised much further abroad.

Kootenai, for example, was recommended to those splendidly bearded Englishmen, A. S. Hill, a wealthy lawyer and Member of Parliament, and Lord Lathom, when they first came to the Canadian west in 1882 to investigate the prospects for large scale investment in cattle ranching. Their return the following year aroused much interest in the Fort Macleod area, and created considerable curiosity and comment. The Fort Macleod *Gazette* recorded the travellers' arrival and their activities in considerable detail. From the issue of September 14, 1883, here is the entry which reveals the party's arrival and some of the interest which they evoked in the community:

> The Earl of Lathom, Messrs. Stavely Hill and J. R. Craig, all of the Oxley Ranch Co., passed through here on Friday last on their way to the Kootenai Lakes; the two former gentlemen spent several days at the Lakes, enjoying the unsurpassed fishing and hunting which can be indulged in under the wing of the experienced guide and hunter J. G. Brown. They will go through the mountains to British Columbia, thence to the Northern Pacific Railway, and back to Helena, where Mr. Craig will meet them.

For Kootenai, the commission to lead the party through the mountains was the first of many similar contracts. It gave him an opportunity to make contact with the new investors in the Canadian west, and to indulge in the kind of talk about places and things of mutual interest that is one of the pleasures of the trail. In turn, the travels of the Oxley group through the Waterton Lakes gives us a glimpse of Brown and an indication of his life. A. S. Hill describes meeting Brown, and although the account lacks detail, it reflects the observations of an alert Victorian traveller who took the time and trouble to record what he saw or heard:

> Early in the afternoon [of Monday, September 11, 1883], we arrived in sight of the house of Kootenai Brown, an old settler who had been there for many years, and who in the autumn previous had been recommended to me as a man who could show me and tell me all about sport in that part of the mountains; we had little difficulty in getting across the stream, as this eastern end of the lake meanders about and no direct trail was visible. But everything is known in the North-West, and the proprietor had heard of our probable visit to him, and sighted us from the hill, and came down and guided us in. He was a wild Indian-looking fellow, in a Slouch hat and curiously constructed garments and moccasins. He told us that he had come across eighteen years ago from British Columbia to hunt buffalo, and after wandering about for some years had settled in this place where he had been for the last four years.... Brown was occupier of the log hut belonging to Kanouse, in which he lived with a rather delicate wife and some children. He had seen something of service with the British army, but with his long dark hair and moccasins had not much of the European remaining about his appearance.... We had a pleasant tea and talk with Brown over the campfire, and arranged for his assistance at the rate of five dollars a day for himself and his horse, to go with us about the mountains for two days and take us for a day's fishing if the weather was calm enough to allow of a very rickety boat venturing out on the lake; and after this he should set us on our way into the Kootenal Pass and see us on the right trail for one day's journey.[13]

Apparently the party, like many others since, had little luck with their fishing or hunting. In his journal entry for the following day, Hill records starting off on horseback around 8:00 in the morning with Brown for a ride up Goat Mountain (now called Mount Vimy). "The only thing we came across," he said, "was a jackass rabbit which Brown shot with his rifle, and a chicken."[14] The same tone of disappointment marks his entry for Thursday, September 13, 1883:

Bull trains on the 240-mile-long trail from Fort Benton to Fort Macleod. For a decade the river port was supply point for what is today southern Alberta-Saskatchewan.

Below: Main street of Fort Macleod in the early 1880s. Because of flooding, in 1883 the Fort was abandoned and a new one built about two miles away on the east bank of the Oldman River.

With the exception of a coyote which the dog chased, as we were riding out, we did not see a head of big game during our stay at Kootenai....[15]

Very disappointed, the group set out the next day to continue the journey through the Rockies to the Northern Pacific Railway. Before he left, Hill photographed the lakes and what are now the Cameron Falls, as well as Brown seated before the rude cabin. The picture shows a dark-haired man of medium height and build, with a long straight nose, piercing eyes and firm lips, dressed in a buck-skin jacket, before a crude but sturdy cabin surrounded by the typical paraphernalia required by men who earn their bread through hunting and trapping. Before the party left, Brown, to commemorate the visit, presented Lord Lathom with an arrowhead he found during the unsuccessful sortie to "Goat Mountain."

The next day, Friday, September 14, 1883, the party, with "five pack horses, four saddle horses, and Brown on his cayuse," set off for the mountain pass that would lead them into British Columbia. Before leaving Hill reported:

Kootenai Brown came out very strong on the subject of packing, and was learned in the various kinds of knots, and in his criticism of inferior artists and in all matters of packing – straps and cinches he was clearly a connoisseur.[16]

Hill's tribute to Brown's ability as a packer was the first of many. Later that day, the group "found some good grass at the foot of what was obviously about to be a steep climb, and as Brown seemed anxious not to get far more than one day's ride from home, we camped at the edge of a wood of burned spruce, with a good view of the hills and some snow."[17] The next morning Hill, Lathom, and the others in the group said farewell to Brown, and at 10:15 started up a steep slope. Brown returned to his smaller world in the simple cabin, and to his sick wife.

The British party's brief visit to the lakes in the autumn of 1883 high-lighted the relative isolation of the place and accurately pinpointed Olive's illness. Her absence from the photograph of Kootenai taken by Hill is significant, for it suggests either that the illness was serious or that Brown, with the diffidence of many squaw men, did not have his wife appear in public before strangers. Illness, however, is the more likely reason. Marie Rose Smith, who first met Brown soon after the second Riel rebellion, claims, probably correctly, that Olive's illness stemmed from a difficult confinement, the birth of Kootenai's only son, Leo:

> Her only help was a Stony Squaw, and from this birth she never really recovered. Brown didn't realize how sick his wife was, even when she tried to tell him. So between sickness and loneliness, with only Indians for company, she kept getting worse and worse and the care of three children was too much for her. [18]

Loneliness is the key word in Marie Rose Smith's account, and loneliness indeed was undoubtedly a paramount factor in Olive's well-being. A pretty but, apparently, not a robust woman, she missed the carefree conviviality of the Métis community. By the autumn of 1883, the year of Leo's birth according to Marie Rose Smith, the Indians no longer came to barter their furs, race their horses, play cards, or compete with Brown in shooting contests. By then, too, Kanouse had returned to Fort Macleod where he purchased a blacksmith shop and began a new career in business. [19]

The loneliness of the mountain valley was thus only occasionally punctuated by periodic visits of Mounted Policemen, or stockmen employed by the large ranches on the lookout for Indians who were killing cattle on leased territory. One of the most frequent visitors was Archie Rouleau who, according to Marie Rose Smith, was a scout employed by the North-West Mounted Police and stationed at the detachment on the Kootenay River. His coming provided the entire family with a welcome change. [20]

Apart from visits from men such as Rouleau, life for Brown's family revolved around the incessant need to fish or hunt, maintain equipment and horses and, periodically, trips to Fort Macleod. It is through the latter that we are able to focus upon Kootenai during this very domestic period of his life, and to catch a glimpse of a pattern of living which Brown and nameless other pioneers evolved through experience and necessity.

The excursions to and from Macleod were not merely journeys of necessity; they were also opportunities to pay social calls upon ranchers en route and to exchange information about an endless variety of subjects. Frank White, for example, who kept a diary while employed at the Cochrane ranch, noted that Brown called there on October 25, 1884, en route to Macleod and that he passed through on the return journey six days later.

On the return visit, White noted that Brown had his children with him and that one of the little girls had a stiff neck.[21] It was during a similar excursion that Brown met John D. Higinbotham, a pioneer druggist then fresh from Guelph, Ontario. He gives this portrait of Kootenai:

> One of my earliest visitors after opening business in old Fort Macleod, was John George Brown, better known as Kootenai Brown. He informed me that, after seeing our advertisement in the Macleod Gazette, he had taken the first opportunity to ascertain whether I was related to a Dr. Higinbotham who, in 1857, had been placed in charge of a group of young subalterns – Kootenai having been one of the number – who were being sent to India to join their regiments. He had nothing but good to say for the kindly medical officer and I much regret that I could not at the time establish a connection.[22]

The Fort Macleod *Gazette* reported Kootenai's visits to town with touches of local colour that are the hallmark of country newspapers. One entry in the issue dated November 14, 1884, reads:

> J. G. Brown, from the Kootenai Lakes, was in town last week. Mr. Brown informs us that he rode from the lakes to Macleod, a distance of fifty miles, in his shirt sleeves, and even then he was uncomfortably warm while trotting along. The lake generally freezes over about the first of November. This year, however, it is yet open, with no sign of freezing. Although numbers of geese and ducks have left for the south, thousands still remain and as yet show little inclination to go. With skating on the Red River at Winnipeg and in the more easterly portion of the Territories, we have considerable reason to feel proud of our western country.
>
> Those who are fond of a fish diet have had the ample opportunity of gratifying that taste. J. G. Brown, of the Kootenai Lakes, brought in a variety of fish this week. Salmon trout, white fish, and pike. One big fellow of the salmon fero species weighed ten pounds, one weighing about six. It is needless to add that these fish were delicious.

While the size and weight of the catch are enough to make the most ardent fishermen envious, the figures also serve to indicate the tremendous abundance of the lakes before the era of organized sports fishing began. More important, they reveal why Brown was able to provide for his fainily with only periodic visits to Fort Macleod.

Brown's trips to Fort Macleod were not mere pleasure jaunts. They were calculated ventures determined by the necessity of obtaining food staples, clothing, medicines, perhaps consulting a doctor and obtaining cash for furs or fish. Nor were they always the pleasant jogs that the *Gazette* suggested. The fifty miles of countryside between the Fort and Waterton Lakes passed through rough territory requiring frequent crossings of ravines and streams. From spring through to autumn mosquitoes, horseflies and gnats provided a constant if unwelcome escort for all travellers following the faint trail to Fort Macleod. When Brown's children accompanied him to the old Fort, the time-worn combination of anticipation and boredom which all parents experience and must cope with were added to the normal hazards of the journey. Every trip required constant vigilance against weather, breakdowns of wagons, accidents to passengers, horsemen or animals. The land gave no quarter and help in case of emergency was rarely, if ever, available. The point is made in the *Gazette* of March 21, 1885:

> J. G. Brown, who came to town yesterday (March 20, 1885) nearly lost a horse by drowning in the Kootenai River. He crossed the ice on the 12th, and was leading his horse at the end of a long lariat, when the animal broke through into fourteen feet of water. A rope was thrown around the horse's neck, and with the assistance of the police and a team, he was dragged out. Still another argument for bridges.

Such accidents were accepted as an integral part of pioneer life, more perhaps in Brown's case than for people who followed a more orthodox pattern of existence. During this period Brown journeyed to and from Fort Macleod, stopping at the Cochrane Ranch or at police detachments selling or exchanging fish, obtaining information, and passing along observations of his own. W. F. Cochrane's diary and letters provide a glimpse of Kootenai making his rounds at this time. A diary entry for January 26, 1885, for example, notes specific details in balance sheet fashion:

> Kootenai Brown came down with some fish and stayed all night. We took 100 lbs. of fish from Brown to be paid for in trade.[23]

Writing to J. M. Browning, the Secretary of the Cochrane Ranch in Montreal, the same information is given a lighter touch:

> Old Kootenai Brown came down from the Lakes the day before yesterday with a lot of fish going to town. I took some from him in trade for beef and flour. They are mostly spendid white-fish many of them 5 and 6 lb. weight. He reports the snow very deep above.[24]

Cochrane duly noted Kootenai's return on February 3:

Kootenai Brown came back and went on to the Math. Dunn cabin. I gave him some beef in trade for his fish and sold him some for $2.00. He left his two sacks of flour to take next time.[25]

In the early spring we again catch a glimpse of Brown and get a brief revelation of cattle ranching in those early days:

Kootenai Brown came down to see about getting the job of holding the bulls in the mountains.[26]

The next entry carries the story a step further:

Kootenai started for home this morning (April 3, 1885,) and found a 2 year old heifer mired at Spring Coulee and came back and I went up with him and pulled her out. And he came back with me.[27]

Such co-operation was typical of the frontier, and characteristic of the man.

It was during one of Brown's periodic trips that his domestic life, almost Rousseau-like in its natural simplicity, was forever shattered by Olive's unexpected death. The date and circumstances of her passing are clouded by inaccuracy, and a suggestion by Marie Rose Smith of neglect on Kootenai's part.[28] It seems clear, however, that Olive's death occurred sometime between the autumn of 1883 after Lord Lathom and Alexander Stavely Hill passed through the Waterton Lakes, and the spring of 1885 when Kootenai was caught up by other dramatic developments in the region. Kootenai buried his Métis girl on the western shore of the lower lake almost directly opposite the original site of Kanouse's cabin, facing the rolling sweep of the plains beyond Mount Vimy and the towering block of Chief Mountain.

With Olive gone the immediate problem of the children faced Brown. Here again accurate information is scanty. According to Marie Rose Smith, Brown took the three children to Fort Macleod where he sought advice about their future from the great pioneer missionary Father Lacombe.[29] Ultimately, through advice from friends and with Father Lacombe's help, Brown was able to place his son Leo in the mission school at St. Albert, a small community near Edmonton, Alberta.[30] The eventual disposition of the girls is not clear, nor is it known whether either of the girls ever again returned to her father.

Brown, on the other hand, kept in touch with his son who came down to the lakes to stay with his father, and who wrote occasional letters that are characterized by a touch of respect

that goes beyond the formality of an exchange. Once fragment-
ed, the family never reunited, and no male issue through Leo
perpetuated Kootenai's name. Leo, who married in 1899, produced five daughters. He died November 29, 1916, only months
after Kootenai's own passing.[31] How Brown took Olive's death
can only be surmised, although Marie Rose Smith pictures him
a heart-broken man bitterly blaming himself for being away
when Olive died.[32] The need to provide for his children must
have presented him with an immediate challenge, however, and
prevented him from dwelling upon the event at their expense.

At the same time, Brown's domestic misfortune also must
be seen against the panorama of serious political and social
unrest within the Territory. Whether he was aware of the nature
or the extent of the developments which increasingly exercised
authorities and settlers alike cannot be stated with certainty, but
undoubtedly he knew through trips to Fort Macleod and as a
result of talks with Cochrane and other ranchers that they were
greatly exercised about the possibility of an Indian uprising in
the area. When the storm of rebellion ultimately broke, it drew
Brown into a round of activity that completed his rehabilitation
and materially helped to minimize his sense of loss.

Chapter 10
Chief Scout: Rocky Mountain Rangers

In the spring of 1885, Kootenai Brown, perhaps in an effort to offset the impact of family misfortune, went on an extended hunting trip through the mountains. While he was away events far beyond the Waterton Valley reached a dramatic climax, the results of which quickly radiated to the remotest corners of the Northwest Territory, eventually impinging upon Brown himself. Politically, the spring of 1885 was an ominous one in the Canadian west. Louis Riel, the Métis firebrand, had returned from his exile in the United States and was gathering support for himself and for his demands that the Indians and half-breeds should be given a better deal by the Canadian government.

His platform, if it can be described in such terms, demanded more liberal treatment for the plains Indians, scrip and land patents for the Métis, responsible government, modification of the homestead law and, surprisingly, construction of a railroad to Hudson's Bay to serve the needs of white settlers on the prairies. Essentially, Riel's program was moderate. It represented the tip, as it were, of the iceberg of apprehension and unsettlement that was caused throughout the northwest as the Canadian Pacific Railway thrust its way across the prairie. The railroad represented the vanguard of civilization, and civilization to the Indian and Métis meant destruction of their culture, with extinction or assimilation as their ultimate fate. When it eventually broke out, the Second Riel Rebellion was the last stand of the people who represented the prairies against those who represented the plough.[1]

Although the southwestern corner of the District of Alberta was remote and far removed from the Red River country, centre of the disturbance, the effects of Riel's return, even at so great a distance, were clearly felt. By March 1885, the Indians around Fort Macleod, particularly those on the Blood Reserve, were becoming restive. Many ranchers in the region became very perturbed by the situation and most feared that an uprising was bound to occur. Their fears were expressed in a variety of ways. The newly-formed South-Western Stock Association agitated for increased protection, while J. R. Craig, manager of the Oxley Ranch Company, removed his family to the comparative safety of Fort Macleod. Such caution, however, was not typical and most ranchers did not consider that the situation warranted such extreme action.

The Fort Macleod *Gazette*, in fact, hotly and positively denied a report which appeared in Eastern Canada that women and children were flocking to the Fort for protection. According to the editor writing in the issue of April 25, 1885, only "two or three ladies whose husbands are obliged to be away from home a great deal have moved to town, but with the exception of these the ladies of the Macleod district are staying quietly at home, and are not as much afraid as the author of the report, whoever he may be."

Despite the editor's indignation and the variable reactions of individuals, the gravity of the situation in the region was underlined by the obvious lack of real military or police strength and by a marked increase in the shooting of cattle by Indians. There were roughly 500 Mounted Police in the whole of the Canadian northwest, and the inability of the small contingent in the Fort Macleod area to cope with Indian depredations to stock caused numerous complaints and added to the fears of local residents.

Some of the feeling which existed in the ranching country of southwestern Alberta is reflected by W. F. Cochrane in his letters to his father and to the Secretary-Treasurer of the Cochrane Ranch Company:

There is a great deal of uneasiness about the Indians, who it is expected may break out any day. Riel's runners are in their camps, and it seems doubtful what they will do. Dunlop [the ranch foreman] was at Stand Off Friday [April 3, 1885,] and thought it looked a serious threat that he hurried home, and I went immediately into town and got some rifles and ammunition, as we were not in very good shape here for any trouble. I got them at [I. G.] Bakers, so I will have a bill of theirs this month that will cover the $75.00. We ought to make every effort to get more protection here from the Government. It has been taken for granted that we will never have any trouble with the Indians, because we have not had any yet. But we are sleeping on a volcano that may break out any time, and there are enough Indians to clean us all up before help came if they were minded. The police have not enough men to give any help outside of Macleod and we will have to look after ourselves. It is not considered safe to be alone on the prairie now and if the halfbreeds have any access north we will be pretty sure to have trouble here.[2]

Cochrane's preparations to defend the ranch were typical. To him the property and the Company's interests came first, and his reflection of the situation mirrored that philosophy. His lack of confidence in the Mounted Police, and preparations made locally to meet the emergency, stand in marked contrast to the attitude reflected by the editors of the *Gazette.* These points of view are manifestly expressed in a letter dated April 12, 1885:

I suppose [that] you are all pretty anxious about [us] here. I do not think we will have any trouble with our Indians but will do everything to be prepared. If there should be an outbreak it would be impossible to hold the ranch on acct. of position, and the amt. of hay stocked here, but Dunlop does not intend to connect himself with the militia or anybody, but get all the men he can from across the line if necessary, hiring them as cowboys, and act independently in the interests of the company.... We have our horses here in the pasture ready for anything that may turn up.... I do not believe Capt. Stewart will be able to raise much of a corps here.[3]

Cochrane' s sceptical reference to Captain Stewart and the raising of a local supplementary defence force evades the recognition that there was a real necessity to buttress the Mounted Police during the period of emergency. Captain John Stewart, to whom Cochrane referred, formerly served in the Princess Louise Dragoon Guards in the East, and, as the owner of a ranch bordering the Blood Indian Reserve, was very aware of the potential danger of an uprising.

While Cochrane, whose large holding was nearest to the Waterton Lakes, thought primarily in terms of his property, others such as Kootenai Brown and Stewart took a very different initiative. Stewart, for example, made a hurried trip to Ottawa in March 1885, and on the 25th of that month saw the Minister of Militia and Defence, Adolphe P. Caron. In a letter dated the same day, Stewart recorded the gist of their discussions, and formally put down his scheme to raise a body of volunteers in the Fort Macleod area to supplement the existing forces in the District of Alberta. His proposals were explicit. A Provisional Cavalry Force of 150 officers, non-commissioned officers, and men drawn up from "ex-Mounted Police of one or two terms of service in the west, together with Englishmen, Canadian Montanians, who have been leading a Nomadic life and whose home is the prairie," would be raised to patrol an area bounded

Two of Brown's friends in Fort Macleod were C. Wood, above, editor of the *Macleod Gazette*, probably standing in the doorway, and Harry "Kamoose" Taylor, below, doffing his bowler in front of his hotel in Fort Macleod.

His nickname is a Blackfoot word meaning "wife stealer," earned because he stole an Indian girl. He was one of the first arrested by the NWMP for peddling whiskey but later became a businessman. His hotel was renowned for its list of 25 rules which included "Baths furnished free down at the river, but bathers must furnish their own soap and towels; Assaults on the cook are strictly prohibited; All guests are requested to rise at 6 a.m. This is imperative as the sheets are needed for tablecloths; Candles, hot water and other luxuries charged extra, also towels and soap; Towels changed weekly."

on the north by High River, on the east by Medicine Hat, and to the south by the International Boundary Line.[4] Stewart's suggested conditions of service were equally precise.

Each volunteer, irrespective of rank, was to supply his own horse, bridle, saddle, saddle blanket, and lariat. Officers were to bring their own uniforms, that of an undress cavalry officer, while other ranks were to use "their own serviceable wearing apparel."[5] Three days after Stewart submitted his proposals in writing, he received permission to proceed with the scheme. Caron's reply was brief and to the point: "Authority is given to raise four (4) Troops of 'Rocky Mountain' Rangers, on basis and conditions contained in report submitted by Captain Stewart to me."

In addition, Caron the next day wired Major General F. D. Middleton, the officer sent out to quell the rebellion who was then at Qu'Appelle, informing him that Stewart had been given authority to raise four troops and that "he [Stewart] says he can give you [Middleton] fifty mounted men in ten days."[6] Stewart, on receiving ministerial approval, immediately returned to Fort Macleod and set about the business of recruiting, equipping, and training the volunteers.

Despite Cochrane's pessimism, three troops totalling 114 men were quickly raised. Whatever equipment was needed to convert them into a fighting force was procured locally, and in a surprisingly short time was assembled for training.[7] In its issue of April 18, 1885, the *Gazette* reported:

> The Rocky Mountain Rangers had their first muster on Wednesday morning [April 15, 1885,] and have been drilling since then. The men have been got into very creditable shape, considering the short time they have been drilled. The Military headquarters are at the old C and N. Co.'s office.

The paper further reported that the active service detachment of the Rangers was to move into police barracks immediately. On the same day Stewart, in a wire despatched from Calgary, informed the Minister of Militia and Defence about the state of preparation of his force:

> Organization complete; withdrawn Police from Macleod; have put fifty men and mounts in garrison at request of Commandant. One hundred Rangers on duty at important points.[8]

The speed with which the unit had been organized and put into the field underlined the seriousness with which the residents of southwestern Alberta regarded the Indian danger.

As the new cavalry unit began assembling and training, tensions in the Fort Macleod region increased daily. On March 31, 1885, a special messenger arrived from Calgary with ominous news of trouble in the north. Fighting had broken out on March 26 at Duck Lake where the Métis under Gabriel Dumont had ambushed a force of Mounted Police, compelling them to abandon Fort Carlton and retire to Prince Albert.

Almost simultaneously, Cree Indians from the Little Pine and Poundmaker reserves further west looted and pillaged the Hudson's Bay Company premises and other buildings at Battleford. Such news, brought by messenger because the telegraph had not yet reached Fort Macleod, electrified the white settlers in southern Alberta. Precautions, dramatized by Captain Stewart's trip to Ottawa and the formation of the Rocky Mountain Rangers, began at once. Superintendent John Cotton, the officer commanding the North-West Mounted Police in Fort Macleod, records in his *Monthly Report* that the picket was doubled on April 2, and "that Indians have warned half-breeds to leave here and place their cattle in a safe place."[9] Two days later the Force's big guns, nine pounders, were readied, ammunition checked, and a messenger despatched to Calgary. Preparations at Fort Macleod reached their peak on April 5:

Men told off under charge of Sergeants and places allotted to them in case of attack. Mounted pickets told off and everything in readiness for any emergency. Supt. Cotton and Capt. Dewey visited Blood Reserve, found the Indians excited and unsettled. Had interview with good results. Night guard strengthened to 16 men, and 2 non-commissioned officers. 20 rounds of ammunition served to each man.[10]

The dry tone of the Police diary belies the general feeling of excitement and uneasiness that prevailed in the community and throughout the general area. As the Rangers drilled, as Snider arms were issued to the Pincher Creek home guard, as Superintendent Cotton and the Indian Agent Pocklington continued to visit and talk to the Blackfoot tribes, urging them to remain calm and aloof during those unsettled days, the whole area was transformed by the emergency. The efforts made to meet the situation were regarded with mixed feelings. W. F. Cochrane certainly remained sceptical of the actions taken in the Fort Macleod area. Writing to his father, Senator Cochrane, he diagnosed the situation in bleak terms:

> There does not seem to be very much confidence put in Stewart, and he has some unpopular men in with him.... I do not think he will get many men. He does not seem to know exactly what to do himself....
>
> Everybody says why don't the Govt. send cavalry and act agressively against the half-breeds. All this infantry militia amts. to nothing.... The Artillery except the lightest of field guns had better be left at home. What is wanted is a light mounted force that can follow and catch up to their [the Métis and Indians] camp, and so fight them where they will have to stand and defend their families. And to make no place safe for them to leave the squaws.[11]

While Cochrane's words, written on April 18, expressed the feelings of many other ranchers in southwestern Alberta, he was less than fair to Stewart. Indeed, the Rocky Mountain Rangers were precisely the light mounted force that he visualized.

Two days after writing to Montreal, Cochrane's diary contains a brief but significant entry: "Drove out to ranch. Met Kootenai Brown at Kootenai ford."[12] While Cochrane remains silent about the encounter, there can be little doubt that the two men exchanged news and discussed the tense situation caused by Riel's return to the Northwest Territory. From that brief encounter Brown once more comes into clear focus. His reaction was immediate and decisive. Without hesitation he immediately set course for Macleod, covering the distance of some 40 miles in little more than a day. Kootenai's arrival was promptly recorded in the Fort Macleod *Gazette* of April 25, 1885:

> J. G. Brown, of the Kootenai Lakes was in town this week. He has been hunting in the mountains, and did not hear that any rebellion was in progress until last Monday [April 20, 1885]. Mr. Brown says that the game is fairly plentiful in the mountains. There are good numbers of sheep and goats. The snow in the mountains is very deep, and we may expect pretty high water.

In another report in the same issue, and more significant than the reports of game and snow conditions reported by Brown, appears this item:

> The Mountain Rangers have secured a valuable addition to their strength in the person of Mr. J. G. Brown, of the Kootenai Lakes, a well-known hunter and scout. He will act as scout for the Rangers who are to be congratulated on having secured his services.

His rate of pay was that of a Trooper – seventy-five cents a day.[13]

When Brown joined Number One Troop of the Rocky Mountain Rangers his action was neither precipitous nor unpremeditated. No longer bound by the responsibilities of a growing family, he seized the opportunity to serve the community and, simultaneously, to earn more money. Involvement with the Rangers enabled him to forget his loss, and, in its own way, was reminiscent of his service with the Eighth Regiment many years before. The difference, however, was enormous.

Number One Troop had a strength of 42 officers and men, and its composition mirrored the ranching society. The officers, as in England, represented the leading elements in the community, but with one great difference: the discipline was different, and the rigid deference which marked the division between officers and other ranks in the British Army did not exist. Although the Troop included Stewart, by then elevated to the rank of Major, as well as Captain Lord Boyle (later the Earl of Shannon), a Lieutenant James R. Scott, and Second Lieutenant the Honorable H. Boyle (Lord Boyle's brother), it was a comparatively informal, carefree group brought together only for the duration of the troubles. John D. Higinbotham, the tenderfoot apothecary from Ontario, catches some of the easy-going attitudes of the volunteers in his description recorded on April 13, the week before Brown joined the Rangers:

> Each man provides his own mount. The Government supplies saddles and carbines. Their remaining outfit, furnished by themselves, consists of a sombrero, or a broad-rimmed felt hat with a wide leather band, coat of "Montana broadcloth" or brown duck (from which they have received the nickname "Canvasbacks") lined with flannel, a shirt of buckskin, breeches of the same or Bedford cord, a cartridge belt attached to which is a large sheath-knife, and the indispensable leather chaps. Top boots with huge Mexican spurs complete the equipment. Discipline is quite unknown to them; a Mountie told me that he heard one of them, during drill today [April 13, 1885,] call out to his commander, "Hold on Cap., till I cinch my horse." [14]

From Higinbotham's description, it is clear that the essential basic equipment which Stewart so carefully laid down in his written submission to Caron, the Minister of Militia, while present, was intermingled with practical everyday western dress. Kootenai, in his buckskin shirt, his wide slouch hat, his knife and rifle, and the natural ease with which he sat in the saddle, added his own particular touch to what was already a colourful group of men.

Within a day of Brown's joining the Rangers, the unit held a mounted parade.[15] The next day another followed during which the sixty men who turned out were issued blank cartridges and instructed in skirmishing. During the parade, Superintendent Cotton of the N.W.M.P. inspected the men's remounts and decided which were to be taken when the unit went out on patrol.[16]

Further drills were held on April 27 and 29. On the latter day the volunteers, again sixty strong, "paraded and received ammunition," and at 10 o'clock in the morning marched out of Fort Macleod heading east.[17] Their destination was Coal Banks, a point near what is now the city of Lethbridge, Alberta; their assignment, to guard the CPR telegraph line gradually making its way towards Fort Macleod from Coal Banks, and the properties of the North-West Coal Company which operated a narrow gauge railroad between Lethbridge and Dunmore. The Ranger's departure was viewed with mixed feelings by the residents of Fort Macleod. Not unexpectedly, the *Gazette* waxed enthusiastic in its description of the event:

> The active service corps of the Rocky Mountain Rangers under Captain Stewart, left for the Coal Banks at noon on Wednesday. Leaving the barracks where they were vigorously cheered, they rode down past I. G. Baker and Co.'s store in half sections. Quite a large crowd was assembled, and as they passed the above point, they were given a rousing send-off, with a long drawn tiger at the end of it. In front was Major Stewart in command, and on either side of him, J. G. Brown and A. A. Vice, the two scouts, both of them men who have seen plenty of Indian warfare, and who will take a scrimmage as a duck takes to water. Both these scouts too have the advantage of being able to talk the Blackfoot language quite fluently. Next came the men flanked by Captain Boyle and Lieut. Scott, then transport wagons, and last, a rear guard.
>
> The corps is composed of a particularly fine body of men, and as they moved past armed to the teeth with Winchesters, and waist and cross-belts jammed full of cartridges, there was but one opinion expressed regarding them, and that was that they would make it extremely unhealthy for several times their number of rebel half-breeds or Indians, should occasion require. Combined with the order which they had obtained by their brief period of discipline and drill was that free and easy manner and action, which is so characteristic of a border corps and which attaches to them a charm not felt in the rigid movements of the strictly drilled military of the east.

A contemporary sketch by J. D. White in the *Canadian Pictorial and Illustrated War News*, June 20, 1885, pictures the volunteers moving off, with Brown and Vice flanking Stewart, their tanned faces almost hidden beneath the brims of huge stetsons which, according to the accompanying note, were strapped on for "grim death." John D. Higinbotham's description portrays a colourful group cantering off across the countryside:

Around many of their necks were silk handkerchiefs, which, besides being an embellishment, prevented the irritation of their coarse brown duck or "Montana broadcloth" coats. Over parts of the same material were drawn a pair of chaps [leather overalls]. Cross belts pregnant with cartridges, a "sixshooter," sheath knife, a Winchester slung across the pommel of the saddle, and a lariat coiled at tree, completed the belligerent outfit, mounted on bronchos good for sixty to a hundred miles a day, they soon disappeared in the distance; a loud clanking of bits and jingling of their huge Mexican spurs, now gave place to the rattling of transportation wagons. [18]

Cochrane and others viewed the Rangers departure with less enthusiasm. Writing to his father on April 26, he noted the impending departure of the troop in more pessimistic terms:

There are sixty men of Osborn Smith's Winnipeg battalion in Macleod, and I believe Stewart's troop are to move tomorrow. They are to patrol between the Coal Banks and Cyprus Hills. I think there will be a good many of them lost down there. [19]

Cochrane was convinced that the despatch of the mounted force from the immediate vicinity of Macleod, despite the presence of ground troops in the town, was an error, and considered Superintendent Cotton of the N.W.M.P. a coward who could not be depended upon. [20] Much of his pique can be attributed to the very success which Stewart achieved in raising Rocky Mountain Rangers, something Cochrane did not believe could be done, and the impact of the enlistments upon the local labour force:

On acct. of so many men having joined Stewart's troop and the police scout force etc., they are pretty scarce and wages are running high. Dunlop has raised his wages to $50.00 from the first of this month [June 1885]. This is a little earlier than we hoped would be necessary, but we cannot afford to lose our men, and they are doing a long days work now. Breakfast at 4.30 a.m. and supper at 6.30 p.m. Stable work done before breakfast. [21]

As the district settled down uneasily to await the outcome of the action, Cochrane's feelings about the disposition of the mounted troop and the Police bordered on the bitter:

Cotton has taken all his available men down to join Stewart. I do not think it is right to leave this district unprotected. [22]

For Brown and the other men in the field, such views were put completely out of mind. Before them were the open spaces of the plain, and their senses quickened to the possibility of a skirmish with Indians, Métis, or both. It is not difficult to picture Brown putting all of his experience and fieldcraft to use, consulting with Stewart and the other officers about possible dispo-

Rocky Mountain Rangers in 1885, Chief
Scout Kootenai Brown in the lead.

sition of men, horses, and equipment, telling stories, or relating his experiences with the Sioux in the Dakota Territory. Indeed, one of the fears in the Northwest Territory was the possibility that Indians from south of the border would cross into Canadian territory to join in the hostilities. The Rangers were therefore charged to patrol the border area to offset, if not to prevent, such an occurrence from taking place.

Once the Rangers reached Lethbridge they were split into two groups. One proceeded north to patrol the area to the east of High River; the other, Number One Troop, continued eastwards towards Medicine Hat which it reached without incident and "In first class trim."[23] For Brown, the return to the vicinity of Medicine Hat was a time of memory and rediscovery of things past.

During one of the patrols, he returned to the scene of his first encounter with the plains Indians almost 20 years earlier. There, together with other Rangers, he "found two Indian skulls and extracted five bullets out of the old cottonwoods on the creek bank."[24] The patrols which radiated out of Medicine Hat were otherwise uneventful, long arduous affairs that interlocked

with the operations of Mounted Police patrols from "A" Division in Maple Creek, and Métis volunteers under Jean Louis Legare whose zone of operations extended from the Cypress Hills to the Manitoba border.[25] The strategy underlining the Ranger disposition were summarized by Superintendent Cotton in his *Annual Report*:

> Major Stewart made Medicine Hat his headquarters, his outposts extending along railway and telegraph lines and northward towards Red Deer River. My outposts [ie. Cotton's police] connecting with Major Stewart's most westerly detachments, thus keeping up a complete chain of patrol and daily communication along the important frontier line....[26]

Only one incident, which occurred at the end of May, caused a flurry of excitement among the troop, and a flush of anxiety in Fort Macleod. On May 31, the telegraph which had only reached Macleod on the 22nd, broke the dramatic news "that one Ranger had exchanged shots with Indians 30 miles this side [ie. west] of Medicine Hat."[27] While Macleod braced itself for the worst, a strong party of police under Cotton and the police surgeon, Dr. Kennedy, left Macleod for Lethbridge intending to carry on towards Medicine Hat to look into the

147

affair.[28] As it turned out, shots were exchanged between one Ranger, Jackson by name, and a small band of Indians who promptly fled in the direction of the border. At the time of the encounter the situation still seemed to be at the flash point, for Stewart reported that the Ranger patrols had covered a good deal of territory and that Brown and Vice, the two scouts, considered that a great number of Indians were prowling about.[29]

Actually, the real climax of the rebellion was reached several days earlier when, on May 15, Louis Riel was arrested. News of his apprehension did not reach Fort Macleod until May 17, and a good deal of its significance was lost in the general feeling of uncertainty which still strongly prevailed in the south. Reports of restlessness amongst the Indians continued to filter into the community, and the Police, supplemented by the Rocky Mountain Rangers, continued their patrols. Uncertainty about the possible behavior of the tribes continued to maintain tensions. J. R. Craig, manager of the Oxley Ranch, and certainly one of the most cautious men in the Fort Macleod area, catches the sense of the situation in his account of ranching:

> Although the scene of conflict and the general uprising was several hundred miles from us in the Macleod district, yet we were all in great peril if the rebels had been successful in even one engagement.
>
> We were in the midst of three of the most powerful Indian tribes of the North-West, the Blackfoots, Bloods, and Peigans, who were well armed and ammunitioned. They outnumbered us ten to one.... If there had been one victory by Riel's followers nothing could have restrained the tribes around us from an uprising.[30]

Gradually calm returned to the prairies; the cooler and wiser counsels of the old chiefs, Crowfoot and Red Crow, aided by the persuasiveness of Father Lacombe and the Rev. John McDougall, prevailed and the Blackfoot confederation did not succumb to the overtures of hot-blooded younger men. As for the shooting incident between the Rocky Mountain Ranger Jackson and unidentified Indians, which caused a momentary shiver of apprehension through southern Alberta, investigation suggested that it occurred as a result of an accidental crossing of the border by American redskins.[31] Such an accident was certainly not difficult, for many of the original monuments marking the "plains section" of the 49th parallel were merely mounds of earth, many of which had deteriorated greatly since the original survey of 1872-1874. By mid-June 1885, since there were "no

American Indians across the line frontier," Number One Troop of the Rocky Mountain Rangers was ordered home.[32]

With their arrival at Fort Macleod the adventure ended. Their return evoked a variety of responses. W. F. Cochrane merely noted "Mountain Rangers back" in his diary entry for July 8.[33] The North-West Mounted Police fired a salute with a nine pounder gun to acknowledge their return.[34] It was left to the *Gazette* to give the fullest account of the occasion:

> On Tuesday afternoon [July 8, 1885,] the Mountain Rangers returned to Macleod after three months of ardurous duty on the frontier between here and Medicine Hat. We have frequently referred to their services.... We suggested last week that there should be some public recognition of their services, and on Wednesday it was decided to present them with an address of welcome. The original intention was to visit their camp some two miles below the town for this purpose, but, as it was rather late in the evening it was decided to postpone the matter until the next day when it was arranged to have the troop paraded in town.
>
> In accordance with this arrangement the men were drawn up in a line opposite the post office at twelve o'clock, and the address was read by Mr. Wm. Black [Secretary of the South-Western Stock Association]....[35]

The picture of Brown and the other Rangers drawn up, their horses and equipment still showing signs of the trail, remains symbolic of the time and a fitting informal climax to their efforts. Celebrations marking the return, dancing at Bates and Genge's Saloon, dinner at "Kamoose" Taylor's unique hostelry, the Macleod Hotel, where table cloths doubled as bed linen, rounded off the occasion.[36] Whether Brown participated in the fun can only be a conjecture, but it would not be amiss to see him taking part for he enjoyed gay times and a good drink.

Within ten days of their return, the Rangers were paid off and disbanded. For his service of 77 days with Number One Troop – April 23 to July 10 1885 – Brown received $118.50.[37] It was, to all intents and purposes, the formal end of the adventure. The precipitousness of the discharge, however, caused a certain amount of dissatisfaction amongst the Rangers and in the community of Fort Macleod. As a result, at the end of July the town's citizens and the Mounted Police held a banquet and ball to show their appreciation of the corps' service. According to the Police report it was a splendid affair and a great social success:

> One hundred sat down to the banquet, the chair being occupied by Lord Boyle. Over fifty white ladies present at the ball.[38]

At the dinner, Stewart, the Ranger's commanding officer, spoke about his men's performance, saying that it was bad luck that the unit was not involved in any action:

> He then went on to say that in this district a body of Mounted men could be raised superior to ANY CAVALRY IN THE DOMINION. He challenged the Eastern press to take this statement up and deny it.[39]

The mood and attitude expressed upon that occasion were not dissipated in the euphoria of the moment. Stewart left almost immediately for Winnipeg to take up grievances over pay, and to appear before the War Claims Commission which was about to start its hearings.[40]

As for Brown, it is doubtful if he attended the glittering affair honouring the Rangers. After such a long absence, and because of his sudden decision to go directly to Macleod immediately after encountering Cochrane, there was the need to return to his cabin to see if all were intact. Then, too, the banquet and ball were held long after the Rangers were paid off and disbanded.

Without direct ties at Fort Macleod there was no need for Brown to linger for social purposes. Only final arrangements for his children's well-being may have required his presence, but even that possibility in an era when large-scale bureaucracy and welfare agencies were still unknown, is doubtful. Instead, we see him catching up on the events in the Fort Macleod district, talking to his many friends – Kanouse, his former partner, Higinbotham the druggist, "Kamoose" Taylor, and many others whose names have not sifted down into the records – buying supplies and equipment for the long winter months ahead. Eventually, after being paid off, he mounted his horse and returned to the mountains and lakes he cherished, to resume a life lonely but tempered by the surroundings and his own preference.

While Kootenai resumed his way of life, Stewart's efforts on behalf of his men continued. In the autumn they bore fruit when the Rocky Mountain Rangers service in the Northwest Rebellion was officially recognized, and the 114 volunteers were made eligible for the North-West Medal.[41] At the end of the year the harsh conditions of service and the haphazard arrangements which characterized the Ranger's disbandment were further recognized:

In addition to the Rocky Mountain Rangers, members of the North-West Mounted Police were very active during the 1885 Riel Rebellion, especially Steele's Scouts, below. Under their legendary leader and the most famous of all the Mounties, Superintendent Sam Steele, opposite, they were part of a force which pursued Big Bear. His braves had massacred seven white men and a policeman, captured Fort Pitt and fled with nearly 50 men, women and children captives. After a 70-day pursuit the captives were released. Seven Indians were later hanged for their part in the massacre.

Thanks to the exertions of Major Stewart at Ottawa, the way is now clear for the issue of scrip or land warrants to the Rangers. The names are now on file at Ottawa, and upon application the scrip or warrant will be issued. The application must be made personally or by some person armed with the power of attorney.[42]

Under the legislation each volunteer was entitled to receive 320 acres or $80.00 in scrip. Kootenai, like most of the Rangers, chose the half section, and thus obtained his "second homestead" in the south half of Township Nine, Range 25, west of the Fourth meridian.[43] Earlier in the autumn, under provisions of Army General Order 10405, October 13, 1885, he applied for the North-West Medal, listing himself as a single man. When he eventually received his award, it was inscribed on the edge with the words "J. G. Brown, Chief Scout R.M.R." He was then 46, vigorous, knowledgeable in the ways of hunting, trapping and trading, but clearly in need of finding himself in what was obviously a rapidly changing society.

Chapter 11

Return to Waterton Lakes

When Brown returned to his cabin on the eastern shore of the middle Waterton Lakes, his solitary life was punctuated only by visits to the nearby North-West Mounted Police detachments at Big Bend and Kootenai some 10 miles away, to the Cochrane Ranch and, less frequently, to Fort Macleod or Pincher Creek.[1] He made little or no use of his gratuity, the half section of land granted him for serving with the Rocky Mountain Rangers. Apart from grazing a few horses and a small number of cattle on the property, Kootenai took no steps to develop it, or to use it as a springboard for greater economic endeavour. The lure of hunting, and demands for his services as a guide or a packer stifled any real attempt to work the grant systematically for profit.

Then there was always the necessity of supplementing his larder with fish, wild fowl or game since town was distant and commodities expensive. Living alone has its obvious drawbacks, not least of them being the lack of companionship and help. What Brown may have felt or experienced during those initial months after his return from service with the Rocky Mountain Rangers can only be conjectured, for it is a period in his life to which he rarely, if ever, referred. The intimation is that it was a difficult, and possibly even an unhappy time, for during the spring following his return to the mountains he succumbed to a serious illness.

When living alone, the danger of falling victim to an accident or sickness is inevitably greater than for those whose lives are passed in the presence of others. On the frontier, in a remote corner of the Northwest Territory, serious illness meant courtship with death. Only luck and the friendliness characteristic of the west saved Kootenai. His plight was discovered by W. F. Cochrane who happened to look in on Brown while searching for stray cattle for the spring round up. Cochrane immediately did what he could to help Brown, then set out for Fort Macleod as quickly as possible. The rest of the story is told by the Fort Macleod *Gazette,* March 9, 1886:

> It is with the most sincere regret that we announce the rather serious illness of Mr. J. G. Brown, of the Kootenai Lakes. Mr. W. Cochrane of the Cochrane Ranch, came in for Dr. Kennedy, who went out to visit him at his ranch at the Kootenai Lakes. It was deemed advisable to bring him to town, and Mr. Cochrane drove him in, and secured his admission to the police hospital, where he now is. Mr. Brown indeed found a good samaritan in Mr. Cochrane. Mr. Brown is deeply grateful for the kindness he received from him as well as from the doctor, and all at the barracks. We trust that Mr. Brown will soon recover sufficiently to take his post as a hospitable host at his place on the Kootenai Lakes.

Brown's admission to the N.W.M.P. Hospital, initiated by Cochrane, was also made possible because of his service with the Rangers, and his acquaintance with Kennedy, the Assistant Surgeon for the Force. The fact that Cochrane and Kennedy undertook journeys of almost 100 miles in the spring when travelling conditions were at their most difficult, confirms the serious nature of Kootenai's illness, and the kind of men they were.

John R. Craig, the manager of the Oxley Ranch, notes in his reminiscences that Kennedy travelled over 30 miles from Fort Macleod to attend a patient seriously ill with bronchitis, and that in the process "he had to cross two unbridged rivers swollen with the June rains and the melting snow of the mountains."[2] Craig's observation epitomises social conditions which prevailed in that southern section of the District of Alberta – the District was established 1882 – during these years and which Kootenai, single though he was, had to accept as a natural part of daily life:

> ...there was no amelioration in the social condition. The few families were separated by many miles – there was less than one family to a township of thirty-six square miles. Social gatherings happened but seldom. A dance in Macleod at the Christmas season, the annual stock meeting, or a visit to the round up, filled the year's entertainment, varied occasionally by a visit from a Governor-General, a Cabinet Minister, or some other more or less important functionary.[3]

As a loner, such rare occasions were even more remote for Brown than for the majority of other white settlers in the region.

The episode of his illness impressed itself upon Brown. Physically tough, vigorously active for his 46 years, the experience served as a forceful reminder that living alone could be dangerous. Kootenai's solution was simple and characteristic of the frontier. Sometime after his recovery, he consoled himself by taking a Cree wife, becoming, in plain terms, a squaw man.

There are many stories about how Brown met and persuaded Isabella – he referred to her in conversation as "Nichemoos" the Cree equivalent of "dear"; in his diaries he called her "the woman"; and in his will, "Isabella" – to remain with him at the cabin by the lakes. The most romantic claim is that Isabella was an Indian princess, but supporting evidence is a will o' the wisp. At the other end of the spectrum is the statement that Kootenai received Isabella in exchange for five horses.

Rose Marie Smith, herself a Métis, who knew the woman soon after she came to Waterton with Brown and remained there until her death in 1935, records that Kootenai met Isabella during his service in the vicinity of Medicine Hat with the Rocky Mountain Rangers.[4] Mrs. Smith and Archdeacon S. H. Middleton, an Anglican clergyman with long service on the Blood Indian Reserve, both claim that the marriage ultimately was solemnized by Father Lacombe during one of his periodic trips to southern Alberta.[5] Church records, however, do not substantiate the claim, and the lack of evidence strongly suggests the much more frequent common law arrangement which characterized early days on the plains. Unlike many similar unions, however, Brown's lasted.

The contrast between Olive, the young Métis girl, and Isabella was startling. Olive, from the evidence of Brown's memory and other references, was a beautiful and lively woman; Isabella, as photographs taken in her later years show, was plain to the point of homeliness, squat, and patiently stolid. Olive had shared Brown's tastes to an extent unusual in the semi-nomadic Metis society of the Red River region; Isabella, by contrast, constantly and consistently deferred to Brown. To Isabella, Kootenai was the main focal point in her life. Intellectually she shared none of Brown's interests and held him in awe because he could read and write. Although she understood English, she never learned to speak the language so that one barrier between herself and Kootenai, and between her and the increasing stream of visitors to the cabin, was never pierced. While these shortcomings may have made Brown restive, perhaps even exasperated, he never let his feelings stray into his diaries, or rise to the surface while in public. As the years passed and as the number of visitors rose, the stocky, silent figure in the background watched impassively, carrying out her duties with an awareness that never intruded into Kootenai's schedules. One visitor, an observant young Scottish girl who visited Brown a number of times in 1914, describes Isabella's presence in the household:

> His wife made tea and served it, but that was all we ever saw of her. She seemed more of a servant. We could understand that as he was so highly educated.[6]

Brown was then 74, and the master-servant relationship may very well have been exaggerated by circumstances and a youthful eye accustomed to very different standards. Despite their different backgrounds and interests, Isabella was an admirable frontier companion, a reliable partner upon whom Brown became increasingly dependent. She was, as Marie Rose Smith notes, an excellent shot, and very much at home in the out-of-doors, often accompanying Kootenai on hunting trips through the mountains which lasted for weeks and which ranged as far afield as the magnificent reaches of the Flathead country:

> Oftimes the Browns travelled in the mountains with pack horses. Jack Street was with them, prospecting and hunting wild game...for he was an excellent shot and energetic in keeping the pot full. Mrs. Brown was splendid at tanning skins and curing meat. She also was a good shot herself, bringing in many prairie chickens, partridges, ducks. While Street and Brown hunted for big game, this woman kept the camp fires burning so there was always a hearty meal awaiting them on their return.[7]

Whenever Brown went away on business, or for the pleasure of a trip through the mountains with other companions, he did so with equanimity, knowing that Isabella would maintain herself and the cabin faithfully and without a qualm.

After Brown brought Isabella to the cabin by the edge of the Lower Waterton Lake, his life resolved itself into a variation of his previous routine. He went to Fort Macleod less frequently. More and more of his time was spent hunting and guiding, for the flow of visitors to the lakes continued to increase once it became known that Kootenai enjoyed company and was a good host. A high proportion of those who came were Métis: Marie Rose Smith and her husband, William Gladstone, "Frenchy" Riviere and others. And every so often Isabella's relatives would appear silently and unheralded, set up their tents in the vicinity of the cabin, remain for a time, and then just as silently disappear.

156

Two of Brown's favourite hunting companions were Achilles (Archie) Roulean and John Street, both members of the N.W.M.P. from the nearby detachments. Through them, and through his contact with the Force established as a result of service with the Rocky Mountain Rangers, Brown's reputation as a scout, guide, and packer became firmly established. The connection with the Force enhanced his reputation in the Pincher Creek-Fort Macleod District. As more and more people discovered the beauties of the lakes and mountains in that corner of Alberta, demands for his services rose accordingly. Craig, the Oxley Ranch manager, reflects the feeling of residents and visitors alike when he wrote about the area:

> There is no fairer land in the Territory than the Pincher Creek District. The country is gently undulating and covered with rich pasturage. When the sod has been broken there is exposed alluvial soil.[8]

In such surroundings, with Chief Mountain brooding over the prairie and the three lakes (Upper and Lower Waterton and Lake Maskinonge) beckoning, Brown's knowledge of the mountain trails and abilities with gun and horse brought him numerous commissions and an ever-widening circle of acquaintances amongst the early residents in the district, men such as John Herron, F. W. Godsal, and Major Stewart, the moving spirit in the Rocky Mountain Rangers organization.

But the need to earn a living remained constant, despite almost idyllic surroundings and a large circle of convivial friends. Accordingly, and indeed because of his friends, Brown gained employment from the major source in his immediate vicinity, the North-West Mounted Police. The officers and men of "H" Division knew his worth as a scout and packer, and because his lakeshore cabin was located near the Force's grazing reserve along the Belly River, adjoining the southwest corner of the Blood Indian Reserve, Kootenai was the logical choice to look after police mounts.

Accordingly, in the summer of 1888 he was employed throughout the summer as a packer at a rate of $60.00 per month.[9] That formal connection with the Force, while useful in terms of supplementing his income and providing some of the commodities that were otherwise not so easily available through selling or exchanging fish, unexpectedly gave Brown an opportunity to revisit scenes of his first days in the Canadian West.

Kootenai Brown, seated at right, outside his cabin at Waterton in October 1883. His solitary life was broken by visits to Fort Macleod, 50 miles away, and to the NWMP Post at Big Bend which was "only" 10 miles away.

Mounted Police duties were responsible for a brief but memorable return to Wild Horse Creek, where for a short time he had been a law enforcement officer 23 years previously.

The reason for Brown's return to the scene of his civil service and prospecting days was rooted beyond personal desire, or the immediate duties required of him at the local Police detachment where he was employed. The unsettled state of the Kootenay Indians, coming so soon after the Métis rebellion on the prairies, caused considerable concern within the provincial and federal administrations, and quickly resulted in the appointment of a three-man commission to investigate and report on the prevailing state of tensions.

In June 1887, accordingly, the three appointees – Lt. Col. Herchmer, the N.W.M.P. Commissioner, Dr. Powell, Superintendent of Indian Affairs in British Columbia, and Kootenai's old friend, A. W. Vowell, then Gold Commissioner and Stipendary Magistrate of the Kootenay district – visited the area and decided that the situation there was sufficiently unsettled to warrant Mounted Police protection. As a result, a force of 77 men under the command of Superintendent S. B. Steele – the redoubtable Sam Steele – Officer Commanding "H" Division at Fort Macleod, was despatched to the scene of the most serious disturbances. Order was quickly reestablished by Steele and his men, with a marked decrease in gambling and drunkenness amongst whites and Indians.

Visible proof that the Police were determined to remain became evident when winter quarters built of logs, and located on the imposing bluff strategically overlooking the confluence of Wild Horse Creek and Kootenay River and commanding the trails to Tobacco Plains, the Crow's Nest Pass, Moyie and the Columbia Lakes, were established.[10] The location was a mere five miles from the old diggings, and very near where Brown and his partners unsuccessfully prospected for gold.

With law and order restored, the Mounted Police were no longer required, and on June 6, 1888, Steele and his men were ordered to return to Fort Macleod. Brown, who joined the detachment at Wild Horse a few days after the recall, was sent to the Division expressly to help with the return, and was put to immediate use in preparation for the trek home. It was a strenuous time for Kootenai, as Steele recorded in his *Annual Report*:

Having been informed on the 29th June, that the trail through the Crow's Nest Pass had been cleared by the working party, who were then returning, I sent Interpreter Berland, an experienced Packer, to examine and report upon the trail. He returned on the 22nd [of July] having made a rapid ride to the vicinity of the Summit and reported the trail in good order, which I reported to you, and also informed you that I sent Packer Brown with the Police pack train loaded with oats and biscuits, as far as the Summit, with instructions to carefully "cache" a days supply for the division at intervals of one days march, the last "cache," to be made sixteen miles from the lower lake, on the Old Man's River.... Packer Brown performed the work of "caching" the provisions satisfactorily.[11]

Reveille sounded at daybreak on Tuesday, August 7, 1888, and at 0530 a.m. with "the object for which the Police had been sent to the district...the preservation of peace and the restoration of friendly relations between whites and Indians having been attained," the column of officers, N.C.O.'s, and men of "D" Troop, three employed packers and 54 pack animals hired locally for the transfer, set off for Fort Macleod.[12] As one of the packers, Brown attended to the loading of animals, kneeing them in the bellies, tightening cinch straps, adjusting equipment, chivying the column along the trail, and constantly surveying the changing terrain, remembering, perhaps even reliving, his earlier trip when responsibilities were fewer and prospects precarious.

Whether he saw his old friend Vowell at Wild Horse remains conjectural. His stay was short, his duties manifold. In addition, there is no indication that the Commission members were in the vicinity during the latter days of the Mounted Police presence. Probable or not, any possible reunion between Brown and Vowell could only have been one of contrasts, with memories of early days interposed between the different status and experiences of the two old friends. Vowell represented the world of officialdom and calculated development of a rugged land in the virtuous orthodox Victorian sense; Kootenai epitomized the unbridled initiative and comparative freedom and colour of the unorthodox, restless wanderer who put his faith in the land, its animals, its savages (civilized or otherwise), and his own initiative.

For one, it meant security after service and an acknowledged place in the society of Victoria; for the other, it meant a continuous abrasive contact with life and, through survival, transformation into a personality, a local character representing a vanishing way of life. At the end, Vowell's orthodoxy and loneliness — he never married — was swept away by suicide; for

Brown, the reward was death through old age and a contribution to the creation of a natural and enduring monument.[13]

Once underway on the trail, the move, despite the inevitable variations of hard work and difficulty, proceeded on schedule and with little incident:

> The "cache" of oats and biscuits left by Packer Brown were found all right, with the exception of two sacks of oats, which had been taken and "cached" near at hand, to be taken away when the division had passed; but fortunately the oats were found in time to be of service to the division. [14]

"D" Troop as a result reached Fort Macleod August 17, 1888, traversing the Crow's Nest Pass without difficulty or delay. Much of the credit for the relatively easy passage must go to Brown because of the judicious locations which he so carefully selected for the journey. Because of the mountainous terrain and limited forage, Brown's phase of the operation was paramount in order to ensure a quick, trouble-free passage through the Pass. Subsequently, the Fort Macleod *Gazette*, September 13, 1888, reported that "the trip was made successfully in eight days to Lees Lake," and that "the transport consisted of about 80 pack animals...composed of Mounted Police trains and two trains belonging to Messrs. Galbraith Bros." In an earlier issue, that of August 20, the paper briefly noted that Kootenai Brown had come from the Kootenay district of British Columbia with "D" Troop.

The rapid and successful return of the Mounted Police from Wild Horse did not end Brown's employment with the Force. There was plenty of work at the Force's Reserve on the Belly River, not all of it easy as the "H" Division Monthly Report for September makes clear:

> On the 25th [of September] Packer Brown attached to "D" Division had his leg broken while handling some horses at the herd.[15]

It was an unfortunate accident, for it came at the best time of the year in terms of hunting, and at a time when preparations for the winter reached their peak. Fortunately for Brown, it occurred relatively near his cabin, and after the initial matter of setting the fracture, he could be transported to the Lakes and given over to the care of Isabella. Since there are no details extant of the nature of the break, or the extent of treatment required, this period of Brown's life must be pictured as a brief but frustrating convalescence for a man of 49 as energetic and active as Kootenai.

By spring he was certainly up and around again, active as ever, riding over the prairie at the entrance to the mountain valley, fishing, visiting the Police detachment at Kootenai, hunting if the need required. At the beginning of June 1889, he was re-employed locally by the N.W.M.P., but at a reduced rate of $40.00 per month.[16] The duties were the usual ones of packing or working new mounts, and the summer passed without incident. Steele, in his June report, noted that "Kootenay Brown left on the 8th in charge of the herd as Constable J. Street was required to break-in bronchos."[17] The temporary employment ended on September 2, and almost immediately Brown, together with Street who took his discharge from the Force in mid-August, went on a long hunting expedition through the mountains.[18] In a sense the expedition was a form of celebration for both. It marked the end of service for one and signified complete recovery from the injury of the previous year for the other.

Since the two men, who were close friends, did not return until well into October, the interval provided a springboard of experiences and change that lessened the length and rigours of the winter months. Little news of Brown emerges from the pages available to the researcher. There are no entries in the Fort Macleod *Gazette,* and Cochrane's diaries are silent. Both point to a quiet interval in a rude but warm cabin, deep in snow swirled up by the strong winds characteristic of the Waterton Lakes, punctuated by visits to and from the Police detachment, prolonged visits by Street, until at last early summer arrives and Kootenai once more is taken on strength by the Mounted Police as a temporary employee. This time Brown's pay was pegged at $60.00 a month, suggesting that his recovery was acknowledged, and his responsibilities greater.[19]

As in previous summers, Kootenai's duties were the usual ones of overseeing the police herd, breaking horses, packing for local patrols, and advising about the terrain whenever called upon. In August, however, Brown, by force of circumstances, was thrown into close contact with one of the public figures of the day.

Because of his experience as a guide and packer, because of his knowledge of the mountains, and because of his proven reli-

In 1887 as a consequence of Indian unrest in southeastern B.C., Sam Steele and 75 men were ordered to the area. They built a police post on the bank of the Kootenay River about three miles from Wildhorse Creek where Kootenai Brown had been a provincial policeman 22 years earlier. They quickly settled the unrest and left in 1888, Brown leading the way as a packer.

A small community which grew up around the post was named Fort Steele in honor of the commanding officer. It became the most important community in East Kootenay, above, but was doomed in 1898 when bypassed by the Crowsnest Pass Railway. Over the years Fort Steele became more and more derelict. Then in 1961 the community was declared an historic park and an ongoing restoration program started. Today, tens of thousands of visitors a year see the restored NWMP post, below, and many other exhibits.

ability in earlier service with the N.W.M.P., Brown was detailed to accompany Mackenzie Bowell, then Minister of Customs in the Macdonald government, on a journey through the Rockies. Bowell was in western Canada on an inspection tour of customs posts and facilities, and on arrival at Fort Macleod he and his party were provided with a Mounted Police escort for the next stage of their journey into British Columbia. The monthly Mounted Police report, which records the journey, is succinct to the point of aridness, and lacks any touch of colour:

The Hon. MacKenzie Bowell, Mr. Parmalee, and a police escort and a pack train consisting of Sgt. Waite in charge, Packer Brown in charge of the pack train, six constables acting as escort, servants, cook and assistant packer, 11 horses and 11 pack animals, tents, and camp equipment was supplied from here as well as blankets and waterproof sheets for the Minister's Party. The Hon. the Minister, Mr. Parmalee, and Capt. Young all rode horses especially selected from both divisions. The whole party with the exception of the Hon. Mr. Bowell left here on the 29th; he joined the party at Pincher Creek on the following morning. They will proceed via the Crow's Nest Pass to British Columbia.[20]

No account of the journey is to be found in the Bowell Papers, and in the absence of any records, we cannot fix any impressions which may have registered upon the future Prime Minister. Yet it is not hard to conceive of the party enjoying their journey through the mountains, marvelling at the scenery and the wild life, impressed by the natural ease and skills with which Kootenai and the Mounted Police escort handled their horses and equipment. Equally, it is not inconceivable that during the trip – it took over two weeks – Brown and others of the escort spoke feelingly, and with the authority of experience, about the need to take steps to preserve wild life and prevent the land from being pre-empted by settlers and large scale ranch leases at the expense of the people of Canada.

Such talk was almost inevitable under the circumstances, particularly since Banff, which had been established only five years previously, was in the general area of their route and provided a pointed and relevant example for the politicians in the party. They, on the other hand, were aware of the other aspect of the case, the matter of raising and allocating funds for such purposes through departmental estimates and parliamentary approval. What is certain, is that the journey through the mountains certainly helped to create a receptive climate of opinion in the minds of Bowell and his companions, so that when the time came for action, impediments at the political level were minimal.

Eventually, the party, riding their specially selected horses, arrived safely in Revelstoke, and on September 16, Bowell telegraphed Superintendent Steele at Macleod to that effect as well as to inform him that the Police escort had started on its return journey.[21] The Fort Macleod *Gazette,* September 25, 1890, which reported the group's safe arrival, slyly described the sortie as "a somewhat adventurous journey." After all, it was not often that a small pioneer newspaper in the far west of Canada could take direct advantage of a small dig at politicians who actually ventured so far and so daringly from the wilder shores of the Ottawa and Rideau Rivers. By way of contrast, Steele reported the escort's return in terse, characteristic terms:

> The party under Sgt. Waite detailed to escort the Hon. the Minister of Customs and party through the Crow's Nest Pass into B.C. returned on the 4th instant [i.e. October] and neither men or horses at all the worse for the trip.[22]

Two days after the escort reached Fort Macleod, Kootenai was stricken from the Mounted Police local employment roll, and soon after returned to the lakes where Isabella patiently waited. For Brown, the severance with the Force at the end of his summer employment was permanent. He may have been employed briefly on an *ad hoc* basis, but that probability is unlikely for there are no entries in the N.W.M.P. central pay ledgers. In a sense, Brown's trip through the Rockies with Mackenzie Bowell, and his permanent severance of employment with the Mounted Police marked the end of the "frontier" period in Kootenai's life.

From this point the pattern and order of his existence were steadily eroded by the advance of ranchers, railroad and farmers, each of which left their imprint upon the land and all who drew their sustenance from it. Southern Alberta was no longer the frontier outback. By 1890 it was simply a land still empty of people, no longer an area where adventure went hand in hand with the unknown, a region underdeveloped but full of promise for those strong enough to take advantage of all its bounties. Significantly, yet by sheer coincidence, Brown's trip through the mountains and the subsequent changes which followed so rapidly coincided almost exactly in time with what the historian Frederick Jackson Turner has determined to be the end of the American frontier.[23]

Chapter 12

Oil and a "Stampede of Speculators"

As Brown and Isabella resumed their lives in the autumn of 1890 and prepared to contend with winter, the changing pattern of social and economic conditions in southwestern Alberta began to intrude more pointedly into their affairs. On the last day of the old year, Kootenai, for reasons known only to himself, transferred his title to the land granted him as a gratuity for his service with the Rocky Mountain Rangers to a man named McArthen [sic, possibly McArthur].[1] What prompted Brown to do so is not clear but his actions, taken in the context of change, strongly suggests that he either could not, or did not want to, take time and trouble to develop his holding into a viable economic unit. By then it was becoming apparent that most small ranches were marginal propositions unable to compete successfully with the large cattle companies and Brown, aware that his land was of marginal utility and lacking in capital, may have decided to take advantage of a reasonable offer. He did not, however, forsake the lakes or a stake in the area.

Early next autumn, Kootenai arranged for a "homestead for SE 1/4 Sec. 31 Tp. 1-29-4th on 23 September 1891 and patent was issued to him on 16th Dec. 1892."[2] Much more advantageously located near the junction of Pass Creek and the Lower Waterton Lake, the quarter section included a fine hay meadow and sufficient grazing for Brown's horses, and provided timber enough for a new cabin. In the wider sense, Kootenai's actions reflected the sort of thing that other small operators attempted. The large cattle firms at the time were doing their best to propagate the idea that the southern part of Alberta was suitable only for ranching on a major scale, for they feared and resented the small independent operators because they were liable to revert to mixed farming if competition in the cattle business proved too difficult.[3] The antipathy to settlers was most vociferously and consistently voiced by Dr. McEachern, manager of the Waldrond

Kootenai Brown in 1885. Beside him is Jerry Potts, another remarkable frontiersman who as a warrior and a scout had no equal. Son of a Scots fur trader and a Blood Indian woman, he engaged in many battles, including killing a man who had murdered his mother and half-brother, and leading the last major confrontation between Indian tribes in Canada. It took place in October 1870 at present-day Lethbridge when the Blood-Blackfoot Indians were attacked by Crees and Assiniboines. For Potts and his people it was a resounding victory. At the site a cairn notes: "Final loss estimated at 300 to 500 Crees and 40 Blackfeet. It was the last great battle."

In 1874 Potts was hired at $90 a month by the North-West Mounted Police when they reached what is today Alberta on their westward trek but couldn't find Fort Whoop-Up. Potts led them to the Fort and to an island in the Oldman River where they built Fort Macleod. He remained with the Force until his death in 1896 and was buried with full honors at the NWMP Cemetery in Fort Macleod.

To the Mounties, Pott's most amazing attribute was his sense of direction. Without a compass or landmarks he found his way over the trackless prairie in winter and summer. Superintendent Sam Steele summarized his ability: "As scout and guide I have never met his equal, he had none in either the Northwest or the States to the south."

Ranch, who became very unpopular during the so-called "Waldrond war on settlers."[4]

Despite such pressure and propaganda from the major interests, the Federal Department of the Interior opened the land in the vicinity of Lees Creek to settlement. Mormons in the area, who had come up from the United States to avoid harassment because of their religious and social beliefs, soon made formal application at the Dominion Lands Office in Lethbridge for select sites. That spring C. O. Card, the president of the Mormon settlement at Lees Creek, left for Salt Lake City, Utah, to arrange for extensive emigration the following year.[5]

By the autumn of 1890, just as Brown was returning from his trip to Revelstoke with the Mackenzie Bowell party, many of the new settlers had arrived and were already successfully cultivating the land. Their efforts, particularly in the use of irrigation, soon impressed everyone, including Superintendent Steele, the officer commanding "H" Division at Fort Macleod, who often visited with C. O. Card and his family.

The Mormon community at Lees Creek became the nearest point of population to Brown, and there is no doubt that he watched the influx with interest and alarm. The discipline and order of the newcomers' community organization, characterized by a common centre within easy reach of houses, corrals, gardens, church and school, were new and impressive. Their influx, in turn, was symptomatic of the rapid increase in population in Alberta.

According to a N.W.M.P. census carried out in 1891, the population of whites and Métis in the region was 18,322; in 1895 the total had risen to 28,783, an increase of 57% in less than four years.[6] Proportionately, the actual increase in Alberta was higher than in the Northwest Territory as a whole. In 1891 the Mounted Police count put the population at 52,230, while in 1895 the total rose to 75,506, an increase of roughly 40%.[7] With the coming of the Mormons to southern Alberta, civilization began to impinge inexorably upon Brown and the Waterton Lakes. In 1899, too, the first Dominion Geological Survey party under J. H. Selwyn entered the area, a portent of what was to come.[8] As the numbers of people in the region rose, the number of visitors to the lakes increased correspondingly as the new residents discovered the charms and beauty of the mountains.

The establishment of the Mormon settlement did not mean that demands for Kootenai's skills as a hunter, packer, or guide rose in proportion to the growth of the new community. The people, though hospitable and hard working, soon gained the reputation of being rather sharp in their business details, and their strict code prohibiting gambling or drink stood out in a society which still considered both a natural part of the open range life upon which it was premised.

Of more immediate seriousness than the social idiosyncracies of the Mormons, however, was the impact of the growing population upon the natural resources of southern Alberta. Game grew steadily scarcer, and the streams and lakes in the region soon showed signs that they were in danger of being fished out. Such reports, amongst them Kootenai's and those of his hunting companion, Jack Street, soon caused the old timers in the region to become thoroughly alarmed.

Symptomatic of such changes and their implications for men such as Brown, was the discovery in 1889-1890 of oil in the mountain valley above and to the west of the main Waterton Lake. Change and all that it meant was thus dramatized by the find, and the frenetic attempts to exploit the resource were revealed to Kootenai in the most immediate sense. The discovery of oil in that southwestern pocket of the Northwest Territory was neither new nor dramatic compared with the subsequent history of black gold in Alberta.

The Kootenay and Stoney Indians were long aware of the presence of the thick, dark strange-smelling seepages along the stream running from what is now Cameron Lake, and Brown himself first learned about them from the bands around the time of the second Riel Rebellion.[9] In that respect, it can be said fairly that he was the first of the Alberta petroleum pioneers. Certainly, he was the first white man to exploit the seepages by collecting the oil for use as a lubricant for his wagons, as a medicant for his horses, and possibly even as a fuel. The discovery and his attempts to use the commodity, however, did not lead to wealth or a change in the order and pattern of his life. Instead, as news of the unusual geological phenomenon began to filter into the growing community of southern Alberta, it created an excitement that resulted in a "stampede of speculators" and a frantic staking of many claims in the general area of the seepages.[10] As always, the Fort Macleod *Gazette* reported upon developments with eager interest, tracing the fortunes of exploration, field operations, and financing in considerable detail. Thus, in its issue of October 3, 1889, there is the authoritative note that an expert had reported favourably upon the oil discovery:

Mr. Osborne...representing the Standard Oil Co., visited the oil fields.... He says there is no doubt in the world that there is oil in the Kootenay country and expresses the greatest confidence that it will be found in paying quantities.

That authoritative pronouncement quickly galvanized local speculators and developers, many of them Brown's friends, into action. On October 31 the *Gazette* carried the following news:

There was a large meeting of claim holders in the Kootenai petroleum fields on Saturday evening. Some fifty claim holders were present or represented.... The following gentlemen were then selected to act for the rest: For Macleod, A. R. Springett; for Pincher Creek, J. Herron; and for the North, A. Patrick.

Various attempts to exploit the "Kootenai petroleum fields" followed, the most spectacular of which was the formation of the Alberta Petroleum and Prospecting Company, a local body with a share capital of $5,000, divided into 250 shares of $20.00 each."[11] A prime reason for the local effort, as a "claim holder" put it in a letter to the *Gazette's* editor, "the big companies haven't been jostling each other in their efforts to get the property."[12] As it turned out, all attempts to exploit the discovery were unsuccessful. By the end of 1891, as the *Gazette* made clear in its issue of December 3, Alberta's first oil boom had petered out:

Boring operations are at a standstill in the Kootenai oil regions. There seems to be great uncertainty as to when work will commence. Two holes have been sunk a short distance.

Throughout this period of fluctuating speculation and unsuccessful development, the Waterton area received a certain measure of added notoriety and publicity through the visits of various well-known southern Alberta residents, and the inspection of the oil seepages by Dr. Selwyn, Director of the Canadian Geological Survey.[13] During the course of staking claims and drilling, what are now Cameron Lake and Cameron Creek became known locally as Oil Lake and Oil Creek, colourful enough descriptive designations reflecting the feeling of the time, but singularly inappropriate in terms of a successful strike.

Indirectly, Kootenai was involved in the most successful attempt to exploit the seepages. He occasionally employed William Aldridge, a Mormon from the nearby settlement, to help with heavy work around the cabin, and it was Aldridge who devised a system of trenches designed to lead the oil into pits or into strategically placed barrels. Aldridge then sold the unrefined crude to the ranchers and settlers in the district for a dollar a gallon.[14] Apart from Aldridge's continuing efforts to bring the commodity to market, the "Kootenay petroleum fields" boom was short-lived. As so often has been the case in Alberta where the climate of development has changed as rapidly as chinooks, in the meteorological sense, the attention of developers and speculators soon shifted elsewhere.

To Brown and other residents in the vicinity of the lakes, Alberta's first oil boom drove home the danger of people flooding into the mountains and foothills and the resulting impact upon the wildlife and natural resources of the area. Although Kootenai, and others who derived their livings from fishing and shooting, deplored the results, Brown himself must be held responsible to a considerable extent for the influx of newcomers and for the consequences which stemmed from their coming.

He not only publicized the presence of oil in the vicinity of the Waterton Lakes, but was equally instrumental in arousing dreams of riches through his reports, invariably overdrawn, of the presence of minerals discovered while on his numerous expeditions into the mountains. Thus, the *Gazette* of September 22, 1892, carried a long editorial on Brown and the remarkable quality of a quartz sample he brought from the "Kootenai Lakes" which assayed at $40 silver, $2.90 gold, $2.07 copper, and contained traces of lead. Taken from a ledge six feet thick and some 4,000 feet long at high level, the sample was calculated to represent a discovery with a potential worth of a million dollars. Such accounts are the stuff of dreams, and such are the few glimpses we have of Kootenai during this period in the history of southwestern Alberta.

While the reports about Brown's doings are limited, there is little doubt that the influx of population and the growing scarcity of fish and game were responsible for an attempt to investigate the possibilities of finding a compatible life elsewhere. In the autumn of 1892, Kootenai, together with two

In 1865 when Kootenai first saw the prairie the land was home to buffalo herds which stretched for hundreds of miles. Within 20 years the animals had been slaughtered virtually to the last one. When the CPR was completed in 1886, its freight included hundreds of tons of buffalo bones. The pile below in 1884 consists of only skulls.

unnamed companions – Street was almost certain to be one of them – headed north to territory reported to be teeming with game.

When the party ultimately returned to Fort Macleod in the early summer of 1893, Brown described their experiences to his friend, C. E. D. Wood, editor of the Fort Macleod *Gazette*. The account subsequently reappeared in the June 16, 1893, issue of that paper. Stripped of its journalistic colour, Kootenai's report gives a glimpse of a changing landscape, and reveals a tantalizingly brief touch of the man, his character of expression, and his humour:

Starting on the 1st September last, he with two companions, a small band of cayuses, and no less than thirteen dogs, departed to clean out the fur-bearing animals in the country around Vermillion Lakes. A considerable amount of trouble was experienced on the road up, until the vicinity of Edmonton, owing to the lack of water. After meeting and vanquishing successfully various wire fences, in which the party got tangled up entirely against their will, on several occasions, Edmonton was finally reached. Delayed there for a week by a snow-storm, a start was made for the Vermillion Lakes, which were reached on the 7th November. From Ft. Saskatchewan up the settlers got gradually more scattered, and the petty annoyance to sportsmen and travellers, in the shape of wire fences, also got beautifully less, their places however, being taken by numerous half-breeds and Indians, also on the hunt, who were, if anything – still taking a sportsmans view of life – worse than the wire fences. Having finally arrived, the party went to work and constructed a log shack and started to follow out the objects of the expedition – hunting and trapping – but, to use the words of our informant, "it was a fizzle, sir, a rank fraud, and it cost me two hundred and fifty good elegant dollars to find out; why! if it hadn't been for rabbits, we'd have starved, and, upon my honor, down here I felt ashamed now to look a jack rabbit in the face. The combined effort of the three of us, and the cayuses, and the 13 dogs, only resulted during the whole winter, in one black-tail deer, and that was positively the only game of any size we saw, the rest of the bag during the trip included 40 foxes, 10 coyotes, 3 lynx and a dozen minks, and that was the result of a season's hunting by three men, who are by no means novices, in a country that [we] were told abounded in game."[15]

The trip was a financial as well as a hunting failure and Brown, as reported, returned "a poorer and wiser man since his excursion" convinced that "any sportsman on the lookout for sport had better strike off into the Rockies, for there he can find plenty of game whereas in the bush country where we were, he's liable to spend his time travelling around looking for the tracks of game that he'll never see."[16] It was the last time that Brown ventured away from his beloved mountains and lakes.

Kootenai's return to Waterton Lakes, his report of conditions to the north, and his discussions with friends such as John
Herron, C. E. D. Wood and others, reinforced the growing feeling amongst many of the older residents that definite steps had
to be taken by the central authorities to prevent the southwestern
pocket of the district from being completely ruined. The climate
of opinion thus created at last moved F. W. Godsal, a rancher in
the Cowley district and one of Kootenai's many friends, to write
to William Pearce, Superintendent of Mines in the Federal
Department of the Interior, who was stationed in Calgary.
Spurred on by Brown, Godsal came immediately to the point:

> I believe that some years ago in an official report you recommended that
> the Crows Nest Pass Kootenay or Waterton Lakes, etc., should be reserved as
> National Parks. I wish now in the strongest manner to urge upon the
> Government the adoption of this suggestion without delay.
>
> The Crows Nest Pass and Waterton Lakes have been for years a common
> resort for the surrounding neighbourhood for camping and holiday making and
> there being but few such places in the country, I think they should be reserved
> forever for the use of the public otherwise a comparatively small number of
> settlers can control and spoil these public resorts. Every day that it is delayed
> increases the probability of friction between the Government and settlers that
> may build in these spots. The C.P.R. is now also building their line through the
> Crow's Nest Pass.... I now only wish most earnestly to ask that this may be
> done and I am sure I have the feeling of the country with me.[17]

Written by a man described by one observer as a dreamer,
the letter epitomized the feelings of Godsal, Brown and the
majority of local residents, and put the problem into stark perspective.[18] As it turned out, Godsal's action was decisive "for by
crystalizing into action the wishes of Kootenai Brown [that the]
Waterton Lakes district should be erected into a national park for
the preservation of its natural beauty and its wild life for all time,
resulted in the development of Alberta's third mountain park."[19]

Pearce, upon receiving Godsal's letter, immediately took
action, forwarding it to Ottawa with an unqualified endorsation
reinforced by the observation that "the lands are of no value for
cultivation and of very slight value for grazing."[20] In Ottawa the
two communications resulted in mixed reactions at the administrative and political levels of government. Civil Service caution
in its most reserved form is apparent in a letter written later that
autumn by A. M. Burgess, Deputy Minister of the Department of
the Interior to his Minister, the Hon. T. M. Daly:

There is really some danger that this reservation of parks may be made ineffectual on account of the number of reservations. I am afraid that if they go on increasing the public will begin to think they are not very sacred.[21]

Fortunately Daly, the Minister, took a more enlightened view of the matter, and although the mechanics of enactment proceeded at the magisterial pace more common in Victorian days, his recommendation eventually completed the formalities required to establish a new park:

Upon the strength of Mr. Pearce's approval of Mr. Goodall's [sic i.e. Godsal] suggestion you [Burgess, the Deputy Minister, Department of the Interior] have my authority for making the proposed reservation for park purposes. Posterity will bless us. In memo. to Privy Council incorporate what Pearce says as to land values.[22]

As a result, on May 30, 1895, under provisions of clause 78 of the "Dominion Lands Act," a township and a half was "set apart for a Forest Park."[23] Only the uppermost portion of the Lakes had been surveyed, although the area designated in the Order in Council extended from a point slightly north of the Lower Waterton Lake to the international boundary. Throughout this slow-paced drama, Godsal, Brown, and other southern Alberta residents who were vitally concerned that such an enactment should come into being, were unaware of the legal legislative developments taking place in Ottawa. Theirs was a more basic life, closer to nature and the perennial problems of wrestling a living from that stern yet beautiful land which they all loved. For Brown, however, P.C. 1621, unknown to him at the time, was of great personal significance.

The establishment of a Forest Reserve in the southwestern corner of Alberta confirmed the rapid economic developments that were underway in the region. Brown's own experiences at this time typified the changes taking place and their impact upon his particular way of life. A brief item in the Fort Macleod *Gazette* gives us a glimpse of Kootenai and the kind of activity that was becoming increasingly commonplace:

Kootenai Brown spent a few days in town this week. Mr. Brown has just returned from an extended hunting trip in the mountains, lasting over two months, during which time he, in company with two companions, travelled over a very considerable extent of country in pursuit of the ferocious grizzly, and the agile bighorns whose monster horns are so coveted by the hunter. The trip however, so far as the big game was concerned, was a most dismal failure, no large game such as the party were in search of being sighted. While in the mountains the party visited a large mining camp composed chiefly of

Americans who were busily engaged in mining copper ore which is said to be very rich, and contains a small percentage of silver, and Mr. Brown laughingly suggested that it was the terrific dynamite explosions which are being sent off every little while, and which can be heard with startling distinctiveness for many miles in the mountains, which are primarily the cause of the scarcity of big game in the mountains this fall.... We had intended to interview Mr. Brown at some length regarding his trip, but that gentleman, without any knowledge or consent, packed up on Tuesday morning [October 8, 1895,] and returned to his home in the mountains, our readers thus losing a very interesting account which would undoubtedly have been forthcoming.[24]

The man's mischievous comments and his quiet departure for home were typical of Brown, a combination of humour and independence which were part of his own inimitable character.

While Brown's trip north and his subsequent excursions into the mountains revealed the nature and trend of developments throughout Alberta, they also confirmed his preference for the combination of mountain and plain over parkland. Creation of a Forest Reserve did not yet impinge directly upon his life, and Kootenai' s attention, like that of most residents in southern Alberta, was focussed upon more immediate and spectacular developments.

The real excitement centred upon the Canadian Pacific Railway Company's decision to construct a branch line over the Crow's Nest Pass in order to link the Kootenay country of British Columbia with the rest of Canada. By mid-July 1897, contracts were let for the laying down of 50 miles of track west of Fort Macleod, and the town began to fill up with "rough strangers of the labouring class."[25] Until that time the greatest economic progress had been made in the field of ranching, although the coming of the Mormons had revealed convincingly that grain and root crops could be grown successfully with and without irrigation. After the short-lived oil boom in the "Kootenay petroleum fields," speculative ventures shifted westwards into British Columbia, with the prospect of lead, silver, gold and coal discoveries stimulating the growing population in the adjoining district of southern Alberta.

By the middle of 1897, at least one mining broker, R. G. Mathews, was established in Fort Macleod, and the *Gazette* ran regular comments on the development of Slocan Bay, Ibex Mines, the Black Diamond Company, and a variety of other mining ventures. News of the Canadian Pacific Railway's coming simply added to an atmosphere of buoyancy and expectation in the Fort Macleod-Pincher Creek area. Although the older residents and the editor of *Gazette* surveyed the influx of "rough strangers" with some apprehension, the railway construction brought profit to local merchants and hostelries. Hotel accommodation was soon taxed to the utmost as large numbers of men, almost 200 on one occasion early in September 1897, continued to arrive, and inconvenience went hand in hand with profit as the project, hailed by the *Gazette* "as one of the most important public works in the history of the Dominion" proceeded.[26]

Although Brown was far from the actual centre of operations and development, he soon became aware of the CPR's decision to thrust a line through the Crow's Nest Pass and, like many other residents in the area, soon became caught up in the project.

Construction of the railway indeed provided him with an opportunity to earn hard cash and, simultaneously, to evaluate for himself how the coming of the railroad would affect southern Alberta. His knowledge of the Crow's Nest Pass through employment with the Mounted Police and through his own wide-ranging hunting expeditions, coupled with his known abilities as a packer, were the very requirements for preliminary freighting of goods and equipment before serious construction could begin. By the early autumn Brown, instead of going on his customary hunting trip, was fully occupied in a rather different capacity. The Fort Macleod *Gazette* pinpoints the time and place, and reveals a brief glimpse of the man in a setting familiar in physical terms:

Mr. J. G. Brown, otherwise known as Kootenai Brown, has charge of a pack train on the Crow's Nest road near Wardner, B.C.[27]

The freighting operations were particularly important that autumn and winter, since the entire construction program during the spring break-up period depended upon the basic stocks of food and building material supplies laid down when weather was suitable for freighting operations. This phase of the operation was precisely summed up by Kootenai's friend, C. E. D. Wood, the editor of the Fort Macleod *Gazette*, who enthusiastically visited the construction sites and wrote glowing accounts of the line's progress. Here is one of his reports which appeared in the *Gazette* on January 14, 1898:

There are only about two months in which to freight most of the summer's supplies, as when the spring break up occurs it will be almost impossible to do any freighting for weeks. There are now about 200 teams on the road and about as many more are required. To get in supplies is one of the most important adjuncts to the work of construction and to facilitate operations the distance is divided into two parts, with Wardner as the central point. The freighting of the eastern division is conducted by Strevel and Buchanan and that on the western by Porter Bros. Company [ie. the CPR] is building large warehouses about 40 miles apart, which will be filled with provisions for men and beast. The supplies for the east are distributed from Macleod and those from the west are brought in from Nelson by water to Goat River landing.

It was, by any standard, a large scale operation with approximately 2,000 men employed over a stretch of about 100 miles from the end of track to a point several miles west of Wardner, B.C. That point throughout the autumn and winter continued to be a lively hub of activity as contractors, teamsters, labourers, ebbed to and fro during the course of construction and all the other preparations that building a railroad line entail. CPR records, contrary to the generally accepted story that Kootenai, during this period, was employed by Canadian Pacific, show conclusively that he was never on that company's payroll.[28] It seems clear that he was probably employed by one of the two major firms handling the freighting business along the road, with Strevel and Buchanan, who were responsible for haulage and handling of goods in the eastern division, the most likely employer.

The record of his modest contribution to the extension of a communications system which has been a hallmark of Canadian history has disappeared. But we see him in a setting of mountains checking the pack animals, tightening the straps and ropes that lashed down assorted supplies, riding along the trail to ensure that the way was clear and all of the pack train was intact, supervising unloading at warehouse depots, cursing the weather or slight mishaps, exchanging information and pleasantries with everyone he met.

Although Brown's employment ended long before the sound of blasting and construction faded away and the CPR's operating department took over the line, the period is reminiscent of Kootenai's earlier days in the Dakota and Montana Territories. Turbulent construction camps, with their inevitable quota of quarrels, fights, even murders, and bouts of hard drinking, were a variation on those earlier days when a man often

Rancher F.W. Godsal, top left, and Canon F.H. Middleton, in center at top right, joined Kootenai Brown's fight to have the Waterton region protected as a National Park.

The photo below by the Royal Engineers in 1874 is probably the first ever taken of Waterton.

risked his life for an eight-ounce bottle of Montana Redeye, or of palmy days when Jamaica ginger and essence of lemon ruled supreme.[29]

But construction soon ended and those days of animal pack trains, like the long bull trains which for so long characterized the economic lifeline of southern Alberta, passed into time. Brown returned to his cabin and to the patient Isabella, while the pace of development established by steel tracks snaking over the prairies and through the mountains increased and changes followed rapidly.

Street lighting, stock prices and education increasingly concerned the residents of Fort Macleod, and the *Gazette,* true to its role, faithfully mirrored the new interests, losing in the process some of the intimacy that characterized its pages during the early days. Inevitably, in the course of such changes, Brown's old friends at Fort Macleod were affected. Kanouse, his old trading partner, moved to Fernie, B.C., Archie Rouleau started a livery stable, and many of the men Brown knew while serving with the Rocky Mountain Rangers – Dr. George de Veber, the surgeon for the force, and John Herron of the Pincher Creek district – were busy free-wheeling in territorial politics. Only Brown seemed content to remain at Waterton Lakes, watching the reflection of the mountain's red and green argillites in the waters, and following a daily round that brought him into continuous contact with nature.

Chapter 13
Canada's Unique Civil Servant

The period following Brown's return from packing along the CPR's Crow's Nest Pass line is opaque, with only occasional shafts of stray information that illuminate his life or provide a clue to his thoughts and actions. It is a period highlighted by the accidental death while hunting of Kootenai's close friend and trail companion, "the ex-policeman of very quiet disposition," Jack Street.[1]

Soon afterwards Brown joined the Theosophical Society of America. Whether the action was predicated on a genuine and personal philosophical basis that attempted to explain the nature of God and the universe and man's relations to them, or whether it stemmed from the bitterness of Street's unexpected loss, one can only speculate. On the other hand, Brown's life, marked by its close dependence upon nature's cycles of plant and animal life, made it conceivable that Kootenai would be attracted to an esoteric philosophy that was the very antithesis of the materialism which characterized the advance of civilization across the North American west.

Certainly the Theosophical Society, founded by Helena Petrovna Blavatsky and Colonel Olcott, was organized to help stem materialism and agnosticism which were, in the latter part of the nineteenth century, viewed as threats to the thought of the age. Again, in the Theosophist's view, Christianity and the other great religions of the world had long ago decayed into formalism, becoming in the process detached from their esoteric cores, or centres. In addition, the Theosophical Society was formed to stimulate transcendental research. For the minority of those who applied themselves, and who passed certain tests, Theosophy held out the prospect of an initiation into the central mystery of life itself. Thus, the Society's appeal was widespread indeed.

Brought up in the comfortable orthodoxy of the Established Church in Ireland, married in a frontier Catholic mission staffed by French-Canadian priests, experienced in the free and easy ways of the Cariboo diggings, aware through observation and acquaintance of the disciplined polygamous society of the near-by Mormon community, Brown could draw upon a wide variety of direct and indirect theological experience.

In addition, his contact with the religions of the East, no matter how brief or superficial, during service in India with the Eighth Regiment, made him aware of, and possibly more receptive to, a religious outlook unfettered by the formalism of conventional churches. Certainly by the last decade of the century, Madam Blavatsky's travels and her views were well publicized through lectures and writings – for example, *The Secret Doctrine*, subtitled "A Synthesis of Science, Religion, and Philosophy," – and through a growing number of followers. In Brown's particular case, the arrival of new neighbors in the vicinity of Yarrow Creek precipitated his application to join the Theosophical Society.

Three newcomers, P. M. Pedersen, Edward Pill and A. E. Endersby, endorsed Kootenai's letter to the Society's headquarters at Pasadena, California. His letter, dated June 30, 1898, resulted in his acceptance as a Full Fellow, member at large, and he remained a staunch supporter until his death eighteen years later.[2] Membership did not materially alter his ways. He still continued to enjoy gay company, particularly that of his Métis friends, the Gladstones, the Smiths, "Frenchy" Rivière, and the 20-gallon parties that often took place when they congregated. Marie Rose Smith and others, however, note in their own ways Brown's increasing concern about the after life, and tell of his teasing Isabella with stories that he would return to earth after death in a new form, perhaps as an eagle or some other great bird.[3] The Cree woman, in turn, believed the tales with a deep seriousness that at times bordered on the pathetic. Whatever the state of his conscience and inner beliefs, Brown never permitted them to interfere with friendship, and his circle of friends and acquaintances expanded steadily, mirroring the growth of the community in southern Alberta.

Soon after Brown finished working along the Canadian Pacific Crow's Nest route, interest shifted from the actual matter of railway construction to a renewed search for minerals and oil. Interest in the latter revived, and with its revival Kootenai was again thrust into a direct role in the search for black gold.

The index to the intensity and seriousness of the search is apparent in the increasing number of expeditions for which he was hired as a guide and packer.

For example, in August 1900 he was employed to guide Archie McVittie, a surveyor who was laying out oil claims in the Sage and Kishaneena Creek area west of the Kootenay Forest Reserve for a group of Cranbrook investors.[4] The claims ultimately became involved in litigation, with Brown as one of the central figures. The shadow of coming events, however, had not yet appeared The twentieth century, so optimistically hailed by Sir Wilfrid Laurier and other Canadians, found Kootenai, a vigorous man of 60, extraordinarily active in the physical sense and very much involved in the changes taking place in that southwestern region of plains and mountains.

In spite of the prevailing optimism and additional calls upon his services, there remained still the problem of earning enough money to offset the twin problems of rising prices and advancing age. With the depletion of wildlife, fishing and hunting did not always provide a full larder, and the loads of fish formerly brought to Fort Macleod or to neighboring ranches and always sold or exchanged for other commodities, became less frequent as the yield from the lakes steadily declined. Even the shorter hauls to Pincher Creek or Cardston did not favour Brown for he was caught in the scissors of inflation and lower productivity. The need to find a supplementary source of income thus became increasingly important. In this respect, Brown's wide circle of friends such as John Herron, Dr. de Veber, and others, and his persistence in the interests of the Kootenay Forest Reserve, redounded to his ultimate advantage.

Shortly before his sixty-first birthday he was appointed Fishery Officer in the Federal Department of Marine and Fisheries at the modest annual stipend of $50.00.[5] Brown's appointment was recommended by Frank Oliver, the Member of Parliament for Strathcona, and it came into effect on January 1, 1901. The duties, like the salary, were nominal and consisted of patrolling the lakes during the fishing season and reporting water and weather conditions to the Chief Inspector at Qu'Appelle. Brown retained the post until he was released from the Fisheries branch on March 31, 1912.[6] In the interval, his wages rose to the sum of $2.00 per day in the 1906-1907 fiscal year, and continued at that rate for the periods when patrols were carried out until Brown's severance of service.[7] Basically, the appointment was made to ensure the presence of an official representative in the vicinity of the Lakes in order to deter illegal fishing.

Brown's appointment was thus a conservation measure, the first such action taken in connection with the Kootenay Forest Reserve since its creation in 1895. In the event, the appointment was a timely one, for it barely preceded a new surge of exploratory development within the Reserve, one that put a new impetus upon the perennial see-saw between the conservationists and the free enterprise developers who were more intent upon profit than preservation.

Changes in the mountain valley followed hard on the heels of his appointment. In 1902, John Lineham of Okotoks, who at one time represented Calgary in the Northwest Territories Legislative Assembly, organized a company called the Rocky Mountain Development Company, and soon serious prospecting began along the small stream known locally as Oil Creek. In November, the Lineham Company began to drill in the valley above the main Waterton Lake at a site only five or six miles from Brown's cabin.[8]

The wooden drill rig and the heavy machinery, hauled so laboriously over rough roads and narrow mountain trails by Lineham and his men, immediately became the centre of a community complex that included log bunk houses and a rough dining hall. The site was optimistically christened Oil City, and Brown quickly became a frequent visitor. Drilling progress, however, was slow, with delays resulting from inexperience, faulty equipment and accidents. Eventually on September 21, 1903, oil was encountered at a depth of 1,020 feet.[9] As a result, further capital investment followed in the form of a pump, three tanks with a total capacity of more than 2,000 gallons, and a small refinery.[10]

During this initial period of development, we see something of the operation through Brown's eyes; random observations as recorded in his diaries. Covering the years 1900-1912, the diaries, while lacking the introspection and prescient observations of a Pepys or a Boswell, bring something of Brown's personality and the background of change into sharper, brighter focus. On October 24, 1904, Kootenai notes that he and Isabella "rode to Lineham's and saw lots of oil."[11]

Almost two years later he records the purchase, on credit, of 13 gallons of crude from the drill site.[12] With the site so close to Brown's homestead, it is not amiss to say that curiosity, necessity and, at times, duties as a fisheries officer took Kootenai often to the small huddle of buildings in the valley above the main Waterton Lake. On occasion, as the diary notes indicate, Brown's impassive Indian woman accompanied him, watching the activities of the men and the wonders of the drilling rig, the refinery, with keen interest if not complete understanding. What she may have thought about the enterprise and all that it represented, Brown does not record. Nor did he confide his own feelings about Oil City.

Outside of the Forest Reserve the search for oil was monitored with avid interest. Developments there were not only followed, but were reported in the press with a standard of accuracy that verged at times on the incredible. The August 10, 1905, issue of the *Canadian Gazette*, published in England, is typical:

> In the extreme south-western section of Alberta, five miles from the American boundary line, a thriving town has sprung up recently, populated almost entirely by oil prospectors and those interested in the development of recent discoveries.... The Great Northern [Railway] is building a spur from the south to the new camp of Oil City, and the Canadian Northern is extending a branch south to the same point.

Neither of the railway projects was seriously considered, let alone started. During its brief heyday, however, Oil City became the focal point at the Forest Reserve. Brown himself listed it on his business card, in which he described himself as a "licensed guide, game guardian, and overseer of fisheries...prepared to conduct tourists, hunters or prospectors in any part of the Rocky Mountains in this district." Further particulars, the card noted, were available at the Arlington Hotel, Pincher Creek. For references, Brown listed the Union Bank, the Bank of Commerce, and the Hudson's Bay Company.

By the end of 1904, Lineham's efforts, three holes in all, failed to strike an oil-bearing strata and the hunt was taken up by a new group, the Western Oil and Coal Company.[13] W. I. Margach, Chief Forest Ranger, who visited the site in the spring of 1906, has left a precise description of the site, and a very cat-

Transformation of the prairie took little more than a generation. The unrestricted freedom of Métis traders, opposite in 1874, vanished when tens of thousands of settlers such as those at center on their way to Alberta changed buffalo grass to grain fields which stretched over the horizon.

egorical expression of his philosophy about commercial developments within the Forest Reserves and National Parks:

...I visited the oil fields of Alberta a few days ago and found the Western Oil and Coal Company of whom Mr. J. B. Ferguson is the Manager.... Owing to the development of the oil wells I think the area of the park quite large enough, as, in my opinion, play grounds come second with development of the mineral wealth and industries of the country....

The operations of this Company are the only operations within the boundaries of the Park. I may say the Company have a modern oil boring plant...and have a hole down to a depth of 1711 feet. Oil has not yet been found in a quantity large enough to make this a shipping proposition. In October 1905 a flow of one barrel per day was struck but as the wall of the well caved in and had to be cased off, nothing but pockets have since been found.... 10 men and a cook are employed; the buildings are a cook camp...sleeping camp...office.... The machine was started about the 1st December, 1904 using as fuel one cord wood per day and has run in that time about 370 days.... There are two wells [in another site] one of which the casing has been taken out...the other well is down to a depth of 1496 feet.

There is said to be a flow of oil in this well but a large flow of water making a pressure that the oil will not raise.[14]

As Margach intimated, the new company failed to find oil in commercial quantities. Consequently, operations gradually came to a halt and, by 1908, Department of Interior Forestry officials in Ottawa were able to record that "nothing has been done this year."[15]

Before the boom ended, Brown, a frequent visitor to the drilling sites, became well acquainted with Ferguson, the company manager. Taking advantage of the inflated values in the local area resulting from the Western Oil and Coal Company operations, Brown sold Ferguson the quarter section of land which he acquired in 1891. The actual date of sale is not recorded in Department of Interior files but Kootenai, writing to Howard Douglas, the Commissioner of Dominion Parks, in the autumn of 1911 describes the transaction in precise terms:

Well, he paid me $2000.00 for it. Of course there was an oil boom then. I do not think it is worth much more now, although land has much increased in value since. It is a fine hay meadow and should you in the future have buffalo or other animals in the Park, would be very valuable. There were 157 acres when I sold, since about four acres have been carried away by the Pass Creek [i.e. Blakiston Brook] and the cabin is also gone. What few house timbers are left are no good. There never was a fence of any kind and no improvements.[16]

According to an undated report written in 1909, Ferguson "contemplated making a summer resort or townsite" out of the property.[17] At the time of Brown's writing to Douglas, the federal authorities were considering the possibility of purchasing the land back from Ferguson. Knowing Ottawa's intentions, and knowing the man to whom he sold the quarter section, Brown pointed out to Douglas that the deal would not be carried through easily:

> This man Ferguson is very shrewd. You will find it necessary to be careful in your dealings with him.[18]

But that was in the future, well after the speculation, the excitement and the sounds of drilling rigs in action had died away from the mountains.

At the beginning of the oil boom, well before Ferguson and the Western Oil and Coal Company began operations within the Kootenay Forest Reserve, Brown and other local residents became seriously concerned about the impact of such enterprises upon the area. Discussion went hand in hand with observation as the venture of John Lineham and his associates gave way to that of the Western Oil and Coal Company. Once again it was F. W. Godsal who drew Ottawa's attention to the impact of such developments upon the area, and whose words to the Secretary of the Department of the Interior began the long drawn out process of review which ultimately brought about the transformation of the Kootenay Forest Reserve into Waterton Lakes National Park:

> I am aware that a certain area near the Waterton Lakes in the extreme southwest corner of Alberta was reserved some years ago as a reserve or National Park and I am pleased that my advocacy at the time helped to bring it about. But I have lately visited the vicinity again, and I inform you that the beauty and grandeur of the scenery is unsurpassed, I do not think equalled by anything at Banff. Further, a very large number of people from Pincher Creek, Macleod, Cardston and other towns resort there every year for camping, it being the only place now left for the purpose. It is therefore very essential that the interests of the public should be properly safeguarded at this "beauty spot." Firstly I doubt if the reserve is large enough for its purpose and as the land around is very stony and quite unfit for agriculture or settlement, it can be enlarged without hurting anyone.[19]

In Ottawa, Godsal's letter struck a responsive chord within the Department of the Interior. As a first step in the process of reevaluating the status of the Forest Reserve, the Chief Forest Ranger, W. I. Margach, as already noted, visited "the oil fields of Alberta" in the spring of 1906. Although his inspection moved him to say that "playgrounds come second with development of mineral wealth and industries of the country," that point of view was not shared by the majority of the department's officials. With the obvious failure to find oil in commercial quantities, with the additional pressure to transform and to enlarge the Forest Reserve emanating from such diverse sources as John Herron, by then Conservative-Liberal Member of Parliament for the federal constituency of Alberta, and Geological Survey reports, the climate of opinion quickly and clearly developed in favour of the conservationists.[20]

Brown certainly was instrumental in the creation of a political lobby on behalf of the Kootenay Lakes Reserve. He had known Herron for years, and apart from expressing himself verbally to his friend on the subject of game protection, Kootenai on at least one occasion in June 1905 wrote to his Member of Parliament about the future of the Reserve.[21] As a result of such diverse pressures and opinions, R. H. Campbell, Superintendent of the Forestry Branch, in May 1907 at last directed Margach to report on the number of persons located in the Kootenay Lakes Forest Reserve, and the nature and extent of their properties because "it was the intention to make provision for the proper administration of the reserve."[22] There the matter rested until after the federal elections of 1908. Fortunately for the future of the Forest Reserve and for Brown, Herron was re-elected in the newly-created constituency of Macleod, ensuring that the continuity of contacts and interest established during his first term in the House of Commons continued.[23]

During these years, Brown's fortunes, stabilized through the sale of his land to J. B. Ferguson, continued to flourish. Money received from the sale of the quarter section, however, did little to modify his daily routine. Kootenai's time continued to be taken up with fishing, hunting, looking after horses which he bred or broke, generally with the intention of selling them to the Mounted Police. Isabella was an integral part of these operations, and Brown's diary is spotted with brief, almost laconic items of how the two spent their days. "Rode with woman; brought in 63 horses. She shot an R.G. [Ruffed Grouse]" is a typical entry.[24] A good horse properly broken in fetched a fair price, as Brown's records show. "Sold Stockings to the Police for $125.00.'[25] It was an outdoor life of constant and, at times,

Although oil was discovered in Waterton, fortunately for the future park it was not in commercial quantities. The photo above shows the original pole cable drilling rig in 1902 and, below, the first buildings on the site which became known as Oil City.

strenuous activity, one that would have taxed the energies of a much younger person, let alone a man in his mid-sixties.

Apart from the personal side of Brown's daily affairs, there were his seasonal duties as a Fisheries Officer which required him to issue licences, record water and weather conditions and to report catches. After the division of the Northwest Territory into the provinces of Alberta and Saskatchewan, when the federal Department of Marine and Fisheries placed its field officers on a daily rate of pay, Brown's duties required him to carry out longer patrols, to fill out time sheets, and to forward daily reports during the season.

In 1908 Brown added to these duties and to his income by obtaining an additional appointment with the provincial government of Alberta. The post of Game Guardian simply required Kootenai to sell game licences and to send returns to the Chief Game Guardian, Benjamin Lawton, in Edmonton.[26] For his troubles, Brown received a small commission for each licence sold. Modest in every sense, the appointment as Game Guardian nevertheless was significant for it added to Brown's reputation as a man knowledgeable in the ways of the region's wildlife, and provided him with a formal qualification that looked impressive on paper. Both stood him in good stead when the future of the Kootenay Forest Reserve began to be considered seriously.

While the changes in the Reserve's status were being examined in Ottawa, Brown's normal routine was temporarily disrupted when, in September 1907, he was summoned to appear as a witness in a series of oil claims being heard at a session of the British Columbia Supreme Court in Cranbrook. Kootenai's implication in the case stemmed from the summer of 1900 when he had been hired to guide the surveyor, McVittie, on a claims-staking expedition to the Flathead region of the East Kootenay country.

While Brown's role in the original enterprise was, at best, nominal, his testimony became one of the main points in the case. Indeed, his answers on the witness stand injected a touch of drama into what was otherwise a very technical hearing. Extraordinarily enough, although Brown had worked for McVittie, he supported the rival claimant, John Watt. The presiding judge, however, refused to accept Kootenai's story over the expert evidence given by the other witnesses, both professional surveyors. In his verdict, Judge P. E. Wilson made his point with brutal frankness:

> On this point much has been said as to the evidence of the witness Brown, in contradiction to that of McVittie... I am convinced that McVittie's evidence in this point [the matter of accurate stakings] is correct, and the kindest thing that I can say is that he is mistaken or has forgotten.[27]

Why Brown supported Watt is a mystery. He may well have suffered a lapse of memory, for he was 68. Equally, he may have stuck stubbornly to what he considered to be the rights of the case. There is, of course, always the possibility of a falling out between himself and McVittie, the sort of personal difference that can be magnified by isolation until it reaches an emotional boiling point. Whatever the basis for Brown's stand in the witness box at Cranbrook, it is lost, for Kootenai's diary is silent, and he apparently did not discuss the case with any of his immediate friends. Instead, we glimpse him through the words of the diary at Cranbrook – "Trial at Cranbrook John Watts [sic]" – returning to the small cabin by the lake where he found the "woman's brother."[28] His personal record then returns to the usual matters which he recorded: weather, horses, visitors, mail received from the Fisheries department and books or papers that arrived in the post.

The early years of the twentieth century, punctuated as they were with the excitement over the oil prospecting within the Kootenay Forest Reserve, reveal more of Brown as a person than is intimated in the records of his early life. His diaries, brief to the point of disappointment, show him to be an essentially warm-hearted man, at times convivial even to irresponsibility, surprisingly well read, a thoughtful and considerate neighbour.

Known throughout the district as a good host, the diary entries reveal Kootenai at his hard drinking best. "Had a party...up to 4;"[29] or, "Frenchy here. Whisky all gone. Glad of it."[30] Apart from such revealing items about occasions when close friends dropped in, Brown carefully recorded details of individuals who passed by. Usually, the accounts note the comings and goings of neighbours, Mounted Police patrols and, sometimes, visitors to the Forest Reserve.

When weather forced him indoors, or when opportunity arose, he read widely, and the diaries record a surprising number of newspapers, magazines and books which found their way into the small cabin in the remote fastness of southwestern Alberta. He subscribed, for example, to *The Strand, Tid Bits, Western Home Monthly*, the *Winnipeg Tribune, San Francisco Weekly*, as well as the local papers from Pincher Creek, Fort Macleod and Lethbridge. In addition, he wrote away frequently to the Theosophical Society for that body's pamphlets and for books such as Helena Blavatsky's *Cosmic Consciousness*, as well as to other less specialized publishers for miscellaneous works that caught his fancy.

One visitor to Brown's two-roomed cabin described it as "quite stuffy and crowded with books, trophies etc."[31] The size of his library and his choice of selections often surprised his guests. W. McD. Tait recalls seeing works by Henry George, Tennyson, Carlyle, Poe, W. T. Hornady, Oliver Goldsmith, Swedenborg, Shakespeare, and E. S. Thompson.[32] Brown was generous with his books, lending them without hesitation to his friends or to visitors whom he liked. On April 14, 1907, for example, he records sending "Vicar of Wakefield to Mrs. H. [Hanson]," the Postmaster's wife at Waterton Mills. The books and periodicals were indispensable companions during the long winter nights and periods of harsh weather.

They connected Brown with the sophisticated world which he had deliberately renounced and provided a direct link with the new ideas and rapid developments occurring in a world accelerating into the twentieth century. Sometimes he discussed the new marvels with Isabella and she would accept them because they were conveyed to her by Kootenai. For the rest she remained a simple Cree woman completely devoted to Brown, more of a comfort through her presence than an intellectual companion. "At home all day reading" occurs frequently through the diary, an entry that is neither unexpected nor unusual.[34]

Although Brown read widely, he was surprisingly disinterested in politics. Political matters, in fact, are one of the significant omissions in his diary. The creation of Alberta as a province, the elections of 1904, 1908 and 1911, when his old friend John Herron was successively elected and defeated, are not mentioned. Witnesses such as Tait, Arthur Harwood and others are unanimous in their observations that topics of current interest which excited the country were rarely discussed by

Kootenai. Brown's intellectual interests during the last decade of his life tended towards philosophy. His diary is sprinkled with maxims and jottings that reflect his turn of mind, and particularly his interest in Theosophy:

> The music of the fountains of knowledge is only heard by the ear trained to catch its melody.[35]

Annie Besant is frequently quoted, and occasionally a classical writer such as Ovid, perhaps reflecting the Latin classes of his schooldays in Ireland long ago. In the day to day sense of practical affairs, Brown's abiding interest was the Kootenay Forest Reserve and that region of the Rockies' eastern slope of which it was the centre. That interest came to the fore after the federal election of 1908 and the return of John Herron to the House of Commons.

By that time, the intention of the Department of the Interior "to make provision for the proper administration of the reserve" was fully confirmed and, with the elections over, could be transformed into practical policy.[36] At the local level, John Herron and Brown became prime movers in the process of transforming the Forest Reserve into a National Park. The initiative in the process was first taken by Herron who, because of his close knowledge of the Forest Reserve through his service with the N.W.M.P., his early interest in oil and his work as a stock inspector, not only knew the area intimately, but equally, as the local Member of Parliament, made it his business to be aware of the local residents' concern about the Reserve's future.

Early in the spring of 1909, Herron approached Brown to determine his views and his suitability for the projected post of park overseer. Brown, in turn, although his views about conservation and the future of the Forest Reserve were well known throughout the district, wrote to Herron summarizing his thoughts on the need for adequate supervision within the Reserve:

> A park overseer is required. There have been over 500 people, picnic and tourist, here this season; a great number are here now [August 16, 1909]. Many of them wantonly or thoughtlessly destroy shade trees and leave camp fires burning which are a menace to all of us, the mountains and all things. If I can obtain this office I am willing to put up an office, close to the lake and look after things to the best of my ability.[37]

Herron's action upon receipt of Brown's letter was prompt. He knew the man, and in those early days when patronage in the

195

Federal Civil Service was an accepted norm unfettered by a minimum of boards and competitions, his support was decisive. He promptly forwarded Brown's letter, together with a strong personal recommendation, to the Chief Clerk in the Forestry Branch:

I have known Mr. Brown for the past twenty-five years. He is an experienced trapper and hunter, and thoroughly conversant with every mile of the district in which the Park extends, having resided in its limits (and now owning a homestead) for the past twenty-five years.

No more capable man could be appointed, and I can assure you that if the Park is to be purposely preserved, and wanton destruction of trees etc., prevention of forest fires etc. checked, it is absolutely necessary for a Guardian to be appointed.... If you can do anything for Mr. Brown, I feel sure that he will capably fulfill the duties of any position in which you may place him.[38]

Action on Herron's strong letter of support did not follow as speedily. It was not until late November that the Superintendent of Forestry in the Department of the Interior, R. H. Campbell, submitted a detailed memorandum on the proposed park to the Deputy Minister, W. W. Corry:

It has also been recommended that some person be placed in charge of this park, and the name of J. G. Brown, who lives in that district and who is already, as I understand, game guardian and fishery inspector, has been suggested for the position. I hardly think that any appointment is necessary until the spring, but at that time I consider that it is adviseable an appointment should be made.[39]

In the margin of the memorandum, neatly typed, was the significant word "Approved" and the signature of the Minister, Frank Oliver. Unknown to Brown, his future was thus determined. The significance of his impending appointment, however, was neither realized nor considered by those who were responsible.

At the end of March 1910, as suggested by the Superintendent of Forestry, Brown's appointment as Forest Ranger in the Kootenay Reserve was confirmed and he was duly notified to that effect. A letter from the Departmental Secretary, C. G. Heyes, outlined the terms of the appointment and indicated the nature of Kootenai's duties:

I am to advise you that you have been appointed a Forest Ranger in connection with the Kootenay Lakes Forest Reserve, at a salary of seventy-five dollars...per month, your appointment to date from 1st April 1910. You will work under the direction of Mr. Howard Douglas, Commissioner of the Dominion Parks, Banff, Alberta, and it will be your duty to protect the game and to prevent the occurrence of fires; also to see that no person locates on the Reserve without proper authority, and in general to see that the regulations (a copy of which are enclosed herewith) are duly enforced.[40]

The appointment, obviously, would require a good deal of effort and, more important, foreshadowed increasing responsibilities. Brown acknowledged the appointment on April 10 and by doing so entered into the ranks of Canada's Civil Service. Almost 71, with a world of experience and adventure behind him, Kootenai put aside the carefree existence to which he had so long been accustomed and assumed the mantle of responsibility unusual for both the man and the times. Already something of a living legend in southern Alberta he became, in effect, one of Canada's most unusual civil servants, a fiercely dedicated conservationist in a fringed buckskin jacket and wide-brimmed western hat.

Chapter 14

Kootenai's Living Memorial

Brown's appointment as Ranger in charge of the Kootenay Lakes Forest Reserve immediately thrust him into the mixed world of public relations and public administration. Coming as it did in the spring, Kootenai had little time to prepare himself for the inevitable influx of visitors and for the equally inevitable increase in the danger from fires started by careless campers. His work load increased immediately. Many of his duties were strenuous, requiring him to patrol the Reserve on fire duty, or to check for cattle and horses which strayed into the grounds.

As a result, he often covered between 200 and 300 miles a month on horseback. In addition, there were inevitable journeys to Pincher Creek by horse or democrat to pick up equipment or to obtain supplies, as well as the necessity of writing monthly reports, recording weather conditions and writing up requisitions for work within the Forest Reserve. Since he was the sole Ranger, the duties, particularly during the summer months, were demanding. For a man of 70, Brown's performance during that first year was highly creditable, a tribute to his flexibility and to his physical stamina.

During those first few months, Brown, who took to his responsibilities with zestful vigour, also discovered the frustration of government employment. After the first three months, he wrote with justifiable exasperation to the Secretary of the Department of the Interior to say that he "had not received any pay and [did] not know to whom [he] should apply" in order to correct the matter.[1] When his cheques eventually began to arrive in September, confusion still prevailed, as he was again forced to write to the Department, this time to the Accounting section. His communication is a model of courtly succinctness.

I beg to call your attention to the fact that the cheques made in my favour, my name is written J. C. Brown. Ought to be J. G. Brown.[2]

Apart from these minor trials, Kootenai's work during the first year proceeded surprisingly well. At the end of the summer he could report that about 2,000 people, almost one quarter of them from distant points, had entered the Reserve, a highly creditable figure considering the almost total lack of roads leading to the area and the fact that formal publicity about the place did not exist. Once the tourists were gone Brown's work did not stop.

In November 150 lots were surveyed and laid out and arrangements were made to accept leases from persons interested in taking them up. The same month, a good horse trail was cut along the western shore of the main Waterton Lake to the international boundary where it connected with an existing wagon road in Glacier Park, the adjoining United States National Park. The object of such improvements was twofold: to encourage more visitors to come to the Forest Reserve, and to provide more facilities for those who came. They constitute the high points of Brown's first year as Ranger, and are typical of the improvements he initiated during the years he was in charge of the Reserve.

Such additions, together with various other items, form the gist of Brown's first Annual Report which he submitted at the end of March 1911 to Howard Douglas, the Commissioner of National Parks. In his submission, Brown also made a number of recommendations. They included the suggestions that an assistant Ranger be added to the staff because of the perceptible increase in game, and that a bridge be built over the Waterton River.

Lack of a bridge, he pointed out, meant that access to the park was limited and that during the period of high water each spring, the Forest Reserve, to all intents and purposes, was isolated. In such conditions the ford normally used in crossing the Waterton River became dangerous, a point that Brown dramatized by noting that he and three companions almost lost their lives the previous spring while attempting to get from one side to the other.[3] Kootenai's most important suggestion, however, dealt with enlarging the Forest Reserve:

> It seems advisable to greatly enlarge this park.... It might be well to have a preserve and breeding ground in conjunction with the United States Glacier Park.[4]

At the time of writing, the Kootenay Lakes Forest Reserve covered a rectangle nine miles long and six miles wide, with a segment of the international boundary forming the southern base.

In Banff the suggestions were duly noted by Douglas, the Commissioner, who in turn passed them on to Ottawa. Indeed, Douglas himself had already endorsed Brown's recommendation for enlarging the Forest Reserve. In a covering summary written at the end of 1910, he had put his point firmly and directly:

> I feel very strongly that this park should be enlarged so as to include more of the big game country. And to provide in conjunction with the United States Glacier Park, a large protected area, in which Mountain Sheep and Goat may be allowed to thrive unmolested as it is very evident that this fine region will soon become generally known and frequented by sportsmen.... I was told by Mr. Brown the Forest Ranger that he could drive a team and wagon through the [South Kootenay] pass to the Flathead in Montana, so it can readily be seen how necessary it is to protect the game before it becomes too late.[5]

With such a specific endorsement, the possibilities of expansion must have appeared good to Brown and to his immediate superior in Banff. As it turned out, the government in Ottawa had other plans. Less than four months after submitting his first report recommending that the Kootenay Lakes Forest Reserve be enlarged, Brown's hopes were cruelly dashed when the area of the Reserve was drastically reduced by Order in Council to a mere 13.5 square miles.[6]

What considerations prompted the govermnent to reduce the Kootenay Lakes Forest Reserve's area while simultaneously changing its status and name, is open to question. The change in title, however, is less difficult to explain. Department of Interior officials simply reverted to the name given to the lakes by the first white man to record seeing that long narrow mountain valley, Lieutenant Thomas W. Blakiston of the Palliser Expedition.[7] Logically enough, Blakiston's choice reflected his keen interest in ornithology. Named after that eccentric English ornithologist, Charles Waterton, a man whose feeling for wildlife went beyond his foibles, it was an admirable selection, for Waterton's appreciation of nature paralleled Kootenai's.

To Brown the lakes in their mountain setting were a magnificent example of nature's bounty, and his notes and reports to Ottawa during the last four years of life reflect his love for them. He saw the mountains in terms of their towering strength, the natural habitat of the mountain sheep and goats that travelled their slopes. At the same time, he knew that the heights, while beautiful in their rugged splendour, were also treacherous and could be obscured by cloud or snow storms, dangerous to the point of death, as his friend Jack Stewart discovered. In the same sense, the lakes were surfaces that at one instant mirrored the soft rose and green bands of argillite shale reflected by the evening sun but which, in a brief moment, could be transformed into a turmoil of wind-swept waves "from the south down the gorge in which is the Upper Waterton Lakes."[8]

Blakiston, who described the valley as "a very windy spot," was nevertheless so taken by Waterton's picturesque setting that he remained at the Lakes for two days, sketching the valley and taking bearings on Chief Mountain and other prominent landmarks.[9] G. M. Dawson's comment that the scenery in the Waterton Lakes is not equalled in grandeur by that of any other part of the mountains, however, comes closest to expressing Kootenai's feelings about his chosen home. A report prepared within the Department of the Interior's Forest Branch at the time the status of the Kootenay Reserve was being reconsidered, and which is basic to the establishment of the area as a National Park, amplifies Dawson's comment:

> It is west of the Belly River that the Canadian Rockies possess their greatest attractions. From the Belly River Valley, rises above the pine clad foothills, the outlying range of the Canadian Rockies, the Wilson Range. From the Belly River to the Waterton Lakes, between which it forms the divide its width is seven miles. The culminating point of this range, Mount Cleveland, 10,535 in height, is in Montana, but its most significant peak is its Canadian summit, Sheep Mountain, which though only 7580 feet high, makes up what it lacks in altitude by its situation at the angle of the Waterton Lakes.[10]

Sheep Mountain indeed was Brown's favourite peak, one which he never ceased to admire and one which drew him repeatedly to its slopes during the autumn hunting season. Such excursions, however, became less frequent as age and park responsibilities eroded his energies.

The fact that the Reserve simultaneously had been renamed and converted into a National Park did little to compensate for the sense of profound disappointment which Brown shared with a great number of other southern Alberta residents. His feelings, and the general attitude of mind created by the government's actions, are summed up in his second Annual Report:

> In writing of the Park it is rather difficult to know just how much land and water there is within its boundaries. In the latter part of July 1911, we learned of the reduction of its area, all the lakes and several of the mountains

of great interest being cut out, a matter of much regret and a step extremely unpopular with the people of Southern Alberta.[11]

In making his point, Brown gave the contrasting example of what was being done in the adjoining American park where "thousands of dollars are being expended, miles of good roads built and even Swiss cottages put up in desirable places for the use of tourists."[12] It was a very Canadian comment, one of disappointment and envy, one that was very much shared by Howard Douglas, then Chief Superintendent of National Parks. Ottawa's reduction of the new park, renamed Waterton Lakes National Park, only served to make Brown press the case for enlargement more strongly than ever. His views and recommendations were shared and endorsed unhestitatingly by Douglas, who simply incorporated much of Brown's reports into his own submissions to Ottawa:

> I quite agree with the Report of the Superintendent of Waterton Lakes Park when he refers to the reduction of the area, as this cutting out of the lakes and also a portion of the land situated between this Park and the United States Glacier Park changes the original intention, which was to have this park adjoin the one on the other side of the border and make one huge game preserve. The cutting down of the area entirely cuts out the Waterton Lakes.... I strongly urge that, at least, a portion of the mountain section lying between the two parks be restored, as well as the lakes.... I would like to include in my report the last paragraph of Mr. Brown's report which I agree with in every particular: "In conclusion I might add that the enlargement of this park is greatly desired by the people of the district, and also by the sportsmen here and on the United States side."[13]

There the matter rested, while the pressure of protests, resentment and reconsideration rose steadily within the Department of the Interior until it at last impinged upon the Borden government itself. In that respect, Brown continued to remind his superiors in Ottawa of the need for extension. In his report for the year 1913, submitted as always in the spring of the following year, he again stressed that "there is a very strong feeling that this area is too small, and that it should be enlarged so as to make it adjoin the United States Glacier National Park."[14]

Despite Ottawa's short-sightedness and procrastination in dealing with what Kootenai and other local residents considered to be a vital basic issue, work in adjusting boundaries and consolidating administration within the much smaller Waterton Lakes National Park continued without stop. Brown, not unnaturally, became more and more involved. As acting Superintendent, he was vitally concerned with such important projects as construction of a bridge over Pass Creek [Blakiston Brook], or extensions and improvements to the trail system in the Park.

More and more of his time, too, was devoted to dealing with the increasing number of visitors to the Lakes, and to the rapid development of commercial enterprises within the Park boundaries. By the end of the tourist season in 1913, two hotels were operating within the Park, one of them owned by Brown's close friend, J. F. Hazard, the other by C. F. Jensen who also operated an automobile between Cardston and the Lakes for visitors. As the commercial possibilities of the region became evident, automobiles, which Brown disliked intensely, began to appear with increasing frequency. Despite his antipathy towards them – an antipathy that did not extend to "gasoline launches" – Kootenai realized that once roads were improved "we will have autos from Macleod (60 miles) and Pincher Creek (40 miles)."[15] That comment, confided to his diary in 1911, shrinks into commonplace two years later when he notes that "Messrs. [S. W.] Hill and [C. A.] Thompson Directors Great Northern Railway came here...from St. Paul Minn. in three days in an automobile.[16]

The day of the horseless buggy had indeed arrived and Brown, true to his flexibility of mind, accepted the change. The transition to a new age is nowhere more evident than in a photograph of Kootenai taken at this time by a person unknown. It shows Brown, dressed in a fringed buckskin jacket, wearing a wide-brimmed sombrero, his lean weather-beaten face stern and unbending, seated in what would now be considered a car of glorious vintage, his body erect as though he were riding a horse that required extreme care in handling.

While such evidence of social and scientific change became more apparent in the new National Park, forcing Brown to meet new people and new problems, the transition from a Forest Reserve to a National Park also created administrative difficulties. In order to consolidate the designated area and make it a purely national playground in which commercial enterprise and private property development could be controlled, it was

The flavor of Kootenai Brown's West, as well as that of the NWMP and pioneer settlers, is preserved at restored Fort Macleod and Fort Whoop-Up. As the official NWMP Museum, Fort Macleod, above, includes many exhibits and, in summer, a patrol in uniforms of the 1874 Mounties.

The bottom photo shows part of the inner square of the authentic reconstruction of Fort Whoop-Up. Like Fort Macleod, it is a popular attraction. The flag which whiskey peddlers flew over the Fort is now the City of Lethbridge's official flag.

necessary to ensure that all land within the Park belonged to the Crown.

As it turned out the only property which did not belong to the government was the quarter section sold by Kootenai at the height of the oil boom to J. B. Ferguson, the former manager of the Western Oil and Coal Company. With the creation of Waterton Lakes as a National Park, the need to acquire the property became urgent. On August 30, 1911, Howard Douglas, by then Commissioner of National Parks, wrote to Brown asking him what he considered the land to be worth.[17] Ferguson, who apparently had written to Brown asking if Kootenai were interested in re-purchasing the land, clearly was aware of the old Forest Reserve's change in status, and wished to profit from it. Brown, in a revealing letter, made these points implicitly in his reply to Douglas:

> I think if Mr. Ferguson got say $2250.00 cash it ought to be quite enough. He wrote me, as you will see by the enclosed letter. I also send an answer, which if you like and think it will do any service you can post; if not just destroy it. I do not think it would be acting fair by you for me to answer direct and I might spoil you a deal. A couple of years ago Ferguson offered to sell back to me for $2500. I think he would take $2000.00 cash. He will never be able to get more, if that.[18]

Douglas, in passing along Brown's comments to the Secretary of the Department of the Interior, underlined the importance of the block:

> ...I would suggest that, if this land can be purchased for that amount [$2000.00 as Brown suggested], it would be advisable to take over the same, as a quarter section of land in the centre of the Park Reserve rather spoils the effect of the whole thing. This quarter section is only a short distance from the lots we have surveyed and which are now being applied for.[19]

After a protracted three-handed correspondence involving Brown, Ferguson, and the Department of the Interior in Ottawa, the quarter section finally came into the hands of the Crown in the spring of 1912. Ferguson, as Brown intimated, proved to be a difficult man to deal with and Ottawa was forced to meet his price of $2500.00. The purchase was made at the last instant only because the Parks Branch had ample money in the current year's appropriation."[20] It was an awkward matter, one in which Brown, whose interests were so closely identified with the Park, was involved so ironically as an interested bystander. That the matter turned out in the best interests of the Park and all that

Kootenai treasured, was due more to good fortune than to good management.

Apart from the matter of the final acquisition of Brown's old homestead, the day to day details of administration more than occupied Kootenai's time and energies. Through his diary we see an indomitable old man at his job, devoted to duty, physically tough, meeting time and the severest elements in that hard country head on, asking no quarter. An entry dated February 1913 tells much about Brown and the Park:

> Mr. Reynolds, U.S. Ranger, Messrs. Hazzard and Carpenter here. 32 below zero. Rode and snowshoed west side of park to pass. Miles 20. Reynolds very sick. Up all night with him.[21]

Two days later Kootenai recorded deep snow and a temperature of 10 below zero.

> Rode and snowshoed to Cameron Falls and Creek. Miles 24, with Mr. Hazzard. Measured bridges on Pass C [Creek] and Cameron Falls.... Did not get home until midnight. Bad going.[22]

His work, as the entries indicate, was often tough, requiring stamina and dedication. As the Park developed and became more popular, his administrative duties took up more and more of his time. The long winter nights previously devoted to reading, at times gave way to the demands imposed by Monthly Reports, applications for leases, letters to his opposite number, the Superintendent of Glacier National Park, about destruction caused by herds of elk roaming across the international boundary.

As the surrounding countryside grew more populous, new problems intruded. The Rev. S. H. Middleton of St. Paul's (Anglican) mission nearby, requested permission to establish a summer camp for his Indian school children within the Park bounds, and this decision preoccupied Brown since there were no precedents to guide him. Construction of new bridges, buildings, and cutting new trails required labour which meant that Brown, once again, was required to hire, pay and discharge men for the summer season.

Such duties made him responsible for large sums of money, and in one entry jotted down in December 1913, he noted paying labourers $675.51, and that "the foreman and all of the men went out this morning."[23] Obtaining suitable men was always a problem. The Park was remote, wages outside were higher and

the men, even the drifters who came with little or no money, complained about the length of time it took them to get paid.[24]

Brown himself felt the pinch of rising prices and a fixed salary that failed to take into account the growing responsibilities of the job. He wrote therefore to Douglas, stating his case with customary directness:

> I need scarcely remind you of the greatly increased value of the necessaries of life, and the general need of wages of all employees. Today any labourer can get $2.50 per day and board.... There are many expenses incidental with my position. I am in the saddle every day. I use 3 saddle horses and I have a team of horses to bring in supplies, wood etc. hay etc. What with the shoeing and so on these are large items of expenditure. Under the circumstances as above stated I ask you to recommend the increase of my wages.[25]

Douglas, realizing the merit of Brown's case, promptly recommended a salary increase of ten dollars per month, and the approval by Ottawa became effective on September 1, 1911. The press of duties and rising costs, however, continued, and Brown again wrote to Douglas in the autumn of 1912 asking once more for a raise in pay. One of the reasons behind the request was that he had been released from the Fisheries Service at the end of March, and the loss of income, though small, provided a further spur to his request. It was a revealing letter showing something of the man's nature and the scope of his duties within the Park. Again the comparison with rates of pay and conditions of service in the adjoining United States Glacier Park were brought in as ancillary arguments:

> All the Forest Rangers here both on the U.S. side and in this district get $100.00 per month. They do not patrol more than I do, and have little or no correspondence to attend to. Nor have they the anxiety and responsibility of spending large sums of Government money. More, I have several hundred people to look after in the season. To preserve order, and keep improper persons out, prevent the sale of liquor, gambling etc. etc. And I may say with Truth: and perhaps pardonable pride, that I have done this effectively – I do not ask for or require, an assistant. I have done, and can do, all the work required myself.... I am in the saddle or driving nearly every day. Shoeing and feed cost a great deal.[26]

In his letter, Brown sensibly requested that provisions for a revision of salary be included in the 1913-1914 Departmental estimates, and he reminded the Commissioner of National Parks through the correct channel of the Chief Superintendent's office, of his request in April 1913. Although a memorandum recommending the increase was put forward by Howard Douglas in

May, no action was taken, and Brown's salary remained pegged at $85.00 per month until he died.[27]

While such matters formed a human background to Kootenai's activities, they never consciously interfered with his work or his enthusiasm for the development and preservation of the Park. He was particularly keen on publicizing Waterton Lakes, and constantly turned over ideas about possible ways in which good photographs or evocative advertisements could be used to promote the Park. Early in December 1912, for example, he wrote to Douglas suggesting one of the earliest schemes to publicize and promote Waterton:

> I beg to say that I know of no way the Interests of the Park can be brought forward before the Public than that of well done photos. There is a good Artist in that line in the vicinity, Mr. Riggal, whose photos of here you have seen.... The Annual Reports of 11 – 12 – 13 also might be sent for free distribution.... Photos might be sent to the Field, Rod and Gun...and other magazines of that class.[28]

Whether anything came of such proposals it is difficult to say. Coming so soon after the formation of Waterton Lakes when development in the concrete sense of capital investment for bridges, roads, trails and buildings dominated Ottawa's thinking, such schemes were put well down priority lists. The outbreak of World War I, in turn, effectively squelched any possibilities of launching an organized publicity campaign extolling the natural beauty of Waterton Lakes.

At the personal level, however, Brown became the Park's greatest diplomat. Through letters to organizations such as the Campfire Club of America, through personal contacts with visitors to the Park during which Kootenai made the most of his striking appearance, his soft-spoken tales of wildlife and adventure and his courtly old-fashioned manners, the natural grandeur of the Park was broadcast far and wide. Brown may have lacked the advantages and technical skills of a National Film Board or the Queen's Printer, but in his own way he played his part in projecting what to him was one of the most beautiful areas in the world. In the process, he never missed an opportunity to remind Ottawa that the decision to reduce the Park's area was a major mistake:

> I beg to say that I have been in communication with the Camp Fire Club of America for over 3 years in reference to the establishment of a Game preserve in conjunction with the U.S. Glacier W. L. Park joining us on the

International Boundary.... It is high time that this question was looked into in all its detail. And it seems that there is no way to preserve Game and other desirable animals and birds and fish except the establishment of parks in which the people, the real owners of the land, can in season see and photograph the wild life themselves and employ the short summer that is given to us here – Our neighbours over the line seem to realize this with their Glacier Park of over 1,400 square miles of Mountains, Lakes, and Rivers, a veritable paradise for wild life.... It much surprised the people of Southern Alberta when the Waterton Lakes Park was cut down to its present insignificant dimensions, and the people here live in hope that it will be central to its [indecipherable] former boundaries and enlarged.... All who have been here will agree in saying that this is the beauty spot of Canada. The scenery is simply magnificent – many have said it is far superior to Banff or any of the other Parks. There is no part of this Park that is adaptable to agriculture and very little indeed suitable for stock.... It is an ideal game breeding ground.... I may add that in the last 3 years Game has greatly increased. Goat, deer, sheep, & especially bear are seen.... The turning over of this part of the country to the Forestry Department will not be attended with any good, and with the exception of a few interested stockman can only lead to complications and final loss of income to the country.[29]

Such communications certainly put Kootenai's case for Waterton Lakes clearly into the open, and he was backed by officials within the Parks Branch as well as by the general population in that part of the province. Certainly the improvements within the Park initiated by Brown were well received and publicly acknowledged in southern Alberta's principal paper, the *Lethbridge Herald*:

So well has Supt. J. G. Brown of Waterton Lakes park utilized the $10,000 allowed by the parks branch for the construction of new trails, and the betterment of existing roads and trails that tourists who go back to Waterton Lakes this year will hardly know the place, so vastly have the number of easily available attractions and interest points been increased since the 1913 season closed. Speaking entirely conservatively, the work Mr. Brown has done with the $10,000 placed at his disposal – and by the way, it is not all used yet – has increased the number of attractions that the common garden variety of tourists will visit by fifty per cent.

These improvements [trails to the international boundary, to Lake Bertha, along Cameron Creek to Oil City, and a pier for the Pass Creek bridge] offer a very excellent indication of what Superintendent Brown has accomplished with comparatively limited funds at his disposal during 1913. I submit, therefore, that if the park has been worthwhile in years gone by, and if the automobile and trail trips have been interesting and pleasurable, comparisons of the past with the present are odious.[30]

In many respects, 1913 was the high water mark in Brown's work for the Park. The same air of optimism and satisfaction voiced in the *Lethbridge Herald* quietly intrudes into Kootenai's fourth Annual Report in which he notes an increase of 181 visitors, roughly 10%, and the general improvements in amenities for tourists.

For Brown, the improvements carried out in Waterton Lakes under his supervision became the main forces in his life. His attempts to adapt himself and to become more efficient reveal a dogged patience. To meet the challenge of the post and to speed up the process of dealing with a growing volume of correspondence, Kootenai requested and eventually obtained a typewriter "for Park use."[31] When time permitted or necessity required, or when weather prevented outdoor patrols, he sat at his table doggedly learning how to use the instrument. "Got mail. Practising on typewriter," or "Bad day, cold wet snow. At home practising on the typewriter," are notations scattered amongst more serious items recorded in his diary during the autumn of 1913. At 74, his attempt to master the machine reveal Kootenai as he was, a man flexible in outlook, prepared to adapt himself in order to keep up to date.

Busy as he was with Park matters, Brown still found time to read and to write letters. He corresponded regularly with only two people, his son Leo at Athabaska Landing in northern Alberta, and his old companion of gold rush days, A. W. Vowell, by then living in retirement in Victoria, B.C. The correspondence has not been preserved, and we can only surmise about the exchanges.

In his diary, Kootenai simply notes receipt of letters, or records the date of his replies. Occasionally, he records writing to Marie Rose Smith and to various other people in the vicinity, including a United States Ranger named Dan Doody who lived at Babb, Montana. The rest of his correspondence is taken up with personal matters – banking, writing about Treaty Money to which Isabella was entitled, sending to the T. Eaton Company's mail order department at Winnipeg for felt shoes, khaki overalls, the latest catalogue. Isabella remains a shadowy figure constantly hovering in the background as Brown went about his business or received a steady stream of visitors. Her presence in the diaries is constant but limited, indicative of how important she was in Kootenai's life, and the bond between them which had developed through the years.

Those who came to visit Brown during these years reveal the changing nature of the Park and its growing importance in the development of southern Alberta. Many were strangers visiting Waterton Lakes during the summer, their interest quickened and curiosity aroused by the presence of an active old man often dressed for show in his buckskin jacket, his long silver hair curling from beneath the wide-brimmed cowboy hat, who rode his horse with that nonchalant ease that marks an expert. They came to hear Kootenai spin out tales of buffalo hunts, encounters with Indians and his stories about hunting in the mountains, for he epitomized to them the romance and adventure of the old west. For the rest, the people that Brown enjoyed most were his friends – Joseph Cosley, the United States Forest Ranger stationed at Belly River, Bert Riggal, the photographer and packer, Billy Huddleston, the Gladstones, the Hansons (the postmaster at Waterton Mills – so named because of a small saw mill on the Waterton River which operated until the First World War), W. McD. Tait and his wife, and Robert Cooper who on at least one occasion, came to a porcupine dinner.

Brown enjoyed himself most with them, and to at least one unburdened some of his past in vivid colourful terms. These years constituted, as it were, the Indian summer of Brown's days, a period during which he found a certain inner tranquility, one that remained unruffled by the pressures of administration, the frustration of thwarted dreams about a vast and beautiful natural park untouched by the rapaciousness of man, and the petty details of daily life.

At least one of the small details in Brown's life was settled during this great burst of activity on behalf of the Park. Early in February, Kootenai purchased a frame house from Jensen, the hotel owner, for the sum of $200.00.[32] In May he "moved from my homestead to the Jensen building," a change dictated by the need to be closer to the main developments in the Park and, although Brown would never admit it, because of the dictates of old age.

In some ways it was a significant move for it presaged new developments in Waterton Lakes, and a marked change in Brown's life. The change of residence, however, did not impede or reduce Kootenai's activities. He continued to work at a pace beyond the level dictated by his age, and the fruits of his efforts appear in his *Annual Report* for 1913.

With the coming of the new tourist season in 1914, Brown's life, unknown to him, took a significant turn. In June, his great dream for Waterton Lakes became a reality when the Park boundaries were revised to consolidate an area of 423 square miles.[33] The increase in size authorized by Ottawa was far greater than either Brown or his keenest supporter, Howard Douglas, ever expected, and the modification extended the Park bounds south to the 49th parallel. As a result, Waterton Lakes, in conjunction with Glacier National Park on the United States side, came into being as one of North America's great game preserves, and certainly one of the world's most beautiful natural playgrounds.

Brown himself did not learn of the great change until July 8, 1914. His diary entry for that day makes no mention of his feelings or his thoughts about the increase in size, although he notes writing a personal letter to the Commissioner of National Parks.[34] Obviously, however, the change in size was an important step, and would pose new problems for the local administrator as well as for Ottawa. Some indication of the importance that the National Parks Branch attached to the extension can be gauged from the arrival of P. C. B. Hervey, the new Chief Superintendent from Ottawa, a few days after Brown received the news of the government's decision.

Hervey's meeting with Brown and his inspection of the terrain encompassed by the new boundaries quickly convinced him that Brown could not adequately supervise the greatly enlarged Park. Hervey's actions were rapid and decisive. He returned to Pincher Creek, the nearest railway point, and on August 3 wired J. B. Harkin, the Commissioner of Parks, that a Superintendent be appointed for Waterton Lakes as soon as possible in order to attend to the work projected for the enlarged Waterton Lakes Park. His reason for the recommendation was simple:

Ranger Brown cannot exercise proper supervision over extended area owing to extreme age.[35]

On the basis of Hervey's wire, authorization to appoint a new man followed and, as a result Brown's friend and one time assistant, Cooper, was appointed to the post, effective September 1.

212

Kootenai Brown in 1914 when he was 74. Despite his age, in one day he snowshoed 20 miles in -32°F weather and two days later covered 24 miles. Two years later at 76 he patrolled 174 miles in one month. During the same period he taught himself to type to better keep up with the increasing paperwork.

Kootenai Brown and his second wife outside their Waterton home sometime between 1910-16. The building was also Waterton's first post office, with Kootenai the first postmaster, among his other duties.

With Cooper's appointment, Brown's effective career in Canada's public service came to an end. His great contribution to Waterton Lakes was made, and remained the basis from which Cooper began the development of what has since become one of the jewels in Canada's national heritage. Brown, apparently, did not resent Cooper's appointment and certainly his diary reveals little emotion over his change of status. Cooper, in turn, knowing how much the Park meant to Kootenai, kept Brown on strength as a Ranger. The transition from a post of supreme authority to an ancillary role was thus minimized. Once Brown turned over the typewriter he so laboriously taught himself to use, forms, Park regulations and other paraphernalia of office, he continued to consult with Cooper and to carry out his patrols more or less as usual.[36]

Only one entry in his diary, that for September 10, 1914, betrays any emotion: "gale from south, cold. Feel miserable." Yet the clock was running down and a sense of finality begins to intrude intermittently in the diary in the autumn of 1914. On October 10 he wrote an entry that is quite uncharacteristic:

Birthday, now 74! Snow with wind. Cooper went for mail. None.... No letters, papers, or anything. Good luck for 75!!!

The next day he rode 15 miles on horseback.

Gradually, inevitably, his strenuous activities decreased, while the record of illnesses became more frequent. Though he frequently resorted to whisky, he did so for its warming comfort and for its medicinal properties. Gone were the days when liquor was a prime pleasure, as well as a prime reason for being sick. And while enthusiasm for his work perhaps diminished as his energies declined, Kootenai's sense of humor never deserted him.

On March 17, 1914, he wryly recorded, "Patrick's day and not a drop." As 1914 wore its way into the past, Brown turned more frequently to books, to the writing of letters, particularly to his son and to Vowell, and to following the remarkably varied predictions of the French wartime clairvoyant Madame de Thebes, as printed in various newspapers.[37] The madam's views, ostensibly based upon an ability to contact the spiritual world, appealed to Kootenai, probably because of his own interest in Theosophy. Otherwise the carnage of the Western Front apparently held little interest for him. Certainly any professional interest in the course of the war in Europe does not manifest itself in his notes.

It was the Park which held his attention and at the end of May, normally the time that visitors begin to trickle into the grounds, he could still report that he had patrolled a distance of 174 miles during the month.[38] As the year wore to an end and a new 1916 calendar replaced the old, the distances travelled by horse, wagon, or on foot diminished and the record of the number of patrols carried out grows smaller. Each provide a meagre record of a man carrying out a tenacious rearguard action against the inexorable overpowering enemy, the rapidity of whose approach increased daily. Kootenai fought the approach of senility with the same stubbornness and determination that had carried him through the hardships of the Cariboo, mail runs over the Dakota plains, and his long years in the mountain valleys beyond the Waterton Lakes.

W. McD. Tait recalls these last months:

> I remember how great an effort it was for him to make his patrol as Fire and Game Warden in Waterton Lakes National Park in order that his diary might show some activity every day. It was only a short time then till he lay in bed and we talked together. It was [then] that the more touching incidents of an eventful life came out.[39]

In deference to Brown, Tait has not set down what he describes as "touching incidents," but it is clear from his recollections that Kootenai did not completely unburden himself. He always reserved part of himself from others and there is no evidence to suggest or confirm that even during those last days he deviated from that personal standard. Michael Holland, who knew Kootenai, touches upon that aspect of Brown's character:

> In 1890 I had a small ranch 27 miles from Macleod in the Porcupine Hills.... In those days old "Kootenai" Brown was living near the Kootenai Pass & I knew & liked him. He taught me to throw the Diamond Hitch which I found useful many years later in African expeditions. Kootenai Brown dressed in buckskin & had long white hair which came down to his shoulders. As far as I can remember he had keen eyes and was a first class packer, trapper & hunter. He sometimes brought Latin quotations into his talk & had been previously something of a scholar, but he never spoke to me of his past, & in those days, we did not enquire into the family history of strangers in the West of Canada.[40]

In mid-March 1916, Kootenai fell ill, rallied, and was soon up and around once more. The illness, however, made him realize that the end was near. Calmly and deliberately he wrote to his son, Leo:

> Since your last letter my health has been very bad and it seems only a short time until I have to pass in my checks [sic]. Never mind about this, it is alright, a thing we have all got to pass through.[41]

His thoughts then turned to Isabella, the silent shadow in the background, and he issued careful instructions about her future:

> When you know this [i.e. Kootenai's death] for a certainty, I want you to come here again and take charge of my wife Isabella. I am leaving her what ought to be enough to keep her in shape and help you out for the balance of her life. I want you to take her up home where you live. She will be a good help to you in many ways and will be anxious to join you.[42]

At the end of May he signed his will, witnessed by Cooper and E. E. Haug, in which he directed that all of his estate was to go to Isabella, and sent it in triplicate to the firm of Thomson and Jackson in Pincher Creek.[43] That done, he continued to write letters to Vowell, to Dan Doody, and forwarded a list of property to his son, Leo.[44] On June 8 he rode "with woman in the launch with Danielson dis. [i.e. distance] 10 miles."[45]

It was the last outing, like the final flow of energy characterizing the release of a coiled spring. After missing two entries for June 21 and 22, he wrote in his diary for the last time on June 24, 1916. On July 18 he died quietly, to Isabella's great sorrow.[46]

Epilogue

Kootenai Brown was buried beside Olive on the western shore of the Lower Waterton Lake near the site of his first homestead. In his will he asked that his son, Leo, his old friend, A. W. Vowell, and the Theosophical Society, Point Loma, California, be notified of his death. Brown also specified that he "did not desire the attendance of any clergyman of any denomination at [his] funeral in an official capacity."[1] Despite this provision, his friends insisted upon the presence of a Minister, and Isabella raised no objection to Reverend Gretton, a Protestant pastor from Pincher Creek. W. McD. Tait, who was present during those last moments by the lakeshore, leaves this picture of the interment:

> And we buried him on the shore of Lower Waterton Lake, the place of which he said 51 years before, "This is what I have seen in my dreams; this is the country for me." His will precluded the presence of a clergyman...but we had a service – a service of tribute to a life as we had seen it lived.... Chee-pay-tha-qua-ka-soon [the Indian name attributed to Isabella by Brown in his letter to his solicitor, March 21, 1916,] was the chief mourner, but there were many other eyes moist and hearts heavy.[2]

Photographs taken at the scene show a small knot of people proceeding to or from, for one cannot say which for certain, the burial, some in wagons, some on horseback, some on foot.

News of Brown's passing was, of course, carried by most of southern Alberta's newspapers. With the printing of each obituary began that process which, in the years since, has created an image of Kootenai that bears little resemblance to the vivid reality of his true life. In the years since his death, hearsay and imaginations rampant have promoted Kootenai to army ranks which he never held, sent him to Eton, Oxford, Trinity College, Dublin, claimed Queen Victoria's famous ghillie as his father, pictured him at play with the children of British royalty, invented stories of amorous scandal in the closed society of British Army service in India, cast him in the role of a gambling dandy on glittering

217

Kootenai Brown is buried in the small family cemetery on the shore of Little Waterton Lake. On either side of him are his two wives, although Isobel, his "Nichemoos," the Cree word for "sweetheart," didn't join him until 1935.

Mississippi River boats, and attempted to transform Isabella, that patient Cree woman, into a prairie princess who at one time saved Brown's life. Of those initial notices, as well as those which have appeared subsequently, it was Robert Cooper, the man who succeeded Brown as Superintendent of Waterton Lakes National Park, who gave Kootenai his most fitting epitaph:

> John George Brown, more commonly known as "Kootenai" Brown, died on July 18, after a short illness, at his home in the park. The late Mr. Brown was the first settler in this locality. He was the first ranger in charge of the park, and, in fact, the existence of the park is largely due to his efforts to have protection afforded the game, as he realized that with the number of settlers in the country its destruction was certain.[3]

As for the rest of the story, Isabella, who now rests beside Kootenai on the shores of the Lower Lake, lingered for many years, scanning earth and sky for signs of Brown's return in another form, living near the Park at Twin Butte until her death on April 1, 1935.[4] She never went north to live with Leo as Kootenai desired, for Brown's son was killed in an accident in November 1916.[5] As for Brown's two daughters, the rest is silence.

Postscript

What kind of man was Brown? In the absence of letters and prolonged observation by persons close to him, we can only establish cardinal points about his personality, his interests, his vigour. Amidst the many apocryphal stories about Brown, they stand out like isolated high points on an otherwise uniform plain of unsubstantiated hearsay.

That Brown was physically tough is axiomatic. His years in India, his travels across mountains and plain, those glorious days with the Métis bear ample testimony to his resilience. One recollection, as much as any extant account, shows Kootenai in his chosen role of outdoorsman:

> I [W. McD. Tait] remember Chateau Reid, my neighbour on the Kootenai River, telling some one at round up camp that shortly after he came to the country here – it was about 20 years ago [i.e. circa 1895-1900] – he was hunting on the shore of Maskinonge Lake at the lower end of Waterton Lakes. He heard two shots fired and coming in the direction of the shots he saw a man undressing. Before he got up, the man had walked out on the shore of ice of the lake, and plunging into the water, took two geese and holding them in one hand out of the water, swam back to the shore ice, climbed up and got to land. Before doing this he had built a fire on the shore at which to dry and warm himself, and when Chateau got up he was partly dressed. Brown was the man's name, and J. G. were his initials.[1]

No account can adequately catch the flavour of total effort, the sweat and excitement that were part of every day existence for Kootenai and his contemporaries. Even the most prosaic journey to Pincher Creek, to Fort Macleod, or to a neighbouring ranch on horseback or jolting in a wagon, carried its share of tedium and, at times, a share of danger. All were a part of Brown's life, just as much as the sweep of the landscape, the wild animals he saw, the clothes he wore, or the whisky he drank.

We know too, that Kootenai, by comparison with most of those whom he met or with whom he shared his life, was well educated. Michael Holland speaks of the occasional Latin tag which intruded into his speech, and we have a record of the journals, newspapers and books which he read. There are also the extant papers in his own hand, reports to Major-General de Trobriand, to the Commissioner of the National Parks, and his account of day-to-day activity in Waterton Lakes National Park. They show that he was capable, could express himself clearly and directly, and that he had a sense of service.

Various sources confirm his old fashioned courtesy, his words soft-spoken, and his ability to make his experiences in the west come to life. "To hear him tell of his experiences in this country was something worthwhile" was the way it was put in the *Pincher Creek Echo*. That he was friendly and always willing to help, particularly those unfamiliar with the country, with horses, ropes or packing, is attested to by Billy Cochrane, Michael Holland, and a host of others. At the same time, it is equally clear that Brown was never afraid to use four-square words when the occasion merited. That propensity went hand in hand with a sharp temper, a characteristic which, as the years went by, Brown was able to curb.

In a similar vein, Kootenai was not a man to spurn a strong drink or to shun a good party. In that respect, he was at home in the gay abandonment of the Métis camp or the more boisterous affairs which took place, perhaps too often, when he and his friends got together. That propensity for partying went hand in hand with a robust, earthy sense of humour:

> Talking of strychnine reminds me of an interesting incident that happened once. It would appear that about this time some unprincipled people were manufacturing a thing called strychnine which was epsom salts, salt peter, and something else, I forgot what. When this incident occurred I was camped with a number of white wolfers on the Marias River. A couple of cheechako [tenderfeet] came along and wanted to join us in the business. A large number of cattle had been introduced into the country and wolves were making depredation on calves and yearlings. The owners offered free of charge all the old or poor cows, and with lump-jaw or mange and any otherwise disabled, with enough poison to poison the carcass, to anyone who would use it. These new comers had been lured west by an advertisement of cattle-men offering these inducements. By some fluke some of this imitation strychnine got into the cattlemen's store house and was doled out to the new comers. They had killed a couple of old cows and rubbed in the epsom salts and salt peter, but the wolves ate the bait and got fat. The two fellows came over to our camp one day and brought a large bottle holding nearly a pint of the supposed strychnine they were using on their bait. They said something like this: "Boys we're

new comers here and are not posted on this strychnine Operation. Maybe we're not using it right. Here's the stuff, take a look at it."

The bottle was passed from one to another and each with a big grin passed it on to the next. When it got into the hands of old Bill Martin who was with us that winter also, the old fellow said: "My friends, would you mind if I tasted a little of this?" The cheechako, a little mystified, assented and old Bill taking a big spoon off the table took out a heaping spoonful, and opening his oversized mouth to its full capacity, inserted the poison and chewed it down. He then began to dispose of his property. "You Kootenai," he said, "can have my old Pinto mare, and you Bill Preston my Hawkins rifle, I haven't got anything else to leave and am tired of life anyway." Then he walked over to a bed in the corner and lay down.

We old wolfers knew, of course, that strychnine was never done up in pint bottles and we saw at once that old Bill was putting one over on the new comers. They were greatly alarmed. They implored us to do something, and failing to get any sympathy from us they rushed for a pot of wolf grease and attempted to force it down old Bill's throat. He kicked them off and told them he wanted to die anyway. The dose he took had its effect but it was not killing. After the excitement Bill took a big drink of whisky and we told the new comers what their poison consisted of. They stayed with us that winter and by spring we had made pretty good wolfers of them.[2]

There are enough tales of a similar sort, most of them imaginative reconstructions of the what-might-have-been kind, to indicate clearly that Kootenai liked his jokes, and enjoyed the horseplay which is so often a vital part of a survey camp or a hunting trip, where men are thrown upon one another by the compulsion of isolation.[3] In a milder sense, Brown's humour and his tendency towards hypochondria reveals itself in the recollections of Annora Brown, the daughter of a Mounted Policeman stationed at the Big Bend detachment:

Kootenai came in one day moaning and groaning that he was sick and was going to die. My father put him to bed and gave him a dose of quinine. Next morning he was better and able to continue his drive to Fort Macleod. After that he always called my father "Dr. Brown." His greeting was always, "Hi namesake! How is Dr. Brown today?"[4]

Without much doubt Kootenai's sense of humour and a certain philosophical flexibility were priceless assets for survival on the frontier.

Most recollections of Kootenai Brown are highly favourable. Marie Rose Smith, however, measured Brown in feminine terms, painting him in one instant as heartbroken and full of remorse over the death of Olive, and in the next breath as a man who neglected Isabella and whose eye wandered in the

presence of young white girls. But the latter incidents occurred late in Kootenai's life during his tenure as Ranger in charge of Waterton Lakes, and the intimation through his diary entries is that he sought bright young company strictly for companionship. Isabella, faithful and patient though she was, could never provide that sparkle which Kootenai at times must have longed for to the point of desperation.

The portrait then remains unfinished. Framed by records, official and unofficial, there are the piercing eyes, the long silver hair, the buckskin coat, wrinkles, a wart or two in the delineation of character. Orphan, soldier, prospector, miner, trader, mail carrier, parent, packer, guide, superintendent, and squaw man. Kootenai was all of these and more.

Whatever is missing – the light and shadow of personality, the confirmation of motives, the range and depth of knowledge and interests – cannot be traced with certainty or put down with precision. Brown lived a full and facinating life, and whatever the magnitude of his faults, his contribution through Waterton Lakes to Canada's national heritage remains, like the Shining Mountains, forever bright.

Kootenai's Waterton today

We can only surmise how Kootenai Brown would regard Waterton Lakes National Park as it is today. Certainly it is a very different place from the simple Forest Reserve and rudimentary public playground that he knew so well and did so much to bring into being. Although many of the mountains, valleys, lakes and streams that he ranged over and fished bear different names from those with which he was familiar, they are, essentially, the same as they were in his day when they provided him with sustenance, as well as pleasure. Whether he would approve of the post-World War One geographical place names accorded distinctive peaks such as Vimy or Alderson is open to question. There is little doubt, however, that he would approve of the controlled development that has characterized the growth and general administration of the Park, as well as some, if not all, of its modern amenities.

Most certainly the nearly 200 miles of trails that now crisscross Waterton, making the most scenic as well as the remotest areas accessible to visitors, would be acceptable to Kootenai. In their own way, they constitute a conservation and a safety measure, preventing the wayward misuse of the area and safeguarding the fauna and flora that are the region's greatest assets. The thread of trails, together with campsites located in the Park's outlying regions, are in keeping with the way Kootenai envisaged that it should be used when he first proposed preserving the area. In that respect, he undoubtedly would endorse the use of low power radio transmitters that broadcast useful information about the Park, or alert visitors about possible dangers such as fires or the caprices of weather. Unlike most of those who come to Waterton Lakes, he was only too familiar with the dangers that are ever present in that rugged terrain.

While it is reasonable certain that Brown would accept as inevitable the establishment of a townsite on the shores of the main lake, and that he would take advantage of its many facilities, it is equally clear that his toleration of the community would be limited, perhaps even grudging. Despite his conviviality and his liking for parties, his preference tilted towards the quiet of his cabin. As for the main campsite within the townsite, the spectacle of motorhomes, trailers, and automobiles, together with power outlets, piped water and sewage facilities, he would regard with a certain disdain as keeping nature at bay. In particular, he disliked the horseless carriage. The sight of automobiles disrupting the quiet of the valleys leading to Cameron Lake,

Alberta Government

Waterton townsite includes major visitor services such as accomodation, stores, restaurants, and an over 200-unit campground. Brochures, maps and other material is available at the Information Centre or by writing: Superintendent, Waterton Lakes National Park, Waterton Park, Alberta, Canada T0K 2M0.

Chief Mountain, or Red Rock Canyon, and adding to the pollution of an atmosphere now very different from that Kootenai experienced, would cause him great concern. It is not hard to imagine the language he could bring into play against the roads and parking lots that he felt should best be traversed on horseback or by foot for maximum appreciation. As for the Park's golf course, and the antics of the Richardson ground squirrels as they take cover from players and balls, surely they would be a continuous source of wry amusement.

What he most certainly would endorse is the re-introduction of buffalo to Waterton Lakes. Although the Park's herd is minuscule compared with the numberless mass that he and his companions saw when they emerged from the South Kootenay Pass, the animals reflect what was once a commonplace aspect of the North American plains, and which was such a significant part of his life. The return, too, of wolves within the Park would warm his heart, even though, like so many others during his time, he hunted them with utter ruthlessness. Their presence, although still tentative and uncertain, together with the bison, bring some semblance of natural balance to the region, supplementing Waterton's remaining indigenous wildlife. Kootenai, particularly during his later years when he was becoming engrossed with Theosophical tenets, considered the balance of nature to be an essential part of life.

With growing public awareness of ecological and environmental issues, and with ever increasing numbers of visitors to Waterton, the need to provide accurate information about the Park's plant and animal life has become paramount. Accordingly, the guided trail walks, lectures, films and video presentations that are now regularly available would have Kootenai's enthusiastic support. These information services are an extension of the process he, in his own fashion, pioneered.

Probably the most singular aspect of today's Waterton that would command Kootenai's approval is that it is a destination park. Unlike visitors to most other mountain parks, those who come to the Shining Mountains tend to linger in order to savour their dramatic appeal. Their presence is a confirmation of Kootenai's belief in the area – and a vindication of his contribution to Waterton's preservation for all Canadians.

Bibliography

INTERVIEWS

Freebairn, A. L., Pincher Creek, Alberta, June 23, 1956.

Nielson, (Miss) Lou, Waterton Lakes, Alberta, June 20, 1956.

Smith, Marie Rose, Edmonton, Alberta, July 8, 1956.

Tait, W. McD., Fergus, Ontario, October 29, 1955.

MANUSCRIPTS

British Columbia. Provincial Archives.

Begbie, M. B. Papers.

British Columbia Blue Books, 1865.

Cox, W. G. Papers.

B.C. Supreme Court. Extracts of Evidence. Cranbrook, 1907.

O'Reilly, Peter. Papers.

Canada. Public Archives.

Adjutant General's Office Correspondence, Record Group 9.

Bowell, Mackenzie. Papers.

Caron, Adolphe P. Papers.

Riel, Louis. Papers.

War Claims Commission, Record Group 9.

Great Britain. Public Record Office.

Commander in Chief Memoranda Papers.

Eighth Regiment, First Battalion. Monthly Pay Lists, 1857-1862.

—. Monthly Returns of Officers Services, 1858-62.

Embarkation Returns 1858-1869.

Half Pay and Military Allowances 1847-1855.

93rd Regiment (Argyll and Sutherland Highlanders) Quarterly Pay Lists, 1837-1841.

—. Returns of Officers Services.

Returns of Officers Services, Retired, Full Pay, and Half Pay.

Royal Military College, Sandhurst. Report of the Collegiate Board for Half-Yearly Examination.

Widows' Compassionate and Royal Bounty Letter Books.

Widows' Compassionate List, 1828.

Widows' Journal, Register of Claims, 1827-1835.

Widows' Pensions, 1828.

U.S.A. National Archives and Records Service.

Adjutant General's Office Records, Group 94.

U.S. Army Commands, Department of Dakota Records, Group 98.

U.S. Army Quartermaster Records, Group 92.

U.S. Northern Boundary Survey Papers.

North Dakota. State Historical Society.

De Trobriand, P. R. K. Papers.

Others.

Bates, J. E. D., and Z. W. Hickman. "The Founding of Cardston and Vicinity — Pioneer Problems." No date, Waterton Lakes National Park.

Brown, John George "Kootenai." Diaries and Letter Book. National Parks Branch, Ottawa.

Canadian Pacific Railway Records. Crow's Nest Pass 1897-1898. [Montreal].

Cochrane, W. F. Diary and Letter Book. Glenbow Foundation, Calgary.

Cosley, Joseph. "The Meeting of Kootenai Brown." Unpublished manuscript, no date, Waterton Lakes National Park.

OFFICIAL PUBLICATIONS AND RECORDS

Canada.

Department of Agriculture, Edmonton, Alberta. *Annual reports,* 1908, 1911, 1915.

Department of Indian Affairs and Northern Development. File W3. vols. I and II. U172-23A.

Department of the Interior. National Parks Branch. Commissioner of Canadian National Parks. *Reports, 1904-1911,* Ottawa, 1911.

—. *Reports, 1912-1926,* Ottawa, 1926.

Department of the Interior. National Parks Branch. File W174, vols. 1-10; Forestry Branch File 112630.

Department of Marine and Fisheries. Files 1298 and 2995.

Department of Militia and Defence. *Report Upon the Suppression of the Rebellion in the Northwest Territories.* Ottawa, 1886.

Department of Veterans Affairs. Honors and Awards Division. Ledger of the Militia Force.

North-West Mounted Police. *Annual reports.* Ottawa, 1885-1891.

—. Pay Ledger No. 4.

Royal Canadian Mounted Police. Files 497; 596; 2634 - 1885; 288 - 1888; 764 - 1888; 178 - 1889; 278 - 1889; 985 - 1889; 238 - 1890; G516 - 31; G995 - 10.

War Claims Commission. *Report No. 4.* Ottawa, 1886.

U.S.A.

U.S. House of Representatives, 40th Congress, Third Session. *Executive Document No. 1.* vol. III. Washington, D.C.

NEWSPAPERS AND PERIODICALS

British Colonist.
British Columbian.
Calgary Herald.
Canadian Cattlemen.
Canadian Historical Review.
Canadian Magazine.
Canadian Pictorial and Illustrated War News 1885.
Cranbrook Courier.
Daily Colonist. (Victoria, B.C.)
Daily Times. (Victoria, B.C.)
Fort Benton *Record.*
Fort Macleod *Gazette.*
Helena *Independent.*
Leisure Hour.

Lethbridge Herald.
Lethbridge News.
Maclean's Magazine.
North Dakota History.
Pacific Northwest Quarterly.
Pincher Creek Echo.
Rod and Gun.
R.C.M.P. Quarterly.

BOOKS

Bancroft, H. H. *Works.* Vol. XXXI. *History of Washington, Idaho and Montana 1845-1889.* San Francisco, 1890.

Barclay, C. N. *On Their Shoulders. British Generalship in the Lean Years 1939-1942.* London, 1964.

Berry, Gerald L. *The Whoop-Up Trail: Early Days in Alberta - Montana.* Edmonton, 1953.

Blue, John. *Alberta Past and Present.* 3 vols. Chicago, 1924.

Burdick, U. L. *Tales from Buffalo Land: The Story of Fort Buford.* Baltimore, 1940.

Burgoyne, Captain R. H. *Records of the XCIII Sutherland Highlanders.* London, 1883.

Butler, W. F. *The Great Lone Land.* London, 1873.

Canadian Parliamentary Guide, Ottawa, 1905, 1909, 1910.

Chief Mountain [Archdeacon S. H. Middleton]. *Kootenai Brown.* Lethbridge, 1954.

Collections of the State Historical Society, North Dakota. vols. II and III. Bismarck, 1908 and 1910.

Cornwallis, K. *The New El Dorado.* London, 1858.

Craig, John R. *Ranching with Lords and Commons.* Toronto, 1903.

Fery, J. H. and J. G. Wight. *Cariboo Gold Mines.* San Francisco, 1862.

Freebairn, A. L. *Kootenai Brown and Other Western Poems.* Pincher Creek, Alberta, n.d.

Gard, Robert. *Johnny Chinook.* Toronto, 1945.

Garrioch, A. C. *First Furrows*, Winnipeg, 1933.

—. *The Correction Line.* Winnipeg, 1933.

Gerstle, Mack. *The Land Divided.* New York, 1944.

Goetzmann, W. H. *Army Exploration in the American West 1803-1863.* New Haven, 1959.

Hart, H. M. *Old Forts of the Northwest.* Seattle, 1963.

Harts' Annual Army List, 1848, 1849, 1855, 1874. London, 1848, 1849, 1855, 1874.

Haultain, T. A. *A History of Riel's Second Rebellion.* Toronto, 1885.

Higinbotham, J. D. *When the West Was Young.* Toronto, 1933.

Hill, A. S. *From Home to Home: Autumn Wanderings in the Years 1881, 1882, 1883, 1884.* London, 1887.

Horan, J. W. *West Nor'West: A History of Alberta.* Edmonton, 1945.

Howard, J. K. *Strange Empire.* New York, 1952.

Howarth, David. *The Golden Isthmus.* London, 1967.

Howay, F. W. *British Columbia From the Earliest Times.* Vancouver, 1914.

Jocelyn, Captain Arthur. *Awards of Honour.* London, 1956.

Kane, Lucile M. (ed.). *Military Life in Dakota: The Journal of Philippe Régis de Trobriand.* St. Paul, 1951.

Kelly, L. V. *The Range Men: The Story of the Rangers and Indians of Alberta.* Toronto, 1913.

Kemble, J. H. *The Panama Route 1848-1869.* Berkeley, 1943.

Kerr, J. B. *Biographical Dictionary of Well-Known British Columbians.* Vancouver, B.C., 1890.

Lamar, Howard Roberts. *Dakota Territory 1861-1889: A Study of Frontier Politics.* New Haven, 1956.

Larpenteur, Charles. *Forty Years a Fur Trader on the Upper Missouri.* Chicago, 1933.

Liddell, K. E. *This is Alberta.* Toronto, 1952.

—. *Alberta Revisited.* Toronto, 1960.

—. *Southern Alberta's Roamin' Empire.* Calgary, n.d.

MacEwan, Grant. *The Sodbusters.* Toronto, 1948.

—. *Between the Red and the Rockies.* Toronto, 1952.

—. *Fifty Mighty Men.* Saskatoon, 1958.

MacInnis, C. M. *In the Shadow of the Rockies.* London, 1930.

Martin, Archer. *Mining Cases and Statutes of British Columbia 1902-1907.* Toronto, 1907.

Martin, Chester and Morton, A. S., *History of Prairie Settlement and Dominion Lands Policy.* Toronto, 1938.

Maw, Margaret. *Meet Southern Alberta.* Calgary, 1954.

Nicholson, N. S. *Boundaries of Canada, Its Provinces and Territories.* (Geographical Branch Memoir No. 2) Ottawa, 1954.

Ormsby, Margaret A. *British Columbia: a History.* Vancouver, B.C., 1964.

Otis, F. N. *Illustrated History of the Panama Railway.* New York, 1862.

Phipps, R. W. (ed.), L. A. F. de Bourrienne, *Memoirs of Napoleon Bonaparte,* vol. IV. New York, 1905.

Quaife, M. M. (ed.) *Army Life in Dakota: Selections from the Journal of Philippe Régis Denis de Keredern de Trobriand.* Chicago, 1941.

Robertson, A. C. *Historical Record of the King's Liverpool Regiment.* London, 1883.

Roe, F. G. *The North American Buffalo.* Toronto, 1951.

Royal Artillery Institution. *Occasional Papers,* vol. I. Woolwich, 1860.

Rudolph, I. de M. *Short Histories of the Territorial Regiments.* London, 1905.

Sharp, Paul F. *Whoop-Up Country: The Canadian American West 1865-1885.* Minneapolis, 1955.

Spry, Irene M. *The Palliser Expedition.* Toronto, 1963.

Stanley, G. F. G. *The Birth of Western Canada.* London, 1960.

—. *Louis Riel Patriot or Rebel.* Ottawa, 1954.

—. *Louis Riel.* Toronto, 1963.

Steele, S. B. *Forty Years in Canada.* Toronto, 1915.

Taylor, John Henry. *Sketches of Frontier and Indian Life on the Upper Missouri and Great Plains.* Bismarck, 1897.

Tisdall, E. E. P. *Queen Victoria's John Brown.* London, 1938.

Thompson, J. M. *Napoleon Bonaparte; His Rise and Fall.* Oxford, 1958.

Turner, J. P. *The North-West Mounted Police 1873-1893.* 2 vols. Ottawa, 1950.

Utley, Robert M. *The Last Days of the Sioux Nation.* New Haven, 1963.

Walkem, W. W. *Stories of Early British Columbia.* Vancouver, 1914.

Welsh, Norbert. *The Last Buffalo Hunter.* New York, 1939. Mary Weeks (ed.).

Woodham-Smith, Cecil. *The Reason Why.* London, 1953.

ARTICLES AND THESES

Bletcher, Betty. "Kootenai Brown's Widow Spends Lengthening Days Within the Pine's Shadow." *Calgary Herald*, December 1, 1934.

Buchanan, Donald. "Waterton Lakes National Park." *Canadian Geographical Journal*, January 1953.

Cappock, Kenneth. "Kootenai Brown." *Canadian Cattlemen*, June 1940.

Christie, A. H. "Kootenai Brown Spent Colorful Career in West." *Calgary Herald*, April 13, 1935.

Collins, Robert. "The Place the Gas will Come From." *Maclean's Magazine*, July 1, 1954.

Dempsey, Hugh A. "Rocky Mountain Rangers." *Alberta Historical Review*, Spring 1957.

Flett, Mary. "A Holiday in the Canadian Rockies." *Rod and Gun*, May 1917.

Haug, E. "Kootenai Brown and the Founding of Wonderful Park." *Lethbridge Herald*, June 21, 1924.

Lee, Lawrence B. "The Mormons Come to Canada, 1887-1902." *Pacific Northwest Quarterly*, January 1968.

Liddell, K. "Kootenai Brown." *Calgary Herald*, December 29, 1951.

MacEwan, Grant. "Blazing Trails in the Western Cattle Kingdom." *R.C.M.P. Quarterly*, October 1945; January 1946.

—. "Clad in Buckskin." *The Western Producer*, August 29, 1957.

McCook, James. "Kootenai Brown's Letter." *Lethbridge Herald*, February 24, 1950.

McDonald, M. L. "New Westminster 1849-1871." Unpublished M.A. Thesis, University of British Columbia, 1947.

Mitchner, Alan. "William Pearce, Father of Alberta Irrigation." Unpublished M.A. Thesis, University of Alberta, 1967.

Moore, John F. "A Gay Adventurer of Pioneer Days." Vancouver *Sun*, March 20, 1954.

—. "Kootenai Brown — Pioneer of the West." *Farm and Ranch Review*, June 1955.

Pearce, William. [Recollections]. *Calgary Herald*, December 27, 1924.

Rackette, G. Adele. "Some Incidents in Kootenai Brown's Interesting Life." *Lethbridge Herald*, July 9, 1936.

—. "Kootenai Brown. Colorful Tales of a Western Pioneer." Glacier Park Transport Company *Driver's Manual*. Lake McDonald, Montana, 1949.

Reid, J. H. S. "The Road to Cariboo." Unpublished M.A. Thesis, University of British Columbia, 1942.

Rodney, William. "Explorations of Lt. Thomas W. Blakiston." *Lethbridge Herald*, September 15, 1950.

—. "Kootenai Brown." *Lethbridge Herald*, February 28, 1952.

—. "John George (Kootenai) Brown." *Encyclopedia Canadiana*, vol. II, Ottawa 1957 and 1967.

Smith, Marie Rose. "Kootenai Brown." *Canadian Cattlemen*, October 1949.

Smith, S. B. "The Grave of Kootenai Brown." *Lethbridge Herald*, October 18, 1935.

Steele, C. F. "Adventures of Kootenai Brown." *Lethbridge Herald*, October 18, 1935.

Tait, W. McD. "Fixing the Border Line." *Canadian Magazine*, 1915.

—. "I Remember." *Farm and Ranch Review*, vols. 15 and 16, 1919-1920.

—. "Kootenai Brown Tells Thrills of Early Days in Cariboo Gold Rush. Vancouver *Daily Province*, February 23, 1924.

—. "Kootenai Brown Tells of Buffalo Hunting in Early Sixties. Vancouver *Daily Province*, March 8, 1924.

—. "Trail Blazing Across the Rockies." *Canadian Magazine*, March 1934.

Windsor, John. "Frontier Chef." Victoria *Daily Colonist*, December 18, 1960.

Wright, Dana. "Fort Totten - Fort Stevenson Trail." *North Dakota History*, April 1953.

Anonymous. "Kootenai Brown's Story of Boundary Survey." *Lethbridge Herald*, May 19, 1934.

—. "The Romance of Mrs. Kootenai Brown Born a Full-Blooded Cree." *Lethbridge Herald*, April 1, 1935.

Notes

CHAPTER I

1 The two graves are marked as follows: "Rebecca Churchill Finucane, wife of Morgan Finucane, M.D., died June 5, 1811, age 35"; and "John Finucane, died May 11, 1809, age 60." John's son Patrick served in the Royal Navy; died at Battle of St. Luc, October 18, 1816, age 36.

2 W.O.31/1159, Commander in Chief Memorandum Papers, Ennistymon, May 28, 1857.

3 PMG 10-17, Compassionate List 1828, Pay Warrant July 5, 1829.

4 Capt. R. H. Burgoyne, *Records of the XCIII Sutherland Highlanders* (London, 1883), p. 8.

5 *Ibid.*, p. 18.

6 WO4-553, Widows Compassionate and Royal Bounty Letter Book, p. 301. Also, WO42/4 B538, Clonmel, May 31, 1828.

7 WO42/4/British B538, Dublin Castle, June 7, 1828.

8 WO31/617, Commander in Chief Memoranda Papers, Portsmouth, April 15, 1828.

9 WO4/553, Widows, p 371.

10 *Ibid.*, London, August 13, 1828, pp. 405-406.

11 WO31/617, Commander, Portsmouth, April 15, 1828.

12 PMG 10-17, Compassionate List 1828, July 5, 1829.

13 WO42/4/B538, Clonmel, May 31, 1828.

14 WO31/1159, Commander, Clonmel, June 20, 1855.

15 *Ibid.*, Clonmel, October 21, 1856.

16 *The Daily Colonist* (Victoria, B.C.), September 27, 1918.

17 WO25/803, Services of officers on Full Pay December 31, 1829, 91 to 95 Foot.

18 WO12/9419, 93rd Regiment, Quarterly Pay List, October 1 - December 31, 1839.

19 Cecil Woodham-Smith, *The Reason Why* (London, 1953), p. 23.

20 WO31/1159, Commander, Clonmel, August 25, 1857.

21 *Ibid.*, Clonmel, June 20, 1855.

22 *Ibid.*, Clonmel, June 30, 1855.

23 *Ibid.*, Clonmel, November 13, 1855.

24 *Ibid.*, Ennistymon, May 28, 1857.

25 Letters, Royal Military Academy Sandhurst, Camberley, December 3, 1958 and July 21, 1966.

26 WO31/1159, Commander, Ennistymon, May 28, 1857.

27 *Ibid.*

28 *Ibid.*, Clonmel, August 2, 1856.

29 *Ibid.*

30 *Ibid.*, Clonmel, October 21, 1856.

31 *Ibid.*, Clonmel, December 31, 1856.

32 *Ibid.*, Ennistymon, May 28, 1857.

33 *Ibid.*, Clonmel, July 4, 1857.

34 *Ibid.*, Clonmel, August 10, 1857.

35 *Ibid.*, Clonmel, August 25, 1857.

36 *Ibid.*

37 *Ibid.*, Clonmel, October 29, 1857.

38 *Ibid.*, Clonmel, November 10, 1857.

39 *Ibid.*

40 *Ibid.*

41 *Ibid.*, London, December 7, 1857.

42 WO76/130, Returns of Officers' Service, Eighth Regiment.

CHAPTER II

1 WO12/2608, Monthly Muster Rolls Eighth Regiment 1857-1858, Adjutant's Roll, January 1 - March 31, 1858.

2 A. C. Robertson, *Historical Record of the King's Liverpool Regiment* (London, 1883), p. 135.

3 *Ibid.*

4 I. de M. Rudolf, *Short Histories of the Territorial Regiments* (London, 1905), p. 78.

5 WO17/695, Monthly Returns of Officers Service, Eighth Regiment, First Battalion, February - October 1858.

6 *Ibid.*, Chatham, October 1, 1858.

7 WO25/3505, Vol. IV, Embarkation Returns 1858-1869.

8 WO17/695, Monthly Returns, Camp Bewlee, December 1, 1858.

9 Robertson, p. 145.

10 WO25/695, Monthly Returns, Camp Roohia, November 1, 1858.

11 *Ibid.*, Camp Bewlee, December 1, 1858.

12 WO17/705, Monthly Returns of Officers Service, Eighth Regiment, First Battalion, Fattehguhr, February 1, 1859.

13 *Ibid.*, March 1, 1859.

14 Mary Flett, "A Holiday in the Canadian Rockies," in *Rod and Gun*, May 1917.

15 Robertson, pp. 149-150.

16 Lloyds of London letter, March 20, 1956. Two ships named *Clara* are recorded in Lloyds Registry of Shipping. The vessel on which Brown travelled was newly built, having been completed in Sunderland in 1859 for Teighe and Company. Also WO12/2611, PRO letter, London, February 9, 1956.

17 Robertson, pp. 149-150.

18 *Ibid.*, p. 151.

19 R. W. Phipps (ed.), L. A. F. de Bourrienne, *Memoirs of Napoleon Bonaparte*, Vol. IV (New York, 1905), pp. 400-401. Also, J. M. Thompson, *Napoleon Bonaparte His-Rise and Fall* (Oxford, 1958), pp. 403-404.

20 WO25/839, Part III/1, 93rd Regiment. The date of embarkation was June 21, 1860.

21 WO25/868 (1), Returns of Officers Services 1872, 93rd Regiment. Army Lists show James Montagu retired August 9, 1873 and died April 23, 1883.

22 Robertson, pp. 151-152.

23 *Ibid.*, p. 151.

24 WO12/2611, Pay Lists Eighth Regiment, First Battalion, 1860-61, p. 2.

25 *Ibid.*

26 *Ibid.*

27 C. N. Barclay, *On Their Shoulders. British Generalship in the Lean Years 1939-1942* (London, 1964), p. 17. Also WO33/5, Purchase and Sale of Commissions, pp. 107-174.

28 Harts New Annual Army List 1862 (London, 1862), p. 477.

29 WO12/2612, Pay Lists Eighth Regiment, First Battalion, 1861-1862.

30 *Ibid.*

31 *Harts*, p. 237.

32 WO12/2612, Pay Lists, July 1 - September 30, 1861.

33 W. McD. Tait in *Vancouver Daily Province*, February 23, 1924, p. 23. According to A. W. Vowell's obituary in the Victoria *Daily Colonist*, September 27, 1918, he landed in Esquimalt in February 1862.

CHAPTER III

1 W. McD. Tait, "Kootenai Brown Tells Thrills of Early Days in Cariboo Gold Rush" in *Vancouver Daily Province*, February 23, 1924, p. 23.

2 Kinahan Cornwallis, *The New El Dorado* (London, 1858), p. 147.

3 *Ibid.*

4 Margaret A. Ormsby, *British Columbia: a History* (Vancouver, B.C., 1964), p. 184.

5 *The Daily Colonist* (Victoria), September 27, 1918.

6 *The British Colonist* (Victoria), March 4, 1862.

7 Tait, p. 23.

8 W. Champness, "To Cariboo and Back." An Emigrants Journey to the Gold Fields of British Columbia" in *The Leisure Hour* (London, 1862), p. 203.

9 *Ibid.*, pp. 203-204.

10 F. N. Otis, *Illustrated History of the Panama Railroad* (New York, 1862), p. 139.

11 Tait, p. 23.

12 J. H. Kemble, *The Panama Route* 1848-1869 (Berkeley, 1943), p. 194.

13 *Ibid.*, p. 207.

14 Tait, p. 23.

15 Champness, p. 206.

16 *Ibid.*

17 *Ibid.*, p. 207.

18 J. H. Fery and G. J. Wight, *Cariboo Gold Mines. Notes, Observations* etc. (San Francisco, 1862), p. 3.

19 *Ibid.*, p. 18.

20 *The British Colonist*, February 28, 1862, p. 3. Various issues of the paper between March and the end of June 1862 show that 21 Brown's arrived in Esquimalt aboard various vessels. Only four had the initials "J"; none are listed with the initials "J. G." or the name John George.

21 J. B. Kerr, *Biographical Dictionary of Well-Known British Columbians* (Vancouver, B.C., 1890), p. 53.

22 Tait, p. 23.

23 *The Daily Colonist*, September 27, 1918.

24 Ormsby, p. 186.

CHAPTER IV

1 Margaret A. Ormsby, *British Columbia: a History* (Vancouver, B.C., 1964), pp. 187-188.

2 J. H. Fery and G. J. Wight, *Cariboo Gold Mines. Notes Observations etc.* (San Francisco, 1862), p. 5.

3 W. Champness, "To Cariboo and Back. An Emigrants Journey to the Gold Fields of British Columbia" in *The Leisure Hour* (London, 1862), p. 259.

4 *Ibid.*, p. 246.

5 *The Daily Colonist*, September 27, 1918.

6 *Ibid.* Also J. B. Kerr, *Biographical Dictionary of Well-Known British Columbians* (Vancouver, B.C., 1890), p. 317.

7 W. McD. Tait "Kootenai Brown Tells of Thrills of Early Days in Cariboo Gold Rush" in the *Vancouver Daily Province*, February 23, 1924, p. 23.

8 Ormsby, pp. 186-187.

9 *Ibid.*, p. 187.

10 Tait, p. 23.

11 *Ibid.*

12 Provincial Archives of B.C., M. B. Begbie, *Report to the Colonial Secretary 1862.*

13 Tait, p. 23.

14 *Ibid.*

15 *Ibid.*

16 *Ibid.*

17 Provincial Archives of B.C., A. N. Birch, *Report,* October 31, 1864.

18 W. G. Cox, Richfield, March 27, 1865.

19 Tait, p. 23.

20 Provincial Archives of B.C., O'Reilly Papers, File 1285, Letter No. 9, Kootenay, B.C., June 29, 1865.

21 *Ibid.*, File 1286, Letter no. 12, Kootenay, B.C., July 24, 1865.

22 *Ibid.*, File 1286, Kootenay, B.C., December 6, 1865. Also, *British Columbia Blue Books*, 1865, p. 124.

23 *The British Columbian*, July 15, 1865.

24 O'Reilly Papers, File 1286, Letter No. 17, Kootenay, B.C., August 18, 1865.

25 *Ibid.*, File 1286, Letter no 25, Kootenay, B.C., September 13, 1865.

26 Ibid., Lean's resignation was dated Fisherville, September 12, 1865.

27 Tait, *Vancouver Daily Province*, March 8, 1924, p. 12.

28 *Ibid.*

CHAPTER V

1 Irene M. Spry, *The Palliser Expedition* (Toronto, 1963), p. 168.

2 *Occasional Papers of the Royal Artillery Institution*, Vol. I (Woolwich, 1860), p. 250. Letter from Blakiston to General Sabine dated Fort Carlton, December 15, 1858. See also Spry, pp. 171-173.

3 W. McD. Tait, "Kootenai Brown Tells Tales of Buffalo Hunting in Early Sixties," in *Vancouver Daily Province*, March 8, 1924, p. 12.

4 *Ibid.*

5 *Ibid.*

6 *Ibid.*

7 *Ibid.*

8 *Ibid.*

9 *Ibid.*

10 Lucile M. Kane (ed.), *Military Life in Dakota: The Journal of Philippe Régis de Trobriand* (St. Paul, 1951), p. 51.

11 Tait, p. 12.

12 *Ibid.*

13 *Ibid.*

14 *Ibid.*

15 A. C. Garrioch, *First Furrows* (Third edition, Winnipeg, 1923), preface.

16 *Ibid.*, pp. 168-169. The same incident is recounted in A. C. Garrioch, *The Correction Line* (Winnipeg, 1933), pp. 272-274.

17 *Ibid.*, pp. 169-171.

18 Tait, pp. 12-13.

19 Garrioch, pp. 170-172.

20 *Ibid.*, pp. 170-171.

21 Adam Short and A. G. Doughty (eds.), *Canada and Its Provinces* (Toronto, 1914), Vol. XIX, p. 99. The Manitoba Census, begun in October 1870, revealed a population of 11,963 residents of which 1565 were white, 558 Indians "settled upon the land," and 9,840 Métis.

22 Tait, p. 13.

23 Kane, pp. 240-241.

24 Dana Wright, "The Fort Totten - Fort Stevenson Trail 1867-1872" in *North Dakota History*, April 1953, p. 67.

25 Charles De Noyer, "The History of Fort Totten" in *Collections of the State Historical Society of North Dakota* (Bismarck, 1910), Vol. III, p. 179.

26 W. McD. Tait, *I Remember*, Glenbow Foundation typescript, n.d., p. 21.

27 Kane, p. 240.

28 *Ibid.*, pp. 192-193, and note p. 192.

29 United States Army Quartermasters Records, Group 92, Report of Persons and Articles Hired, Fort Stevenson, D.T., June 6, 1868.

CHAPTER VI

1 Lucile M. Kane (ed.), *Military Life in Dakota: the Journal of Philipe Régis de Trobriand* (St. Paul, 1951), p. 41.

2 *Ibid.*

3 William H. Goetzmann, *Army Exploration in the American West 1803-1863* (New Haven, 1959), p. 406.

4 Robert M. Utley, *The Last Days of the Sioux Nation* (New Haven and London, 1963), p. 7.

5 Kane, p. 22.

6 *Ibid.*, p. 40.

7 *Ibid.*, p. 43.

8 *Ibid.*, p. 48.

9 *Ibid.*, p. 42.

10 United States Army, Quartermasters Records, Group 92, Report of Persons and Articles Hired, Fort Stevenson, D.T., June 6, 1868.

11 United States Army, Quartermasters Records, Group 92, Fort Stevenson, D.T., April 19, 1868.

12 John Henry Taylor, *Sketches of Frontier and Indian Life on the Upper Missouri and Great Plains* (3rd Edition, Bismarck, N.D., 1897), pp. 261-262.

13 Kane, p. 192.

14 *Ibid.*, p. 193.

15 *Ibid.*, p. 322.

16 W. McD. Tait, "I Remember" in *The Farm and Ranch Review*, May 20, 1919, pp. 570-573.

17 *Ibid.*

18 Kane, pp. 287-289.

19 U.S. House of Representatives, 40th Congress, Third Session, *Executive Document No. 1*, Vol. III, p. 35. Terry's *Report* was dated October 5, 1868.

20 Kane, p. 289.

21 *Ibid.*, p. 310.

22 *Ibid.*, pp. 337-338.

23 United States Army, Quartermasters Records, Group 92, Fort Stevenson Post Returns, June 16 - October 31, 1868.

24 United States Army, Quartermasters Records, Group 92, Fort Buford Post Returns, August 17, 1869.

25 Kane, p. 77.

26 *Ibid.*, p. 78.

27 *Ibid.*, p. 200.

28 *Ibid.*, p. 347.

29 *Ibid.*, p. 348.

30 *Ibid.*, p. 361.

31 *Ibid.*

32 *de Trobriand Papers*, State Historical Society of North Dakota, Fort Totten, D.T., April 1, 1869.

33 Kane, pp. 364-365.

34 *Ibid.*, p. 368.

35 *de Trobriand Papers*, April 1, 1869. On March 19, 1869 T. F. Richer wrote a statement in French for de Trobriand while snowbound at Big Coulee stating that Brown was not responsible for the loss of F. Bittner, John Shank, and H. O. Voyles. He also gave an account of the trip.

36 United States Army, Quartermasters Records, Group 92, Fort Buford Post Returns, August 17, 1869. Also Returns dated only as "August 1869."

CHAPTER VII

1 United States Army, Quartermasters Records, Group 92. Fort Buford Post Returns, August 1869.

2 *Ibid.*, Report, Fort Totten, September 1, 1869.

3 Parish Records, St. Joseph of Leroy, North Dakota, p. 136.

4 Lucile M. Kane (ed.), *Military Life in Dakota: The Journal of Philippe Régis de Trobriand* (St. Paul, 1951), pp. 84-85.

5 W. McD. Tait, *I Remember*, Glenbow Foundation typescript, p. 38.

6 Marie Rose Smith, *Eighty Years on the Plains*, Glenbow Foundation typescript, p. 126.

7 Kane, p. 32.

8 *Collections of the Historical Society of North Dakota*, (Bismarck, N.D., 1910), Vol. III, p. 226.

9 John Henry Taylor, *Sketches of Frontier and Indian Life on the Upper Missouri and Great Plains* (3rd ed., Bismarck, N.D., 1897), p. 98.

10 *Ibid.*

11 *Ibid.*

12 United States Army, Adjutant General's Office, Record Group 94, Fort Totten, May 17, 1871, p. 120.

13 *Ibid.*, Fort Totten, December 28, 1869, p. 192.

14 *Ibid.*, Fort Stevenson, May 31, 1872. For his trouble Crofton was charged by Major General Hancock, the officer commanding Dakota Department, and ultimately had to repay sixty dollars to the U.S. Treasury.

15 Quartermasters Records, Group 92, Fort Stevenson Returns, February 1872.

16 *Ibid.*, Fort Stevenson, 1873.

17 *Ibid.*, Fort Buford Post Records, July 1871.

18 *Ibid.*, Fort Stevenson, July 22, 1873.

19 *Ibid.*, St. Paul, July 31 and August 19, 1873. W. McD. Tait, "Fixing the Border Line" in *The Canadian Magazine*, No. 3, July 1915, pp. 214-215, claims that Brown took the job of post-sutler with the United States section of the Northern Boundary Commission, but there are no records to confirm his employment with the Commission during its last days in the field. See also Tait, "Trail Blazing Across the Rockies," in *The Canadian Magazine*, March 1934.

20 *Ibid.*, *Report on Employment at Fort Stevenson, D.T., 1874*, March and June 1874.

21 Tait, *The Canadian Magazine*, March 1934, p. 38.

22 PAC, J. W. Taylor Papers, Letters to the State Department, Taylor to Hamilton Fish, St. Paul, Minn., January 20, 1870.

23 G. F. G. Stanley, *The Birth of Western Canada* (Toronto, 1960), p. 178.

24 *Ibid.*

25 Tait, pp. 51-52.

26 *Ibid.*, pp. 43-45.

27 *Ibid.*, p. 53.

28 *Ibid.*, pp. 46-49.

29 Taylor Papers, St. Paul, January 20, 1870.

30 Stanley, p. 178.

31 Tait, pp. 50-51.

32 *Ibid.*, pp. 45-46.

33 *Ibid.*, pp. 49-50.

34 Stanley, pp. 178-179.

35 Tait, pp. 38-40.

36 *Ibid.*, pp. 41-42.

37 Norbert Welsh, *The Last Buffalo Hunter* (New York, 1939), ed. by Mary Weeks, pp. 200-206.

38 F. G. Roe, *The North American Buffalo* (Toronto, 1951), pp. 471-472.

39 Tait, pp. 53-54.

CHAPTER VIII

1 W. McD. Tait, *I Remember*. Glenbow Foundation typescript, pp. 54-55.

2 *Ibid.*, p. 59.

3 *Ibid.*, p. 54.

4 *Ibid.*, pp. 55-56.

5 Joseph Howard Kinsey, *Strange Empire* (New York, 1952), p. 263.

6 Charles Larpenteur, *Forty Years a Fur Trader on the Upper Missouri* (Chicago, 1933), p. 286.

7 *Indictment Record Book*, United States District Court, First Judicial District of the Territory of Montana, September 10, 1877 - October 4, 1888.

8 H. H. Bancroft, *Works*, Vol. XXXI, *History of Washington, Idaho, and Montana 1845-1889* (San Francisco, 1890), p. 658.

9 *Three Years in California. William Perkins Journal of Life at Sonora, 1849-1852* (University of California Press, 1964).

10 Letter, John Jerome Healy to Tappan Adney, n.p., August 25, 1905, Historical Society of Montana, Glenbow Foundation copy.

11 Tait, pp. 151-152.

CHAPTER IX

1 W. McD. Tait, *I Remember*, Glenbow Foundation typescript, p. 59.

2 Paul F. Sharp, *Whoop-up Country: The Canadian American West 1865-1885* (Minneapolis, 1955), p. 4.

3 *Ibid.*, p. 5.

4 L. V. Kelly, *The Range Men* (Toronto, 1913), p. 93.

5 Tait, p. 138.

6 *Ibid.*, pp. 84-85.

7 *Ibid.*, p. 85.

8 *Ibid.*, pp. 86-87.

9 *Ibid.*, p. 87.

10 *Ibid.*, p. 133.

11 Chester Martin, and A. S. Morton, *History of Prairie Settlement and Dominion Lands Policy* (Toronto, 1938), pp. 90-93. Also, Kelly, p. 140.

12 Tait, pp. 133-134. McEachern was the Chief Veterinary Surgeon for the Canadian government. The Waldrond stretched over the southern part of the Porcupine Hills while the Oxley ranged over the hills around Mosquito Creek. The Cochrane Ranch Company moved into the Belly River area after moving from its initial lease west of Calgary. It was ultimately sold to the Mormon Church.

13 A. S. Hill, *From Home to Home: Autumn Wanderings in the Northwest 1881, 1882, 1883, 1884* (London, 1887), pp. 331-332.

14 *Ibid.*, p. 333.

15 *Ibid.*. p. 337.

16 *Ibid.*, p. 340.

17 *Ibid.*

18 Marie Rose Smith, "Eighty Years on the Plains" in *Canadian Cattlemen*, October 1949, p. 15.

19 Fort Macleod *Gazette*, September 4, 1883. Kanouse bought the business from a John B. Smith.

20 Smith, p. 15.

21 Frank White's Diary in *Canadian Cattlemen*, September 1949.

22 J. D. Higinbotham, *When the West was Young* (Toronto, 1933), p. 252.

23 W. F. Cochrane *Diary*, January 26, 1885. Glenbow Foundation.

24 *Ibid.*, January 28, 1885.

25 *Ibid.*, February 3, 1885.

26 *Ibid.*, April 2, 1885.

27 *Ibid.*, April 3, 1885.

28 Smith, p. 18.

29 *Ibid.*

30 Chief Mountain [Archdeacon S. H. Middleton], *Kootenai Brown* (Lethbridge, 1954), p. 31.

31 *Ibid.*, Middleton claims that one of Brown's daughters died in childhood and is buried in the lakeshore plot. The other daughter, a Mrs. Bedore, he states was living in Quebec in 1954.

32 Smith, p. 18.

CHAPTER X

1 G. F. G. Stanley, *The Birth of Western Canada* (Toronto, 1960), pp. 192-193. Also, *Louis Riel Patriot or Rebel* (Ottawa, 1954), pp. 17-22.

2 Glenbow Foundation. Cochrane Ranch *Letter Book 1885*, W. F. Cochrane, April 6, 1885.

3 *Ibid.*, April 12, 1885.

4 *Report upon the Suppression of the Rebellion in the Northwest Territories in Canada Therewith in 1885* (Ottawa, 1886), p. 76.

5 *Ibid.*, March 22, 1885, p. 77. The arms stipulated were to consist of one revolver, Mounted Police pattern, one cartridge belt with knife attached. Each man was to carry three blankets of NWMP weight and quality. All volunteers were given a daily allowance of 50¢ for rations with utensils supplied by the government. Officers pay corresponded to that in Canadian Cavalry units; N.C.O.'s and men were paid on N.W.M.P. scales: Sgt. Major $1.50 per day; Sergeant $1.00; Corporals, 90¢; troopers 75¢. Stewart proposed a daily expenditure of $2.50 per day for Troopers, including equipment, horse appointments, rations and forage.

6 PAC, Adolphe P. Caron Papers, Ottawa, March 29, 1885, Vol. 199, p. 40.

7 *Report* Suppression of the Rebellion, pp. 74-76. Purchases were made from I. G. Baker; A. Heney and Co.; Qual and Scott; J. D. Higinbotham; G. King and Co.; Snider and Clark; and Tweed and Ewart.

8 Caron Papers, Calgary, April 18, 1885, Vol. 199, p. 78.

9 R.C.M.P. File 2634 - 1885, *Monthly Report Fort Macleod*, April 2, 1885.

10 *Ibid.*, April 5, 1885.

11 Cochrane Letter Book, April 18, 1885.

12 W. F. Cochrane *Diary*, April 20, 1885. Glenbow Foundation.

13 PAC, RG 9, 11F7, 15, Field Pay Lists Rocky Mountain Rangers, April 23 - July 10, 1885.

14 John D. Higinbotham, *When the West Was Young* (Toronto, 1933), p. 319.

15 R.C.M.P. File 2634 - 1885, Fort Macleod, April 23, 1885.

16 *Ibid.*, April 24, 1885.

17 *Ibid.*, April 29, 1885.

18 J. D. Higinbotham in *The Canadian Pictorial and Illustrated War News*, June 20, 1885. The account was erroneously attributed to J. D. Hutchinson but the mistake was rectified in the next issue, June 27, 1885, p. 103.

19 Cochrane Letter Book, April 26, 1885.

20 *Ibid.*, May 5 and 8, 1885. Cochrane's note about the Winnipeg Battalion is inaccurate. Two companies of the 9th Battalion Quebec Voltigeurs arrived in Fort Macleod from Calgary to protect the community and to escort supply trains between the two points. See Fort Macleod *Gazette*, May 29, 1885 and R.C.M.P. File 2634-1885, Reports May 1 and 16, 1885.

21 *Ibid.*, May 2, 1885.

22 *Ibid.*, June 8, 1885.

23 Fort Macleod *Gazette*, May 9, 1885.

24 W. McD. Tait, "Kootenai Brown Tells of Buffalo Hunting in Early Sixties" in Vancouver *Daily Province*, March 8, 1924, p. 12.

25 R.C.M.P. File G995-10 (1946), March 14, 1945.

26 N.W.M.P. *Annual Report* 1885, Appendix C, p. 59.

27 R.C.M.P. File 2634-1885, May 31, 1885. A report dated May 21, 1885 notes installation of telegraph instruments in the Fort Macleod Police Orderly Room with Sergeant White appointed operator. Higinbotham, p. 320, May 24, 1885, states that the public telegraph was established that day in his store.

28 *Ibid.*, June 1, 1885.

29 Fort Macleod *Gazette*, June 6, 1885.

30 John R. Craig, *Ranching with Lords and Commons* (Toronto, 1903), pp. 156-157.

31 N.W.M.P. *Annual Report 1885*, Appendix C, p. 59.

32 Caron Papers, Vol. 199, p. 513.

33 Cochrane *Diary 1885*, July 8, 1885.

34 R.C.M.P. File 2634-1885, Fort Macleod, July 8, 1885.

35 Fort Macleod *Gazette*, July 14, 1885.

36 *Ibid.*

37 RG9, 11F7, 15, Field Pay Lists Rocky Mountain Rangers.

38 R.C.M.P. File 2634-1885, Fort Macleod, July 31, 1885.

39 Fort Macleod *Gazette*, no date visible on microfilm.

40 *The Canadian Pictorial and Illustrated War News*, July 11, 1885, reported Stewart's arrival in Winnipeg on July 6.

41 Department of Militia and Defence, Militia General Order 21, Ottawa, September 18, 1885. Also, Capt. Arthur Jocelyn, *Awards of Honour* (London, 1956), p. 168.

42 Fort Macleod *Gazette*, December 15, 1885.

43 Dominion Land Titles, Land grant no 2518, Department of the Interior, December 15, 1885.

44 Ledger of the Militia Force engaged in the Northwest 1885, certificate no. 2518, Honours and Awards Division, Department of Veteran's Affairs, Ottawa. When seen by the author in 1956 the medal was in the possession of Arthur Harwood, former postmaster at Waterton Lakes National Park.

CHAPTER XI

1 J. R. Craig, *Ranching With Lords and Commons* (Toronto, 1903), p. 260.

2 *Ibid.*, p. 292.

3 *Ibid.*, p. 293. Governor General the Marquis of Lansdowne visited the Cochrane ranch in September 1885 for example. See W. F. Cochrane *Diary 1885*.

4 Marie Rose Smith, "Eighty Years on the Plains" in *Canadian Cattlemen*, October 1949, p. 18.

5 *Ibid.* Also Chief Mountain [S. H. Middleton] *Kootenai Brown* (Lethbridge, 1954), p. 31.

6 Letter from Mrs. Bella Wallace, Three Hills, Alberta, August 15, 1954.

7 Marie Rose Smith, *Eighty Years on the Plains.* Glenbow Foundation typescript, n.d., pp. 129-130.

8 Craig, p. 261.

9 R.C.M.P. File 764 - 1888, Ottawa, June 18, 1888.

10 S. B. Steele, *Forty Years in Canada* (Toronto, 1915), pp. 245-255.

11 *Annual Report N.W.M.P. 1888* (Ottawa, 1889), Appendix G, p. 84.

12 *Ibid.*, p. 85.

13 The *Daily Colonist* (Victoria, B.C.), September 27, 1918.

14 *Annual Report N.W.M.P. 1888*, p. 85.

15 R.C.M.P. File 288 - 1888, Monthly Report, September 1888.

16 N.W.M.P. Pay Ledger, Vol. IV, p. 272.

17 R.C.M.P. File 178 - 1889, Monthly Report, June 1889.

18 R.C.M.P. File 596. Street was released on August 12, 1889 and was recorded as discharged at Kootenay Lakes on October 24, 1889.

19 N.W.M.P. Pay Ledger, Vol. IV, p. 272. Brown was employed June 11 - October 6, 1890.

20 R.C.M.P. File 238 - 1890, Monthly Report, August 1890. Also Fort Macleod *Gazette*, September 4, 1890.

21 *Ibid.*, Monthly Report, September 1890.

22 *Ibid.*, Monthly Report, October 1890.

23 Frederick Jackson Turner, *The Frontier in American History* (New York, 1945), pp. 1-3.

CHAPTER XII

1 PAC, War Claims Commission, RG9 - II A4 - Vol. 27, Fort Macleod, December 31, 1890.

2 Department of Indian Affairs and Northern Development, File W2 - Vol. I, Ottawa, October 10, 1911.

3 S. B. Steele, *Forty Years in Canada* (Toronto, 1915), p. 268.

4 Fort Macleod *Gazette*, September 1891.

5 R.C.M.P. File 278 - 1889, Monthly Report, March 1889. See also Steele, pp. 268-270.

6 Fort Macleod *Gazette*, October 11, 1895.

7 *Ibid.*

8 Department of Indian Affairs and Northern Development, File U172 - 23A, n.d.

9 Report of the Commissioner of Canadian National Parks, 1912-1926. Department of the Interior (Ottawa, 1926), p. 88. The section referred to is Brown's Annual Report 1913.

10 Fort Macleod *Gazette*, October 3 and 31, 1891.

11 *Ibid.*, January 30, 1890.

12 *Ibid.*, February 6, 1890.

13 *Ibid.*, July 30 and September 10, 1891.

14 J. W. Horan, *West Nor'West* (Edmonton, 1945), pp. 99-100.

15 Fort Macleod *Gazette*, June 16, 1893.

16 *Ibid.*

17 File W2-Vol. I, n.p., September 12, 1883.

18 Chief Mountain [S. H. Middleton], *Kootenai Brown* (Lethbridge, 1953), p. 39.

19 Lethbridge *Herald*, June 19, 1937.

20 File W2 - Vol. I, Calgary, September 23, 1893.

21 File U172 - 23A, Ottawa, November 18, 1893.

22 File W2 - Vol. I, Ottawa, December 19, 1894.

23 *Ibid.*, May 30, 1895. Also, Canada *Gazette*, June 29, 1895.

24 Fort Macleod *Gazette*, October 11, 1895.

25 *Ibid.*, July 30, 1897.

26 *Ibid.*, September 10, 1897.

27 *Ibid.*, September 3, 1897.

28 Letter, CPR, Montreal, December 2, 1954.

29 Fort Macleod *Gazette*, February 18, 1898.

CHAPTER XIII

1 Marie Rose Smith, *Eighty Years on the Plains*, Glenbow Foundation type-script, n.d., p. 131.

2 Letter, Theosophical Society, Pasadena, California, November 9, 1954.

3 Smith, p. 129.

4 British Columbia, Attorney General's Department, Victoria, March 21, 1955.

5 Department of Fisheries, Ottawa, February 14, 1957, File 1298, p. 290. Also, Department of the Interior, File W174-1, Waterton Mills, Alberta, February 13, 1911, personal history form filled in by Brown.

6 Department of Fisheries, File 2995, p. 360.

7 *Ibid.*, File 1298, p. 470.

8 The actual site was located on the northwest quarter of Section 30, Township 1, Range 30, west of the Fourth Meridian.

9 J. W. Horan, *West Nor'West* (Edmonton, 1945), p. 101.

10 *Ibid.*

11 Brown's *Diary 1900-1916*, October 24, 1904.

12 *Ibid.*, July 25, 1906.

13 *Calgary Herald*, September 3, 1955.

14 Department of Indian Affairs and Northern Development, File W2 - Vol. I, Calgary, May 4, 1906.

15 *Ibid.*, Ottawa, n.d. [1908-1909?]

16 *Ibid.*, Waterton Mills, Alberta, September 13, 1911.

17 *Ibid.*, Ottawa, n.d. [1908-1909?]

18 *Ibid.*, Waterton Mills, Alberta, September 13, 1911.

19 *Ibid.*, Cowley, Alberta, n.d., 1905.

20 *Ibid.*, Report on Proposed National Park, Ottawa, n.d. [1908-1909?].

21 Brown's *Diary*, June 13, 1905.

22 File W2 - Vol. I, Ottawa, May 27, 1907.

23 *Canadian Parliamentary Guide* (Ottawa, 1910), p. 130. Under the Elections Act of 1902 the district of Alberta was divided into four constituencies: Edmonton, Strathcona, Calgary and Alberta. The Macleod constituency was established by the Act of 1906-1907, and was first contested in the 1908 elections.

24 *Diary*, November 13, 1904.

25 *Ibid.*, June 7, 1906.

26 Province of Alberta, Department of Agriculture, *Annual Reports* 1908, 1911, and 1915. Letter, Edmonton, February 20, 1957.

27 "Judgement of the Supreme Court of British Columbia, November 4, 1907" in Cranbrook *Courier*, November 7, 1907. See also Martin's *Mining Cases and Statutes of British Columbia 1902-1907* (Toronto, 1907), Vol. II, p. 530.

28 *Diary*, September 18, 1907 and October 6, 1907.

29 *Ibid.*, n.d.

30 *Ibid.*, n.d.

31 Letter from Mrs. Bella Wallace, Three Hills, Alberta, August 26, 1954.

32 Interview, W. McD. Tait, Fergus, Ontario, October 29, 1955.

33 *Diary*, April 14, 1907.

34 *Ibid.*, October 20, 1906.

35 *Ibid.*, n.d., 1907.

36 File W2 - Vol. I, Ottawa, May 27, 1907.

37 *Ibid.*, Waterton Mills, Alberta, August 16, 1909.

38 *Ibid.*, Pincher Creek, Alberta, August 19, 1909.

39 *Ibid.*, Ottawa, November 25, 1909.

40 *Ibid.*, Ottawa, March 30, 1910.

41 *Ibid.*, Waterton Mills, Alberta, April 10, 1910.

CHAPTER XIV

1 Department of the Interior, File W174 - 1, Waterton Mills, Alberta, July 1, 1910.

2 *Ibid.*, Waterton Mills, Alberta, September 10, 1910.

3 Department of the Interior, *Reports of the Commissioner of Canadian National Parks 1904-1911* (Ottawa, 1911), p. 63.

4 *Ibid.*

5 Department of Indian Affairs and Northern Development, File W2 - Vol. I, Banff, Alberta, December 31, 1910.

6 P.C. 1388, Ottawa, June 8, 1911.

7 Occasional Papers of the Royal Artillery Institution, Vol. I (Woolwich, 1860), p. 252.

8 *Ibid.*, p. 253.

9 *Ibid.*

10 File W2 - Vol. I, n.d., Ottawa [1908-1909].

11 Department of the Interior, Reports of the Commissioner of Canadian National Parks 1912-1926 (Ottawa, 1926), pp. 81-82.

12 *Ibid.*, p. 82.

13 *Ibid.*, p. 22.

14 *Ibid.*, p. 88.

15 Brown's *Diary*, n.d.

16 *Ibid.*, September 30 and October 9, 1913.

17 File W2 - Vol. I, Edmonton, August 30, 1911.

18 *Ibid.*, Waterton Mills, Alberta, September 13, 1911.

19 *Ibid.*, Edmonton, September 21, 1911.

20 *Ibid.*, Ottawa, March 20, 1912. See also exchanges dated St. Catherines, Ontario, January 26, 1912; Edmonton, February 3, 1912; and St. Catherines, April 1, 1912.

21 *Diary*, February 4, 1913.

22 *Ibid.*, December 18, 1913.

23 Brown's Letter Book, Waterton Lakes National Park, *Monthly Report*, October 1913.

24 File W174 - 1, Waterton Mills, Alberta, July 28, 1911.

25 *Ibid.*, Waterton Mills, Alberta, November 9, 1912.

26 *Ibid.*, Ottawa, May 28, 1913.

27 *Diary*, December 6, 1912.

28 File W2 - Vol. I, Waterton Mills, Alberta, June 1, 1913.

29 Max McD. [sic], "Improving the Waterton Lakes Park" in the *Lethbridge Herald*, January 21, 1914.

30 *Diary*, May 1, 1913 and October 22, 1913.

31 *Ibid.*, November 17, 18, and 20, 1913.

32 *Ibid.*, February 2, 1913.

33 P.C. 1165, Ottawa, June 24, 1918.

34 *Diary*, July 18, 1914.

35 File W174 - 1, Pincher Creek, Alberta, August 3, 1914.

36 *Diary*, September 1, 1914.

37 Brown's Letter Book. Only one letter from Leo Brown is preserved. Dated Fort McMurray, Alberta, November 27, it is respectful and included a photograph, now missing, of Leo's family. The younger Brown wished his father a Merry Christmas, and "many more years of health and prosperity."

38 *Diary*, May 31, 1915.

39 W. McD. Tait, *I Remember*, Glenbow Foundation typescript, p. 151.

40 Letter, Michael Holland, Balcombe, Sussex, July 7, 1954.

41 Department of the Interior, File 1013, Waterton Lakes, Alberta, March 21, 1916.

42 *Ibid.*

43 *Diary*, May 20, 1916.

44 *Ibid.*, June 10, 1916.

45 *Ibid.*, June 8, 1916.

46 *Pincher Creek Echo*, July 21, 1916.

EPILOGUE

1 Department of the Interior, Files 1013 and 3644. Brown first wrote to the legal firm of Thomson and Jackson on March 21, 1916. His Will, witnessed by Robert Cooper and E. E. Haug, is dated May 20, 1916.

2 W. McD. Tait, *I Remember*, Glenbow Foundation typescript, p. 152.

3 Department of the Interior, Report of the Commissioner of Canadian National Parks 1912-1926 (Ottawa, 1926), p. 60.

4 *Family Herald*, April 10, 1935.

5 Files 1013 and 3644. Isabella's Will dated May 5, 1917, refers to "the late Leo Brown" and lists his widow's name as Justine. Also, Chief Mountain [S. H. Middleton], *Kootenai Brown* (Lethbridge, 1954), p. 31.

POSTSCRIPT

1 W. McD. Tait, *I Remember*, Glenbow Foundation typescript, pp. 150-151.

2 *Ibid.*, pp. 56-58.

3 For example: Robert Gard, *Johnny Chinook* (Toronto, 1945); Chief Mountain [S. H. Middleton], *Kootenai Brown* (Lethbridge, 1954); Grant McEwan's various writings; Mary Flett, "A Holiday in the Canadian Rockies" in *Rod and Gun*, May 1917; A. H. Christie, " 'Kootenai' Brown Spent Colorful Career in West" in the *Calgary Herald*, April 13, 1935.

4 Miss Annora Brown, Victoria, B.C., n.d. Personal recollection.

5 Marie Rose Smith, *Eighty Years on the Plains*, Glenbow Foundation typescript, pp. 131-135.

INDEX

and commission 15, 20; and career 17, 18, 32

Brown, Capt. John 13, 14, 20

Brown, John George (ghillie) 9, 217

Brown, John George "Kootenai" army career, intimation of 15; birth 12; and Bowell, Mackenzie 164-165, 168; and broken leg 161-162; and buffalo: disappearance of 107, 108; first sight of 59, 62; hunt 97-104; hunting camp 102-103; stampede 104; and bull boat 62-64; and Canada, return to 97, 118-123; and C.P.R. 176-178; and Cariboo 42-50; and Chagres River 38; character of 8-11, 220-223; and commission 19-25, 33-34; and conservation 11, 108, 174-176, 195, 219; as constable 52-56; and counterfeiters 53-56; and daughters 97, 105, 134; death of 8, 216, 219; and de Trobriand 82-84; and disembarkation leave 32-33; Duck Lake, first sight of 65-66; early life 15-17; education 17, 215; as Ensign 24-25; and Eighth Regt. 26-34; and Ell, Louis, murder of and acquittal 113-117; epitaph 219; and family dispersal 134; and Ferguson's quarter section 205-206; as Fisheries Officer 183, 192; forebears 12-13; as Forest Ranger 195-197, 206-208; Fort Garry trip 62-66; Fraser River, freighting on 49-50; as Game Guardian 192; and Gilchrist fight 48-49; and "Goldtooth" 66; and Higinbotham, J.D. 132; and Hill, A.S. 127, 128; and homestead, transfer of 166; and illness 153-154; in India 29-30; and Indians: first encounter with 59-60, 146; trading with 66-70; wounded by 61; Ireland, departure from 34; and Isabella 155 ff.; and Kanouse, H.A. 122-126, 128, 131, 150, 180; and Lord Lathom 61, 127, 134; as mail contractor 90-96; and mail carriers, murder of 72-73, 77-79; to mainland B.C. 43; marriage 91-92; and Métis: first encounter with 65-66; and buffalo hunt 97-102; and hunting camps security 103-104; and winter camps 104-107; and Mormons 168-169; and murder charge acquittal 115; and Napoleon's tomb (original) 31; and nickname 59; and Northern Boundary Survey party, search for 95; and North-West Medal 150, 152; and N.W.M.P.: packer with 157-161; return from Wildhorse 159-161; severance from 165; and Northwest Rebellion 142-152; as oil case witness 192-193; and Oil City 184-185, 209; and oil expedition 182-183; and oil in Waterton 169-171; in old age 211-216; and Olive's death 134-135; packer, ability as 130, 157-159, 215; and Panama 38-39; and Panama Isthmus 37-39; and Panama - San Francisco fare 39; and parents 12, 13, 15; and pony express 70-73; and ranchers 125-126, 127; reading habits 193-195; and Red River Rebellion 92-93; and RMR chief scout 61, 142-152; romantic stories about 8, 29; and Ruffee, C.A. 71-73, 74-75; and San Francisco 39; and Sandhurst examinations 20-21; and Second Chinese War 30; and second homestead 152; and Sitting Bull 79-84; and son Leo 131, 134-135, 210; and South Kootenay Pass 58-59, 128, 200, 215; stamina of 220; suicide attempt 115; and Theosophy 181-182; and tintype photo 70; and traders, murder of 67-70; and trapping 46-47; and typewriter 210; and U.S. Army 74-97; and Vermillion Lakes 173; and Victoria, B.C. 42; and Waterton Lakes: first sight of 59-60; fisherman at 126-127, 132, 133; return to 109, 118, 122, 153; sells store stock at 124; squatting at 122; store at 123; and Waterton Lakes National Park: acting Superintendent of 9, 199-212; conservation of 174-175; establishment of 11, 175, 195; expansion of 199-200, 202, 212; publicizing of 126, 171, 208-209; and wolfing 109-111, 221-222

THE AUTHOR

William Rodney was born, raised and educated in Alberta. He earned a degree from the University of Alberta, then an MA from England's famous Cambridge and a PhD from the London School of Economics. He was later appointed a Fellow of the Royal Historical Society and of the Royal Geographical Society.

In addition to *Kootenai Brown*, he has written several other books, many articles and radio documentaries. For *Kootenai Brown*, he received the University of B.C.'s Medal for Popular Biography. The book also won an Award of Merit and Distinction from the American Association for State and Local History.

Literary awards, however, are only one aspect of the author's life. During World War Two he joined the Royal Canadian Air Force and survived an operational tour with RAF Bomber Command. This duty was extremely hazardous, with some 50 per cent of air crew being killed in action. During his service he won the Distinguished Flying Cross and Bar.

He is now enjoying retirement, his last posting Professor of History at Royal Roads Military College near Victoria on Vancouver Island.